CONCEPTUAL DESIGN *of* STRUCTURES

PIERLUIGI D'ACUNTO, PATRICK OLE OHLBROCK,
ROLAND PAWLITSCHKO *(eds.)*

CONCEPTUAL DESIGN *of* STRUCTURES

CONNECTING ENGINEERING *and* ARCHITECTURE

BIRKHÄUSER BASEL

CLEMENTINE HEGNER-VAN ROODEN AND MASSIMO LAFFRANCHI
6 **FOREWORD**

PIERLUIGI D'ACUNTO, PATRICK OLE OHLBROCK AND MIGUEL FERNÁNDEZ RUIZ
8 **ON THE CONCEPTUAL DESIGN OF STRUCTURES**

AURELIO MUTTONI AND JOSEPH SCHWARTZ
16 **CONCEPTUAL DESIGN OF STRUCTURES IN PRACTICE, RESEARCH, AND TEACHING**

CHALLENGING GRAVITY

LEONARDO TODISCO
30 **PREFACE**

INTERVIEW WITH WILLIAM "BILL" BAKER, ALESSANDRO BEGHINI AND JANET ECHELMAN
32 **ENGINEERING AND ART – MOVING FORWARD TOGETHER**

ALEJANDRO BERNABEU LARENA
42 **FIVE THOUGHTS ON THE RELATIONSHIP BETWEEN STRUCTURE AND ARCHITECTURE**

INTERVIEW WITH CHRISTIAN MENN AND STEFAN POLÓNYI
54 **THE SIMPLE, ELEGANT FLOW OF FORCES**

PAUL GAUVREAU
62 **DESIGNING BY HAND IN AN ERA OF UBIQUITOUS COMPUTING POWER**

KAI-UWE BLETZINGER, ANN-KATHRIN GOLDBACH AND REZA NAJIAN
70 **FORM FINDING BY SHAPE OPTIMIZATION WITH IMPLICIT SPLINES AND VERTEX MORPHING**

PATRICK OLE OHLBROCK, GIULIA BOLLER, AND PIERLUIGI D'ACUNTO
80 **CONCEPTUAL DESIGN OF STRUCTURES IN THE DIGITAL AGE**

EXPOSED OR CONCEALED

ROLAND PAWLITSCHKO
92 **PREFACE**

INTERVIEW WITH CHRISTIAN KEREZ AND JOSEPH SCHWARTZ
94 **WE ARE THE ONES WHO TELL THE STRUCTURE HOW IT SHOULD CARRY LOADS**

CECILIA PUGA
104 **A DIALOGUE BETWEEN AN ARCHITECT AND AN ENGINEER**

JÜRG CONZETT
114 **CONCEPTUAL DESIGNING**

JEANNETTE KUO
126 **STRUCTURING SPACE**

LEARNING FROM THE PAST

MARIO RINKE
136 **PREFACE**

THORSTEN HELBIG AND FLORIAN MEIER
138 **MATERIAL TECHNOLOGY AND SUSTAINABILITY – VISIBLE AND INVISIBLE INFLUENCES TO INNOVATIVE STRUCTURAL FORM**

TULLIA IORI
146 **TELL ME, PROF., WHAT IS THE USE OF THE HISTORY OF CIVIL ENGINEERING?**

INTERVIEW WITH BJØRN NORMANN SANDAKER AND JOSEPH SCHWARTZ
154 **A CONVERSATION ON STRUCTURAL ENGINEERING, ARCHITECTURE, AND EDUCATION BETWEEN SWITZERLAND AND NORWAY**

INTERVIEW WITH AURELIO MUTTONI AND ROBERTO GARGIANI
162 **TEACHING CONCEPTUAL DESIGN OF STRUCTURES TO YOUNG ENGINEERS AND ARCHITECTS**

COMMON RESPONSIBILITIES

CATHERINE DE WOLF
172 **PREFACE**

INTERVIEW WITH KNUT STOCKHUSEN
174 **CONCEPTUAL DESIGN FOR REUSABLE INFRASTRUCTURES**

INTERVIEW WITH ELLI MOSAYEBI
182 **THE INTERDISCIPLINARY NATURE OF ARCHITECTURE: CHALLENGES AND OPPORTUNITIES BETWEEN ACADEMIA AND PRACTICE**

MIGUEL FERNÁNDEZ RUIZ AND DUARTE M. VIULA FARIA
192 **THE ROLE OF ENGINEERING AND CONCEPTUAL DESIGN ON SUSTAINABILITY**

INTERVIEW WITH LEE FRANCK AND JANE WERNICK
198 **RESPONSIBILITIES OF CIVIL ENGINEERS IN SOCIETY**

MARIO RINKE
204 **CONCEPTUALIZING STRUCTURAL PERMANENCIES**

214 **AUTHORS**
220 **IMAGE CREDITS**

In the early stages of the design process, the function and form of a building are roughly outlined and formulated. However, the importance of the concept is often overlooked, even though it forms the basis of our building culture. Even technically brilliant designs can fail in later stages if a coherent and well-thought-out concept was not developed in the early design phase – some fail during construction, some during operation, and some only when the building has reached the end of its life.

Conceptual design primarily provides a conceptual framework for how a building will be implemented visually, structurally, constructively, and technically. The conceptual design describes the idea and intent at its core. It is the overarching plan, and the execution is the corresponding follow-up. Both steps are interdependent. The key to conceptual design lies in the search for balance – the integration of the aspects architecture, construction and engineering. It is about finding the harmonious relationship between conditions and requirements. In the search for equilibrium between polarities and dualities, designers look for a holistic approach to achieve the balanced goal – the building. It is about the interplay between aesthetics and functionality, tradition and innovation, material and atmosphere. It's about creating a solution in which all elements harmonize with one another and the result is ideally more than the sum of its parts.

The speakers at "The International fib Symposium on Conceptual Design of Structures 2021" and the authors of this book understand and embody these principles of balance and synthesis. They demonstrate the thoughtful and cohesive design behind a building and the issues and challenges that arise. It is about the balanced application of computer-aided calculation methods, which often only suggest accuracy and should be supplemented, if not replaced, by handwork and conceptual thinking. It is also about dialogue and collaboration between architects and engineers. The interaction between spatial structure and structural framework is explored. Intangibles play as important a role as the history of the building and the topographical, landscape or urban context. Likewise, the process of form-finding is influenced by historical and material development, as is the interweaving of the work of generations of engineers and the history and evolution of the conceptual design of buildings themselves. Responsibility to society and ecology is always emphasized – the adaptability of structures and their functional variability as "load cases." The central role played by the pursuit of the right measure and balanced design becomes clear, and one can see how it contributes to the success of high-quality construction, and thus to building culture. This is why the "strong" spatial and structural design of the Kiesoffenhalle on the Attisholz site was the ideal venue for "The International fib Symposium on Conceptual Design of Structures 2021."

This book combines practice, research, and education, linking these areas in a cycle that allows knowledge and experience to grow reciprocally. This book is not a typical record of the conference proceedings of the "Symposium on Conceptual Design of Structures 2021," but instead embodies the spirit of the evolution of the symposium and the succeeding exhibition. The content of the book condenses the underlying dialogues and the discursive phases in between the papers and contributions, which only hint at the layers required for Conceptual Design to be revealed. The selected articles provide a comprehensive, but by no means exhaustive, understanding of Conceptual Design for buildings. You – the readership with a strong affinity for building design – will hopefully be inspired to appreciate this important and complex phase of the design process by immersing yourself in the world of Conceptual Design and the variety of thoughts and ideas that can lead to remarkable concepts and appropriately executed structures.

With this in mind, the Society for Structural Engineering, as co-organizer of the symposium and supporter of the book project, wishes you an inspiring read.

Clementine Hegner-van Rooden, Massimo Laffranchi

PIERLUIGI D'ACUNTO
PATRICK OLE OHLBROCK
MIGUEL FERNÁNDEZ RUIZ

ON THE CONCEPTUAL DESIGN OF STRUCTURES

1 Arup, O.: (1986) Ove Arup & Partners, 1946–1986, Academy St. Martin's, London – New York, p. 9.

The deliberate creation of objects in our environment profoundly influences both the quality of our individual lives and the functioning of society as a whole. The ability of designers to produce impactful, effective, innovative, and inspiring designs holds immense significance for all of us. Central to the design process is conceptual work, the stage at which pivotal decisions are made that ultimately shape the outcome of a project. As highlighted by Ove Arup[1] in the context of engineering, this process defies scientific formalization and eludes precise definitions.

This book offers a pathway for investigating shared traits in the conceptual design of structures, while also providing valuable insights from accomplished artists, architects, and engineers. By delving into their diverse perspectives, projects, and reflections, we arrive at important lessons on understanding, implementing, and teaching this invaluable topic. The following reflections encapsulate our understanding of the conceptual design of structures and serve as a stepping stone for exploring the contents of this book.

An interplay between space and structure

Science studies particular events to find general law. Engineering makes use of these laws to solve particular problems. In this it is more closely related to art or craft; as in art, its problems are underdefined, there are many solutions, good, bad, or indifferent. The art is, by a synthesis of ends and means, to arrive at a good solution. This is a creative activity, involving imagination, intuition and deliberate choice.
— Ove Arup

At its core, the conceptual design of structures relies on the inherent relationship between space and structure. During the initial stages of design, the focus is not solely on achieving structural efficiency or material integrity; instead, it is a question of discovering synergies that transcend traditional disciplinary boundaries. This approach acknowledges that the conceptual design of structures goes beyond technical considerations and encompasses a broader exploration of spatial relationships and human perception. We believe that load-bearing elements should not be viewed as mere technical requirements, but as opportunities to define spatial and formal concepts. Comprehending the inherent physical logic of a load-bearing system allows the structure to be used to reinforce and define the overall design. This perspective highlights the potential for the structure to become an integral part of the architectural vision.

Arranging load-bearing elements in space requires a careful balance of architectural considerations and structural demands. The goal is to harness the architectural possibilities offered by these elements while simultaneously safeguarding their structural performance. An exemplary illustration of this holistic approach is the INES Innovation Center, collaboratively designed by architects Mauricio Pezo and Sofia von Ellrichshausen and structural engineer Luis Mendieta [PAGE 8]. In this project, the spatial configuration of the curved walls located at the four corners of the floor plan and the alternating openings in the slabs create a distinct spatial experience throughout the building. The use of curved walls not only regulates the spans of the slabs but also facilitates the creation of open and intimate spaces while providing lateral stability to the entire construction.

LEFT PAGE Interior view of the INES Innovation Center of the Universidad del Bío-Bío in Concepción, Chile, collaboratively designed by architects Mauricio Pezo and Sofia von Ellrichshausen and structural engineer Luis Mendieta.

The visibility or concealment of a structure is another critical factor that greatly influences the perception of space. Many exceptional buildings were designed with an intentionally hidden structure playing a supporting role in the background rather than taking center stage. One example of this is the Salk Institute, masterfully designed by architect Louis Kahn and structural engineer August Komendant, where concealed Vierendeel beams enable flexible and open horizontal spaces. Conversely, well-known cases exist where the structure assumes a prominent role, becoming the defining element that shapes the space. The Johnson Wax Building, conceived by architect Frank Lloyd Wright and structural engineer Mendel Glickman, serves as a prominent illustration of the interplay between space and structure. Despite the engineers' initial skepticism concerning the feasibility and efficiency of the mushroom-shaped columns in the main hall, this unconventional structural decision proved crucial in creating a captivating impression of space and light that would have been unattainable through a more conventional technical solution.[2]

An iterative, open-ended, and collaborative process

The conceptual design of structures is a dynamic and open-ended process that defies rigid boundaries and follows a nonlinear path. It is an iterative process that demands creativity, consideration of cultural background, sensitivity, and multidisciplinary dialogue. While certain sub-topics within the larger framework can be formalized, the overall process necessitates an exploratory and adaptable approach involving the designers' personal subjective decisions.

During the initial framing phase of conceptual design, the focus is on gathering relevant information, identifying criteria, and understanding any design constraints that may be present. This initial stage involves connecting the available data with the designers' knowledge base. During this phase, a key cognitive process is abstraction, in order to discern the relationship between essential parameters and aspects and to articulate the core design idea effectively.[3] In this early stage, it is crucial for designers to adopt assumptions that serve to simplify and problem-reduction strategies, ensuring a systematic and synthesis-oriented approach to the design problem as a whole. During the subsequent generation phase, designers engage in speculative thinking and produce initial conceptual proposals, often conveyed through sketches, written descriptions, hand calculations, or prototypes, as highlighted by Nigel Cross.[4] This stage enables a wide range of design options to be explored. Once a proposal is defined, it enters the evaluation phase. The design's performance is simulated and assessed against subjective and objective criteria. Although initial proposals may have shortcomings in some respects, they may also exhibit unexpected and valuable qualities worth preserving. Based on this evaluation, the existing idea is refined or discarded, and a new proposal is initiated. This iterative and reflective process – referred to as a "reflective conversation with the situation" by Donald Schön[5] – occurs in the minds of the designers and plays a fundamental role in addressing complex design challenges.

Effective dialogue and collaboration among different disciplines throughout the entire conceptual design phase is key to the success of a project. The synergy between the project designers is a decisive factor in devising any major architectural project, as the new stadium and sports facilities project for the 1972 Olympic Games in Munich impressively demonstrates **[PAGE 12, TOP]**.

---

[2] Giedion, S.: (1996) Raum, Zeit und Architektur, Birkhäuser, Basel, p. 273.

[3] Conzett, J.: (2007) Synthetisches Denken – Eine Strategie zur Gestaltung in Grenzüberschreitungen im Entwurf (Architekturvorträge der ETH Zurich), gta Verlag, Zurich.

[4] Cross, N.: (2006) Designerly Ways of Knowing, Springer.

[5] Schön, D.: (1983) The reflective practitioner: how professionals think in action, BasicBooks, New York.

Conceiving through models and tools

The conceptual design of structures relies heavily on modeling physical reality. Models play a critical role in abstracting, simulating, comprehending, and predicting various design aspects that may otherwise be ambiguous or concealed.[6]

As mediators throughout the design process, models provide designers with insights and the confidence to make informed decisions. Ever since Galileo's publication[7] in 1638, the field of structural design has maintained an inductive-deductive approach that combines empirical experimentation, physical models, and formalized mathematical descriptions.[8] In this context, designers must be acutely aware of the assumptions and limitations that underlie the theoretical foundations of their models. Visual models, such as sketches and drawings, hold significant importance in conceptual design. Drawing on Lawson's observations,[9] it can be argued that designers predominantly rely on visual and diagrammatic thinking as their primary mode of cognition, directly engaging with graphical information, as suggested by Kotnik and D'Acunto.[10] This visual approach empowers designers to comprehend and manipulate information effectively.

A combination of analog and digital models is commonly employed in the contemporary conceptual design of structures. Analog models, such as sketches, hand calculations, and physical models, provide a high level of interactivity, allowing for meaningful associations and interpretations. These models focus on the fundamental aspects of the design, emphasizing simplicity and precision, as noted by Paul Gauvreau **[PAGES 62-69]**. Analog sketching and drawing harness the remarkable potential of the human hand, acting as a bridge between the designer's imagination and the emerging image, as highlighted by Juhani Pallasmaa.[11] Physical models allow design concepts to be tested in a space and provide a tangible connection to the material characteristics **[PAGE 13]**. On the other hand, digital models, including technical drawings, parametric models, renderings, and computer-based simulations, offer enhanced precision and replicability while providing a straightforward way to study the impact of design changes. However, they often require significant data and may limit associations and interpretations. As a result, digital models and computer-based tools are particularly valuable when the design concept has reached a certain level of maturity. In this context, Matthias Rippmann emphasizes the potential of new intuitive digital modeling tools within the conceptual design of structures, particularly those based on strut-and-tie models and graphic statics.[12] These computational tools possess the potential to enhance clarity, speed, and interactivity, opening up new possibilities for designers.

A synergy between form, forces, and materials

The conceptual design of structures relies on the interplay between the equilibrium of forces, the expression of the form, and the effective use of materials. Recognizing this vital relationship is essential, as the form of a building and its structural and material behavior are inherently related.[13] Accordingly, the design process often revolves around how the equilibrium of forces within a structure can be ensured through form and materials. A brilliant example of this concept is provided by the Salginatobel Bridge near Schiers **[PAGE 12, BOTTOM]**, a masterpiece created by Robert Maillart through the innovative use of graphic statics.[14]

---

6 Addis, W.: (2013) "'Toys that save millions' – a history of using physical models in structural design," Structural Engineer 91(4), pp. 12–27.

7 Galilei, G.: (1638) Discorsi e dimostrazioni matematiche intorno a due nuove scienze.

8 Schwartz, J.: (2011) "Teaching," in Co-operation: The Engineer and the Architect, Birkhäuser.

9 Lawson, B.: (1994) Design in mind, Butterworth Architecture, Oxford – Boston.

10 Kotnik, T. and D'Acunto, P.: (2013) "Operative Diagramatology: Structural Folding for Architectural Design," in Rethinking Prototyping, Proceedings of Design Modelling Symposium 2013, Springer.

11 Pallasmaa J.: (2009) The Thinking Hand: Existential and Embodied Wisdom in Architecture, Wiley.

12 Rippmann, M.: (2016) "Funicular Shell Design: Geometric Approaches to Form Finding and Fabrication of Discrete Funicular Structures," PhD thesis, ETH Zurich.

13 Dieste E.: (1996) "Technology and under development," in Eladio Dieste, 1943–1996, Consejería de Obras Públicas y Transportes Junta de Andalucia, Seville, pp. 259–266.

14 Fivet, C. and Zastavni, D.: (2012) "The Salginatobel bridge design process by Robert Maillart (1929)," Journal of the International Association for Shell and Spatial Structures 53(1), pp. 39–48.

15 Engel, H.: (2013) Tragsysteme – Structure Systems (Fifth Edition), Hatje Cantz Verlag, Ostfildern.

16 Adriaenssens, S., Block, P., Veenendaal, D. and Williams, C.: (2014) Shell Structures for Architecture: Form Finding and Optimization, Taylor & Francis – Routledge, London.

17 Otto, F.: (1990) Mitteilung des Instituts für leichte Flächentragwerke: Experimente. IL 25, Universität Stuttgart.

18 Fivet, C. and Brütting, J.: (2020) "Nothing is lost, nothing is created, everything is reused: structural design for a circular economy," The Structural Engineer 98(1), pp. 74–81.

19 Heyman, J.: (2019) "The structural engineer's view of ancient buildings," Journal of Materials and Structures 13(5), pp. 609–615.

Various approaches exist to articulating the causal connection between form, forces, and materials. Form-active structures[15] employ specific geometries to achieve static equilibrium and a smooth flow of forces. These structures often feature curved or double-curved shapes generated through a systematic process of form-finding.[16] The resulting forms are often not only expressive and elegant but also highly efficient in terms of their material utilization. However, even pioneers like Frei Otto acknowledged the challenges associated with this integral structural design approach. While form-active structures provide a certain level of force control, they may struggle to address the functional and spatial complexities typically encountered in building projects.[17] Conversely, vector-active systems[15] rely on linear elements in order to attain static equilibrium. The geometry and topology of these linear members, which are predominantly subjected to axial stress, are key to effectively partitioning forces. Section-active structures,[15] on the other hand, utilize rigid elements like beams, walls, frames, and slabs. The equilibrium of these systems is contingent on mobilizing tension, compression, and shear stresses within the same cross section. Unlike form-active structures, vector- and section-active systems do not necessarily require form-finding, allowing for easier integration of functional and architectural considerations.

Ultimately, it is crucial to acknowledge that most designed objects exhibit static redundancy, presenting an array of potential distinct equilibrium states. This characteristic empowers designers to more precisely manage the flow of forces, which provides a significant advantage during the initial design phase.

Using resources effectively

Structural engineers and architects bear a great responsibility for the significant impact that structures and infrastructures have on the environment and on society. It is, therefore, essential for them to promote the effective use of resources and to support sustainable design practices [PAGES 192-197].

When dealing with existing structures, the preferred approach is to prioritize their reuse and refurbishment whenever feasible.[18] In this context, an outstanding example is provided by the Zeitz Museum of Contemporary Art Africa (MOCAA) in Cape Town, designed by the architecture firm Heatherwick Studio in collaboration with the structural engineering firm Arup [PAGE 15, TOP]. It is important to recognize that existing buildings often possess an unexploited load-bearing potential beyond what conventional calculations may suggest.[19] Hence, before embarking on creating any new construction, the primary consideration should be whether a new building is necessary or whether, instead, an existing structure can be adapted and repurposed. However, embracing the philosophy of reuse brings with it certain challenges and risks, as reliable and complete knowledge of the mechanical properties of an existing structure is never guaranteed. In most cases, it will be essential to employ advanced survey and analysis methods and tools in order to adapt and repurpose an existing structure successfully.

In the realm of new buildings and infrastructure, designers should strive to challenge the constraints of the project brief and to use resources efficiently. This ambition should encourage them to question conventional rules and practices in the interests of developing innovative solutions. The conceptual design of structures should remain unbiased regarding the choice of construction technologies to employ. It should be context-sensitive, seeking to harmonize the functional, environmental, and structur-

TOP Determining the ideal shape of a shell subjected to compressive membrane forces by using a reverse model in tension based on Heinz Isler's "hanging cloth reversed" method. Model developed by Heinz Isler with a cloth impregnated with water and then frozen during the night.

LEFT PAGE, TOP Heinz Isler, Fritz Auer, Frei Otto, Jörg Schlaich, Fritz Leonhardt, Rudolf Bergermann and Knut Gabriel (from left to right) discussing the project of the Olympic Stadium in Munich in 1968.

LEFT PAGE, BOTTOM The Salginatobelbrücke near Schiers, designed by Robert Maillart and completed in 1930, exemplifies the graceful integration of form, forces, and materials.

al requirements of the various structural elements with the properties of the source materials [PAGE 15, BOTTOM]. Moreover, it is important to prioritize the aspects of durability, enhanced deformation capacity, and structural robustness. By adhering to these fundamental principles, designers can minimize the need for continuous construction maintenance and make valuable contributions to the long-term sustainability and resilience of the built environment. Embracing these principles enables designers to actively shape a more sustainable and resource-efficient future, in which structures strongly commit to environmental consciousness and social responsibility.

Our common responsibility

The conceptual design of structures plays a vital role in ensuring the long-term structural integrity and functionality of buildings. To fulfill this responsibility effectively, a profound understanding of theoretical knowledge and practical expertise is essential. While textbooks provide valuable insights, true mastery is achieved through repeated hands-on practice.

A comprehensive understanding of the discipline's history is vital for generating innovative concepts. In this context, history represents an invaluable tool for envisioning the future. As emphasized by Tullia Iori [PAGES 146-153], it is crucial to follow the footsteps of those who came before us, building upon their knowledge, experience, and legacy. Countless structural designers, scientists, and architects who came before us offer invaluable examples. Furthermore, it is of the utmost importance that we embrace the potential and the challenges presented by new emerging materials, methods, and technologies. This requires that we maintain a vigilant and inquisitive mind-set within the realm of the conceptual design of structures. Even the smallest details can hold great significance, and remarkable outcomes can be achieved by paying attention to them.

Addressing existing crises is not merely a necessity but also an opportunity to foster innovation and resilience. Designing with the interests of society in mind requires that we recognize the deep impact our designs have on future generations [PAGES 162-169]. Education and interdisciplinary collaboration are foundational pillars of this pursuit as we strive to create a sustainable and harmonious planet for all.

RIGHT PAGE, TOP Zeitz Museum of Contemporary Art Africa (MOCAA) in Cape Town after the renovation of the 57-meter-high historic grain silo by the architecture office Heatherwick Studio in collaboration with the structural engineering office Arup.

RIGHT PAGE, BOTTOM The METI School, a two-story school building made of earth and bamboo in Rudrapur, Dinajpur District, Bangladesh. The building was designed by the architects Anna Heringer and Eike Roswag, who was also responsible for the technical planning.

INTRODUCTION

AURELIO MUTTONI
JOSEPH SCHWARTZ

CONCEPTUAL DESIGN OF STRUCTURES IN PRACTICE, RESEARCH, AND TEACHING

As authors of this text, we have had the good fortune, following our common education, to spend several decades working in the field of structural engineering, with particular emphasis on conceptual design. Through collaborations on various projects with different architects and professionals and through research and teaching roles at the university level, we tried to pass on our passion for structural design to the younger generations of engineers and architects. We strongly believe that practice, research, and teaching are highly linked in the context of conceptual design of structures. Intending to promote dialogue on the topic of conceptual design, we enthusiastically initiated the fib Symposium on Conceptual Design of Structures 2021 in Attisholz (Switzerland). During our preparation for that conference and during the days we spent in Attisholz, we discussed at length precisely what structural design is – and is not. It soon became evident that there were as many definitions of conceptual design as there were participants at the conference.

The definition of a structure, however, is easier to agree on. The purposes of a structure depend, in fact, on its use and its function. In many cases, load-bearing structures help create architecture by shaping a space or organizing it – this is one of the meanings of the word "structure" in some languages; "to structure a space" is a synonym of "to organize a space." The conceptual design of structures can therefore not be detached from the general activity of architectural design and is often intimately linked to architecture. On the other hand, it is difficult to imagine designing a structure without understanding how it works. Understanding internal forces and learning how to creatively intervene regarding an initial structural choice to increase its efficiency and make it more compliant with other design requirements is not enough if one is to know how to design. Knowing the history of structures – i.e., how they have evolved according to the materials available, the possible construction methods, the ever-changing relationship between the cost of materials and the cost of labor, etc. – and understanding the link between structure and architecture – i.e., how the structure can contribute to creating a space and structuring it, for example – are equally necessary if one is to be able to design.

It is precisely this circumstance that makes the design process so interesting, but also so challenging. Without a high level of competence in one's own discipline, a team player cannot make a good contribution. Being open to the other disciplines is just as important. It is like a team sport. Not everyone has the same talents and abilities for tackling the various tasks, and it is a matter of deploying and positioning the players so as to achieve the best results. It is obvious that the clear allocation of roles and the competence of each individual player on the one hand and good teamwork and communication among the individual players on the other is what makes a successful team. The human aspects also play a role that should not be underestimated: mutual recognition, respect, and trust are elements that are very conducive to the design process. In many of our projects, we have been amazed to discover that, when the aforementioned qualities are

LEFT PAGE Canopy of the Jan Michalski Foundation dedicated to writing and literature at Montricher, Switzerland (with Mangeat-Wahlen architects, Muttoni and Fernández civil engineers, A. Muttoni structural designer): development of an innovative slab structure to better meet the architectural challenges present, a few exchanges of ideas, and sometimes even just one extremely concise sentence, have sufficed to conceive the main design idea and thus the basis for the project. This mutual understanding between the individual disciplines requires a common language. In this respect, graphic statics can make a good contribution to education and practice, and can give architects and engineers a strong intuitive understanding of the load-bearing structures, regardless of their complexity from the point of view of the civil engineers' way of thinking in terms of analytical statics. The methodology is ultimately based on the craft of drawing, and thus on the most fundamental craft of architects (and engineers).

Based on the considerations above, we can now try to formulate a personal definition of conceptual design:

"The term 'Conceptual Design of Structures' denotes the intellectual activity of developing a highly appropriate structural solution – in terms of structural system, shape, materialization, construction method, detailing, etc. – for a given purpose in a defined context. When related to buildings, it follows the programmatic idea of a reconciliation between the disciplines of engineering and architecture through the reciprocal integration of load-bearing structure and architectural design concept, with a unified understanding of the interplay of form and load-bearing capacity. This activity is nurtured by knowledge of the functioning of structures and of construction history – although it should never be limited to uncritically applying already known solutions."

We know that, in the past, great architects learned how to design either by working in the workshops of the great masters, by studying architectural treatises, or by observing and reflecting the masterpieces of their time. In the Renaissance, this was the case not only for great architects, but for all those active in the arts and sciences. Leonardo da Vinci for instance, who was active as a painter, draftsman, sculptor, engineer, scientist, and architect, spent several years in Verrocchio's workshop at Florence. On the other hand, he was a great collector of ancient treatises, which he studied with great care. From the 18th century onward, training took place mainly in schools. This was necessitated by the increase in theoretical knowledge and by the prevalence of theoretical foundations and calculation in the training of engineers. As we know, although particularly important when calculations for structures was performed manually and required very specific knowledge, this later proved to be counterproductive, leading to the professions of architect and engineer becoming separated and to a progressive decrease in the importance of the creative component of the project for the latter.[1]

The importance of theoretical knowledge has not diminished, and academic training is therefore still necessary and indispensable today. However, it is not sufficient: it must be supplemented by apprenticeship with architects and engineers capable of designing, by possessing the curiosity to know and to understand that the most remarkable works shall never diminish, and by the study of theoretical texts, which should always be a source of inspiration and questioning, especially today when all the certainties are so changeable.

Our education

Our common education has strongly influenced our subsequent experiences and professional activities.

[1] Muttoni, A.: (2011) The Art of Structures, EPFL Press.

In my case (AM), the years preceding my university education had contributed to my training as a designer. My older brother studied architecture and started his own design office when I was still in my teens. My predisposition towards manual activities made me passionate about building his architectural models and this brought me closer to the creative activities of architects. I often followed my brother to discussions with colleagues, and I found it exciting that topics assigned to architecture students led to lively discussions and often very diverse design solutions, all with their own logic. My brother was also a subscriber to a journal *(L'Architettura - Cronaca e Storia)* that presented engineering projects, which were often also very exciting. The projects by Morandi, Musmeci and Nervi that I used to discuss with my brother left a mark. The fascination for the design component which could be prevalent even in the work of engineers – in combination with the technical-scientific component, which I also loved – motivated me to undertake the study of civil engineering.

In my case (JS), I had had much less contact with the profession prior to my studies. In my childhood, my technical and handicraft talents were already pronounced and I would build objects with great joy and tenacity – especially with wood – without much external influence. I liked to work creatively, with rudimentary plans made by myself, and I always tried to achieve as much as possible with the little material I had at my disposal, and with a certain cleverness. I am convinced that this constant training, which was carried out independently with great enthusiasm, shaped me for my future profession and helped determine my career choice. In my case, during my civil engineering studies at ETH, I was never in close proximity to architecture. My first contact with real-life cooperation happened during the time of our doctoral studies. I shared the office with AM, and I was thus able to experience how he would study drawings of his brother's projects in the evening, critically analyze them and, after some calculations, would discuss and help develop the projects with his brother on the phone. I then started reading publications and looking at his buildings, and I progressively developed a fascination for the architecture of the Ticino School.

In our common study at ETH Zurich, we had the great fortune to have excellent professors. Pierre Dubas, who taught on metal structures, had an incredible ability to combine explaining very complex differential equations with commentary on many slides showing practical cases, from the general concept to the most minute details, and always tried to highlight the link between theoretical analyses and practical solutions. Hugo Bachmann and Bruno Thürlimann's great merits were, respectively, the former's exhaustive and the latter's extremely rigorous treatment of the functioning of reinforced concrete structures. Perhaps the most important figure, however, was Christian Menn. We were fascinated by his ability to explain the statics of structures so clearly and, at the same time, to convey to us the pleasure of designing a structure. In fact, the discussions we had at the drawing board, where he would ask us to justify our choices, with his improvements made in pencil on our drawings, were very similar to our later experiences in architecture schools. Menn was a very precise, analytical, practicing bridge-builder in the tradition of Robert Maillart, with an extraordinary sense of formal and topological creative will. He was a demanding master lecturer in structural engineering and bridge construction, setting very high standards in everything and never completely satisfied with his own works. For us, Menn, the eternal seeker, was a reflection of the ambivalence and incomprehensibility of the aesthetics in the built structures, but also of the fascination of unattainable perfection. All of this showed us the culturally rich professional world – in addition to the technical one – that was open to us as young prospective students.

Our experience in research and practice

We both chose to continue our education by taking a PhD under the supervision of Bruno Thürlimann, spending more than six years working side by side. Thürlimann was a born scientist par excellence, with a great feeling for practice. He was primarily interested in the practical application of mechanics and limit analysis, and had an excellent command of elasticity and plasticity theory. As an advocate of the use of new design principles taking into account plastic material behavior, he vigorously promoted the development of research in this field. Many things were in a state of upheaval in the 1980s, and both Thürlimann and Menn showed us that in the history of engineering, everything is in motion and will always continue to move on. Thürlimann's way of thinking helped us to more truly understand the actual behaviors involved when dealing with load-bearing structures. We also learned that for simple elements, an extremely rigorous analytical treatment could be accompanied by a graphical visualization with stress fields that were very easy to understand despite the complexity of the analytical analysis. It was therefore a very efficient apprenticeship in exercising intuition regarding the behavior and functioning of reinforced concrete structures.

We took full advantage of the great academic freedom we were given. We were both interested in the design of reinforced concrete structures using the stress fields method, developing and offering exercises and courses to the students. If we could already deal with simple examples for 2D-planar cases rigorously, why not do so with complex structures and in space? This idea came to us upon discovering the approach of Jörg Schlaich and co-workers, who proposed a treatment based on the theory of elasticity but with a solid intuitive component, i.e., the so-called strut-and-tie method.[2]

Based on limit analysis, moreover, we felt we could do better: the functioning of a structure can be selected so that, at the ultimate limit state, it will behave exactly as had been determined in designing it. This bridges the gap between design and analysis, with few limits on creativity during design. Furthermore, it is possible to develop a rigorous method that makes it easy to optimize a structure or to obtain its load-bearing capacity by comparing the two limits inherent to the theory. We soon realized that the stress fields and the strut-and-tie models were two sides of the same coin: both could be used at the same time, making it possible to study equilibrium and determine the internal forces in a very simple way. It was in this context that we appealed to the old and simple method of graphical statics that was in vogue in the 19th century, which made it possible to visualize the stresses and thus the functioning of a structure. This initially resulted in a textbook for students that we drafted with Thürlimann in 1988. Later, when we had already been in practice for some time, a book followed.[3]

We both had the opportunity to join engineering firms as partners – firms where exciting projects would be worked on with the relevant actors in design and construction. The seed that was sown during our studies and research was now able to sprout and bring theory and practice together. Our experience in education and practice was extremely formative. It allowed us not only to "see" the internal compressive and tensile forces in a structure, but also to design a structure with a shape that best met the different requirements, and at the same time to dimension the most severely stressed elements in a simple and consistent way. The design of a structure – independent of the building material – no longer had to go through tedious iterations, passing through a complex analysis and ending with

[2] Schlaich, J., Weischede, D.: (1982) A Practical Method for the Design and Detailing of Structural Concrete, CEB Bulletin No. 150.

[3] Muttoni, A., Schwartz, J. and Thürlimann, B.: (1997) Design of Concrete Structures with Stress Fields, Birkhäuser.

an iterative correction of the shape in the most stressed parts. Instead, it could start with the design of a set of internal forces and continue with the dimensioning of the material required to carry these forces, with the final shape and the required reinforcement as the direct result. This advantage proved to be essential over the years that followed, as we worked intensively with several architects on very different projects.

The awareness that we can largely dictate to a structure how it will work made us agile in the initial discussions with the architects, and ultimately allowed us to influence the holistic design in an active way. Additionally, the realization that the tectonics of loading and carrying can be worked on with the same tools as the tectonics of joining – namely with strut-and-tie models and stress fields – facilitated discourse with architects and often helped in developing simple rules related to the use of the structure to strengthen the architecture. All of this has made it possible to have a pleasant intellectual collaboration with architects, even if the intensity of this collaboration can vary greatly depending on the architect and the task. The following examples represent a selection of our work in this context.

Jan Michalski Foundation, Montricher, Switzerland. The architectural idea behind this project was to suspend small houses that accommodate writers in residence at the foundation from a canopy covering an area of around 6000 m². The structure thus contains the suspension points for the small houses, but it also has the function of creating a space that links them to the library, an exhibition room, and an auditorium. For the canopy, the architects and engineers hesitated for a long time between a grid of beams and a perforated plate: neither solution was adequate to meet the challenges of the project. Following lengthy discussions, we developed an innovative structure. The material – in this case concrete – is arranged according to the stress trajectories produced in a slab by the application of loads towards the supports, here formed by a forest of tall, slender columns [PAGE 16]. This design is derived from the research carried out by the structural designer since the 1980s in the context of the actual behavior of slabs and the analogies with shells, a method based on shear fields. In simple cases [PAGE 22, TOP LEFT, UPPER DIAGRAM], the shear field is fairly predictable. On the contrary, for slightly more complex situations, the shear field describes intriguing paths that may even seem counter-intuitive [PAGE 22, TOP LEFT, LOWER DIAGRAM]. For the Jan Michalski Foundation canopy [PAGE 22, TOP RIGHT], the material was arranged along these paths. The result is a structure that highlights the focal position of the support columns towards which the ribs converge, but which does not exhibit a rigid grid that would be inconsistent with the architectural idea. This project is an interesting example: not only the form, but also the overall structural system can be generated from considerations regarding the load-bearing behavior of the structure.

Bahrain Pavilion Dubai Expo 2020. Christian Kerez consulted me (JS) after first having tried to develop the idea of a spatial structure generated from thin Mikado-like columns with local engineers. The initial approach failed because it had not been implemented as an interdisciplinary collaboration. The architects tried to enhance the spatial quality of the "forest" of bars, whereas the engineers modeled the system as appropriate and carried out conventional verifications, encountering several buckling issues with the slender bars. The more additional bars they introduced and the more they enlarged the cross sections, the more the static problems became apparent. We suggested developing a simple and consis-

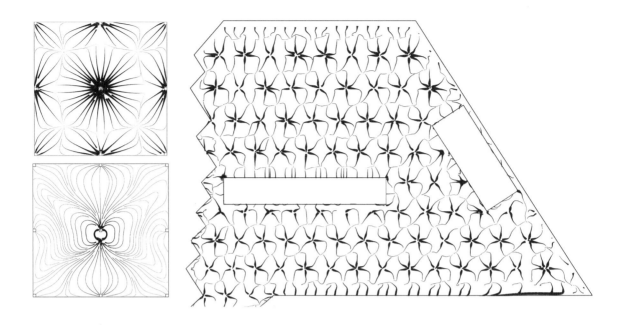

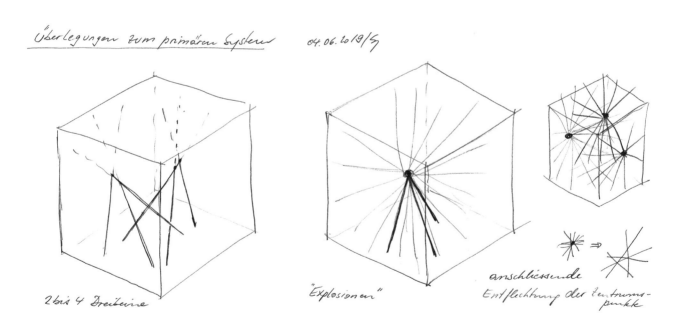

TOP **Canopy of the Jan Michalski Foundation dedicated to writing and literature at Montricher, Switzerland (with Mangeat-Wahlen architects, Muttoni and Fernández civil engineers, A. Muttoni structural designer): a – shear field for simple case and, b – for slightly more complex boundary conditions, c – shear field for the canopy of the project**

BOTTOM **Bahrain Pavilion Dubai Expo 2020 (with Christian Kerez Architects, J. Schwartz structural designer): example where a simple statical concept (represented in the sketch) could solve the complexity of the design problem and could provide rules for the architectural design. Pictures of the final project can be found on pages 102–103.**

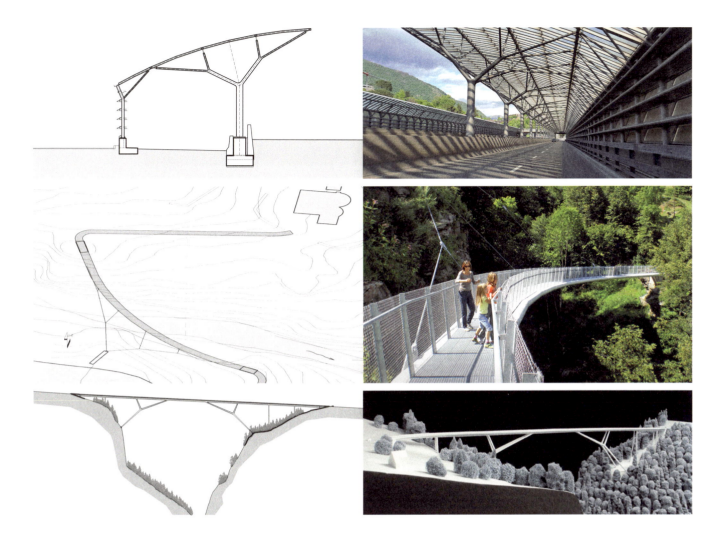

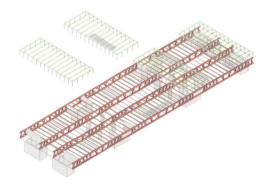

Three examples where the equilibrium with graphic statics was essential to shape the structure and led to a similar structural system for very different structures:

FIRST ROW **Noise protection structure at Chiasso (Grignoli Muttoni Partners civil engineers, A. Muttoni structural designer, Mario Botta architect)**

SECOND ROW **Footbridge Negrentino (Lurati Muttoni Partner civil engineers, A. Muttoni structural designer, Martino Pedrozzi architect)**

THIRD ROW **Design competition for the Tamina bridge (2nd prize, Lurati Muttoni Partner with Fürst Laffranchi).**

FOURTH ROW **Building of the Zug Public Transportation Company (Graber Steiger Architects and J. Schwartz structural designer). Through the stacking of volumes generated by trusses, column-free interiors with maximum flexibility were developed.**

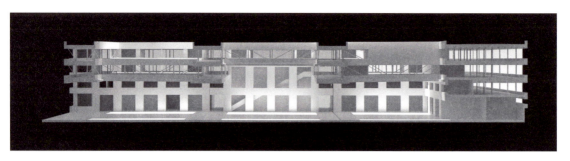

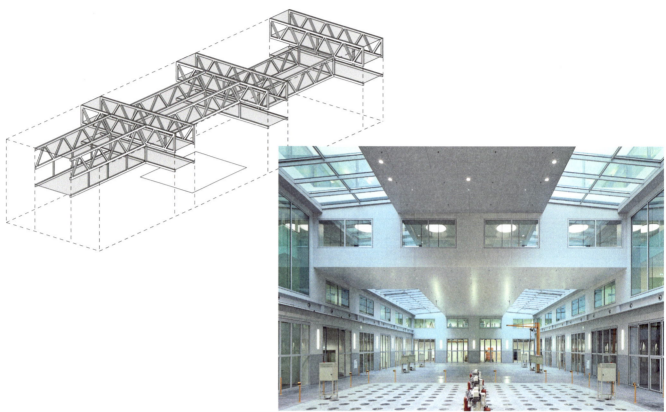

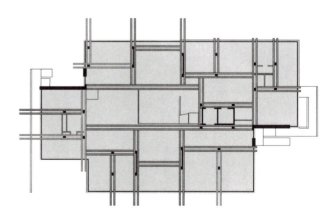

TOP/CENTER Hilti Innovation Center (with Giuliani Hönger Architects and J. Schwartz structural designer) is a multifunctional office, laboratory, and research building which offers a high degree of flexibility of use as well as the possibility of expansion.

BOTTOM Nolax Innovation House 2019 (with Deon Architects, J. Schwartz structural designer): an example in which the spatial structure reinforces the architectural idea and in which synergies have been found between architecture, engineering, and building services

tent concept first. The prerequisite was to establish rules that could serve as guidelines for the design during the discussion with the architects. We proposed developing tripods **[PAGE 22, BOTTOM]** with their highest points located about halfway up the building, their bars extending to the flat roof or to the façades. In addition, these tripods were to be connected by lying bars at their highest points. We then estimated the forces in the tripods, neglecting the buckling of the rods, and realized that these forces were small and required very small cross sections. Subsequently, we used additional secondary and tertiary bars **[PAGE 101]** to stabilize the bars of the tripods and to support the façades and roof beams as efficiently as possible. Second-order theory was used, permitting the yielding and thus even the buckling of individual members.

It was interesting to observe how the structural and architectural design requirements intertwined and how an improvement of the bearing structure often led to a better architectural design **[PAGES 102-103]**. At the end of the process, we had to admit that the simple concept was key to bringing this complex project to successful realization.

Bifurcating Structures. How do you connect a support to a bridge deck or a roof when it has to be supported at several points? This structural theme links these three quite different projects, in the sense that it is the decomposition and bifurcation of forces in space that leads to the structural solution. The first project refers to a noise protection barrier along a motorway over a length of almost two kilometers **[PAGE 23, FIRST ROW]**. Because this infrastructure is located in an urban environment, architect Mario Botta had the idea of designing the noise protection as an avenue of trees. The geometry of the tree-like structure was defined on the basis of equilibrium using graphic statics, enabling simple and effective optimization. The second example is a curved pedestrian footbridge providing access to the Romanesque 13th-century church of Negrentino for people with reduced mobility **[PAGE 23, SECOND ROW]**. The deck is supported on one side only. Running between a concrete block anchored in the rocky massif and six connecting points on the outside of the bridge deck, a system of cables is defined using graphic statics. The third example, strongly influenced by the previous projects, refers to a large bridge with a span of 235 m and with the deck more than 200 m above the valley bed **[PAGE 23, THIRD ROW]**. The idea was to develop the system supporting the deck as a single system with a higher degree of geometric freedom than in classical arch bridges. These three projects show that the same design tools can be used more or less consciously for quite different cases, enabling interesting and original solutions to be developed.

Structuring Space. These three examples illustrate strategies for how to articulate and strengthen various spatial and functional relationships with the structure. The design of the new Building of the Zug Public Transportation Company **[PAGE 23, FOURTH ROW]** ensures multilayered legibility through its differentiated permeable structure, and is thus able to mediate between the different scales of the surroundings. The proposed typology, with its courtyards, roof gardens, and terraces, enriches the workplaces and ensures a consistently balanced supply of daylight despite considerable room depths. By stacking volumes generated by trusses, column-free interiors with maximum flexibility were developed. The Hilti Innovation Center in Schaan **[PAGE 24, TOP]** is a multifunctional office, laboratory, and research building. The aim was to offer a high degree of flexibility of use as well as the possibility of expansion. The project planning team felt that it was important to develop a structural system that would take different and specific spatial situations as a starting point and merges them into a compact whole. The load-bearing structure plays a space-defining role and creates a strong spatial order. For the Nolax House [PAGE 24, BOTTOM] the load-bearing structure and the spatial concept form an inseparable unit with flowing, multifunctional rooms of different modes without circulation zones. Thanks to the cooperation between architects and engineers from the concept phase all the way through to execution, a strong structure was created, the expression of which is further strengthened by the materialization of the wood-concrete composite construction method. These three projects demonstrate successful interdisciplinary collaborations between architects and engineers and a careful design with respect to multiple facets.

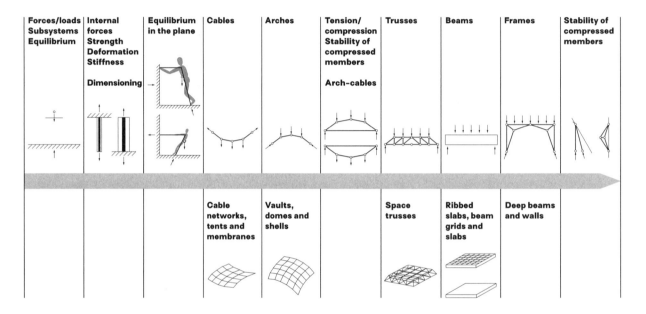

Teaching structural design

Our own teaching in the field of conceptual structural design has always been strongly influenced by our background and by the experience we have gained during a lifetime of research and practice. In our book *Design of Concrete Structures with Stress Fields,*[3] we succeeded for the first time in modeling reinforced concrete structures based on a consistent theory and in a very uniform way. Design and structural behavior could thus be combined into a single unit. At the same time, visualization of the internal forces was a matter of course for both the tectonics of bearing and the tectonics of joining. This also provided the basis for the book *The Art of Structures,* which provides architects and structural engineers with a very visual understanding of the load-bearing behavior of all kinds of structural typologies.[1] This view made it possible to explain every type of structure in a simple manner, not only in such a way that the load-bearing behavior becomes comprehensible, but even making it possible to estimate the necessary dimensions. With this in mind, this book starts with the structural systems which are easy to understand (cable systems, arches, shells), and not with the ones which are easier to calculate with common tools (e.g., beams [PAGE 26 CENTER]). In addition, presenting the functioning of structures offers an opportunity to present built representative case stud-

TOP The so-called path of structures shows in a graphical manner the table of content of the book *The Art of Structures*[1] in which all structural types are studied, from the simplest to the most complex ones.

ies, including the history of construction. We both used this concept as an introduction to structural design, as a powerful tool to introduce conceptual structural design in both disciplinary and interdisciplinary design courses.

Conclusion

Load-bearing behavior generally has a very abstract character. What is not immediately visible offers the magic of being there to explore. "Playing" with the internal forces presupposes understanding them, and perhaps it is oversimplified treatments of beam statics that on the one hand can serve as a powerful and useful tool for engineers, but on the other hand allows them to retreat to a "safe" place and hide behind the question of whether an already given structure "works" or not. What is then missing, however, is curiosity: the never-ending search for understanding, and, very often, the innovative development of load-bearing structures with an overarching objective. This consists of designing an interdisciplinary and unique structure that is also characterized by the engineer's handwriting. In this sense, the awareness that going beyond the familiar and quasi-standardized typologies of load-bearing structures such as beams, columns, slabs, shells, etc., and looking for structures in which the "flow" of the internal forces in space, often actually going beyond known topologies, is an excellent starting point, has helped us a great deal to free ourselves from common approaches to design and, more than that, gave us the confidence to intervene much more directly in dialogue with architects.

Ultimately, from our point of view, this is exactly what true structural design looks like: the development of a structure based on interdisciplinary formulated boundary conditions, from which criteria and synergies can be derived that serve as guidelines and guardrails for the design. In this way, the engineer's work becomes a true intellectual team task at the highest level. The contributions of the different team players can no longer be differentiated, and this results in structures in which the conceptual design and structural engineering concerns fully merge.

CHALLENGING GRAVITY

EXPOSED OR CONCEALED

LEARNING FROM THE PAST

COMMON RESPONSIBILITIES

As a structural engineer, I strongly believe that the conceptual design phase plays a leading role in shaping the performance of structures. This stage is of equal importance regardless of the project's scale, as every project – no matter how simple or small – presents an opportunity for creativity and innovation. From my perspective, conceptual design is not the mere result of a spontaneous burst of inspiration; instead, it arises from diligent, systematic, and ambitious efforts to discover the most suitable solution to a given problem. Inviting parallels with seemingly more artistic disciplines (e.g., architecture, literature, cooking, music, etc.), successful design processes in structural engineering are rooted in contextual understanding, informed by practical experience, and guided by fundamental principles. Combining this foundational knowledge with the latest developments in innovative tools and construction technologies may unlock unexpected results in the field of structural design.

This section contains several essays exploring the relationship between structure and architecture, as well as collaboration among professionals in the conceptual design stage. The discussions range from specific cooperations between artists, architects, and engineers to broader examinations of design principles and educational approaches. While the texts address various topics, they collectively emphasize the importance of informed decision-making, interdisciplinary collaboration, and the pursuit of innovative and well-integrated architectural and structural designs.

The interview featuring Janet Echelman and the engineers at SOM (Bill Baker and Alessandro Beghini) gives an exemplary picture of the interdisciplinary collaboration involved in crafting visually captivating net sculptures. These lightweight artistic pieces enable fluidity and scalability, while meticulous craftsmanship ensures seamless integration with buildings, guaranteeing a harmonious fusion of art and architecture.

Alejandro Bernabeu also explores the relationship between structure and architecture, presenting five ideas that shed light on their interconnectedness and the design process. The author emphasizes the potential of structure to be an opportunity for design improvement rather than an obstacle. Through artistic references and real-life projects, this text delves into the transformative power of structure, its capacity to shape space, and its role in optimizing designs. It also highlights how major structural requirements, such as high-rise buildings and large spans, can inspire innovative design solutions.

The role of structural design teaching in collaboration between architects and engineers is then explored in a roundtable discussion between engineers Christian Menn and Stefan Polónyi, invited by Joseph Schwartz at ETH Zurich. The discussion highlights the importance of bridging the gap between science and art in the two disciplines, as well as the need for architects and engineers to work closely, highlighting the importance of understanding and visualizing forces in the design process. The discussion emphasizes the value of communicating a sense of structural form to students and integrating architectural and structural considerations into the design process at an early stage.

Paul Gauvreau's essay advocates for the power of hand drawing and calculating as design tools. These apparently "old-fashioned" tools promote simplicity (which is consistent with low construction cost) and reflection, and avoids unnecessary complexity, leading to an improvement in designers' abilities to create. The challenge is to find the right balance between hand and computer for optimal design outcomes.

In their work, Kai-Uwe Bletzinger, Ann-Kathrin Goldbach, and Reza Najian investigate the design of new structural forms inspired by historical precedents using advanced computer methods for structural design, such as form finding through shape optimization.

This section ends with an essay by Patrick Ole Ohlbrock, Giulia Boller and Pierluigi D'Acunto on the role of computation in the conceptual design of structures. The text explores the complex and ambiguous nature of structural design, highlighting the iterative process involved in the generation and refinement of design concepts.

Covering a range of subjects, the essays presented in this section collectively enhance our comprehension of the intricate and uncertain characteristics of structural design. Undoubtedly, they emphasize the importance of making well-informed decisions, fostering collaboration across disciplines, and striving for inventive architectural and structural designs.

Leonardo Todisco

ENGINEERING AND ART – MOVING FORWARD TOGETHER

WILLIAM "BILL" BAKER, ALESSANDRO BEGHINI AND JANET ECHELMAN IN CONVERSATION WITH ROLAND PAWLITSCHKO

RP SOM and Janet Echelman have realized some very exciting projects with net structures, through a collaboration that goes back several years. What was the first project, and how did you get together?

AB We met Janet more or less coincidentally in 2013 while working on a project in West Hollywood, where we were designing and engineering a building complex with two hotel towers [PAGES 32, 36 TOP, 38]. There was a requirement for a piece of public art as part of the development, and our client hired a curator who engaged Janet to be the artist for a work that would be suspended between the two towers. At the same time, we were doing a deep dive on graphic statics and on the geometry of equilibrium – topics which also relate to Janet's work. We are still very interested in understanding the geometry of equilibrium, and Janet's art is a kind of vehicle to do that. Her artworks are beautiful sculptures, but also beautiful structures.

JE From the time I was selected to create this artwork, I began meeting very regularly with SOM's structural engineering team of Alessandro Beghini, Mark Sarkisian and Bill Baker. I already had a conceptual artistic idea: I wanted to create a dream catcher inspired by what we know about the state of dreaming. So I began research on the mapping of brainwave activity during periods of REM sleep and dreaming, and at the same time looking at the craftsmanship of Native American dream catchers, which can consist of many structural layers.

RP Janet, can you tell us more from your perspective about the design process with the engineers?

JE I found our exploration process exhilarating. SOM would share a wide variety of possibilities of what the structural layers could look like, and where they could be positioned with respect to the building. I started to sketch various ideas and send them back to Alessandro and Mark. They did markups on top of my drawings to show what worked or what had to be changed. After receiving SOM's sketches, I redrew and redraped the forms with a new geometry. We finally had four vertically stacked structural layers. This was the first time I had done a multilayered structure, which opened up a whole new range of aesthetic and expressive opportunities.

What's been unique for me in working with SOM is that we have a genuinely collaborative process. We are both pushing ourselves forward in order to open new doors and find the most elegant solutions to simultaneously achieve our aesthetic and structural goals. It's a very iterative and collaborative process.

RP Alessandro, can you describe the structure of the *Dream Catcher* in brief?

AB Principally, in the sculptures we have designed together so far, we are dealing with a horizontal structural layer of ropes and the colorful sculptural nets draped underneath. The uniqueness of the *Dream Catcher* is that some of these colorful nets are hyperbolic paraboloid forms connecting two structural net layers. This creates a direct relationship between all four layers, which are positioned at different heights between the two supporting towers, making the structural behavior more difficult to simulate. Wind forces do not just affect one structural layer; the wind is tensioning and slackening all of the layers in different ways. We did a number of numerical simulations just to understand how the forces would be redistributed on the different structural layers and how each would perform overall. We very quickly realized that we were dealing with very complex engineering challenges.

BB The way we form-find the geometry is reminiscent of the Olympic Stadium in Munich and of the methodologies established in the 1970s that are still valid in a way – for example, force-density. When you look at these roof structures, you're seeing a representation of the forces at the same time. You see the beauty of an honest structural expression. It's similar with the *Dream Catcher:* This structure shows very pure shapes and forms with so many layers, also intellectual ones. And the thing is, it's completely honest; you can't cheat at all.

RP Janet, you first worked with bronze-casting, but later became drawn to knotted fiber mesh. Why

PREVIOUS PAGE *Dream Catcher,* West Hollywood, California, USA, 2017.
SOM worked closely with artist Janet Echelman to create this mesh sculpture suspended above a public plaza at the Jeremy Hotel in West Hollywood. The 27-meter-tall sculpture is inspired by what we know about dreaming. It features brainwaves that can be electronically recorded while dreaming.

TOP *Everywhere the Edges,* performance installation at Princeton University (in progress)
With this project, engineers Sigrid Adriaenssens, Bill Baker, Alessandro Beghini and artist Janet Echelman want to explore structures that are in motion with the human body. Up to six dancers move simultaneously in, on, under, around and with a large net sculpture in an experimental dance.

are you so interested in lightweight structures? What makes them so fascinating?

JE   Lightweight structures fascinate me for multiple reasons. One is that lightweight structures enable fluidity and softness that allow for movement. It's that fluidity and the way our brains recognize the potential for movement and change of shape that makes the structures so mesmerizing. In addition, I just find them incredibly beautiful. These lightweight structures also make it possible to achieve monumental scale that enables an immersive art environment wider than our peripheral vision. Bigger is not necessarily better, but I'm trying to create an environment where you can get lost in the art and feel a sense of awe. Highly elegant and efficient structures enable the work to retain their delicacy at a monumental scale. This is critical for my work to function at the scale of the city, especially when it needs to be durable and resilient in all kinds of weather conditions including hurricanes, winds, ice storms, and snow.

RP   If you look at the detailing, are there any references to the fishing industry?

AB   From an analytical perspective, we know the mechanical properties of the ropes and, essentially, we are assuming that these ropes are connected to each other like in a structural net. The structural analysis we perform is really the same as in the design of any other structure. We look at the structural net as a continuum: we have various linear elements, such as ropes and chains, in the analysis model that are connected to each other. We look at the connection details and develop them in a later stage. These connections are rope splices, which are part of the long history of traditional maritime craftsmanship.

There are so many beautiful ways to splice a rope, especially when you consider different colors. We can harness the technology of the weaving industry and the fishing net industry. In the end, we use existing technologies to fabricate ropes and nets. Therefore, our specially made scale models or maquettes became very important – to be able to test the nets, to have the right number of meshes or the form that we expected. We learned a lot from these maquettes. It was a feedback loop to adjust our numerical computational model.

RP   If you attach nets like this to a building, do you see very large horizontal forces appear? And what do the transitions between the ropes and the house look like?

AB   Where the ropes are attached to the building, we typically have a chain or a steel wire with a steel ring that collects the ends of the ropes. In addition, there is typically a steel anchorage attachment element on the building. The chain or wire at the corner of the sculpture would connect to the steel anchorage system. The forces occurring at the end of the sculpture are significant, but not nearly as significant as the forces that we design buildings to withstand. Of course, if the building is a two-story wooden construction it may cause a problem, but in cases of a taller concrete or historical brick building, this is usually not a problem. We pay special attention to creating a smooth transition that ensures that the sculpture merges seamlessly and, in a sense, invisibly with the building. So, you will never see a large unsightly connection detail to the building that would distract from the sculpture. For the project in West Hollywood, as the architects and engineers, we could detail the building at the connection point around the sculpture. We were able to integrate the chain into the building: It disappears in the exposed slab edge and is connected to a steel plate that is cast inside the slab. At existing buildings, we try to conceal the chain in order to give the impression of effortlessness.

RP   How about *Earthtime 1.26* that you and Janet were able to install in Munich **[PAGES 36 BOTTOM, 40/41]**? A connection to an existing building was not possible.

AB   In Munich, we had a lot of restrictions on where to place the support points because the site was between an historic church, a castle, and entrances to a subway station. We cooperated with a Munich-based architect and engineer. At the end of the day, you have to work with the location and make the best of it. In Munich we couldn't touch any building because they are all historical. We could only use ballasts – very large concrete blocks that pedestrians barely notice, because they focus primarily on the sculpture floating above them. We came up with the most elegant solution possible, so even though the supports are more massive than sculptures at other locations, it's honest.

RP   Janet, are there other collaborations with structural designers?

JE   We are also doing collaborations in academia. For example, we are working at Princeton University to explore new ideas in a kind of basic research. The engineers Sigrid Adriaenssens, Bill Baker, Alessandro and my team are working with the choreographer Rebecca Lazier and a team of dancers **[PAGE 34]**. We're exploring how we can create structures that move and transform with the human body. It's one thing to bring one dancer into a net, but then it's a completely different thing to work with two or even three dancers who are all moving at the same time. This is a very complex

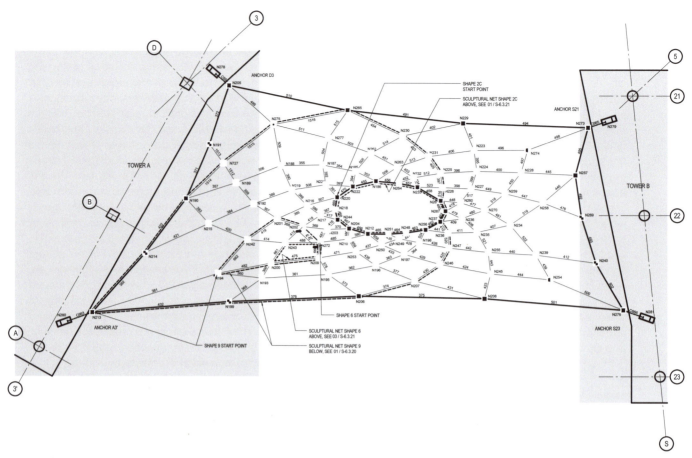

TOP *Dream Catcher,* West Hollywood, California, USA, 2017. This overview plan shows how ropes and nets are connected. When looking at the structures, one simultaneously sees the forces.

BOTTOM *Earthtime 1.26,* Munich, Germany, 2021. The connections are part of a craftmanship that goes back to the traditional way of the marine industry to splice a rope. For the realization of the project, existing technologies to produce ropes and nets were used.

engineering research endeavor. And we're also collaborating with scholars at MIT, Caitlin Mueller and John Ochsendorf, to develop new computational design tools that will enable us to design aesthetically while understanding how to keep the structure in equilibrium.

RP   What material are the ropes in your artworks usually made of?

JE   My earliest sculptures were made of dyed cotton and silk. Today, we are using a variety of highly engineered fibers: Aramid fibers, UHMWPE (Ultra high molecular weight polyethylene) with a physical polyester sleeve as a UV-protection, PTFE (Polytetrafluoroethylene), or high-tenacity nylon, because of its expressive range of color. We work with material engineers in the development of those fibers and their structural and color potential. The different color impressions are created by the combination of physical color within the yarns combined with projected colored lighting at night.

RP   How does SOM determine the structural design of the sculptures?"

AB   Regarding the form-finding software for the structural net, we use a code developed in-house that leverages the API (Advanced Programmer Interface) of existing structural software. The form finding process is based on the force density method. The code was developed using Matlab and reads and writes data from the S-Frame structural software. The S-Frame software is then used for the analysis of the structural ropes for the sculpture. The form finding of the sculptural net is done with a different custom piece of code that interfaces with Rhino for the input/output. The structural net software is completely different from the custom proprietary software Janet's studio developed to design her net sculptures. Basically, our models are precisely about the structural properties and behavior of the ropes, while Janet's models characterize the visual appearance of the sculpture.

RP   Is the arrangement of the structural ropes only possible in the way ultimately executed, or is there also some room for variation here?

AB   Janet's studio has collaborated with computer scientists and engineers to develop custom software that can simulate the soft-body dynamics of the sculptural net materials with a high degree of physical accuracy. The latest version of this software is capable of simulating nets with millions of small segments very quickly, allowing for rapid iterations and fine-tuning of the sculptural forms. The software also incorporates the constraints of the fabrication process in the simulation, including twine diameter, stiffness, weight, and specific looming constraints. This restricts the input parameters of the simulator to help ensure all the form-found nets are also buildable.

Regarding the structural net material, we typically use either single braid ropes (e.g., plasma 12 strand) or double braid (e.g., DV composite). For the rope arrangement, there are multiple solutions. However, every solution is defined by several rules. Some connections are very hard to fabricate. For example, it is hard to splice four ropes together at a single point. And the "cells" in the structural rope layer should not be triangular, but polygonal, to provide more geometric adjustability during installation. The cells can be a four-sided or a five-sided polygon. A triangle is very hard to stretch and has no flexibility, while a polygon gives you a lot of flexibility and adjustability. Steel ropes can be accurately sized and manufactured in precise lengths, and their static properties are also very well known. In contrast, the ropes of Janet's sculptures are hand-spliced, and their fabrication is very different from steel cables. In this manual fabrication process, the final rope lengths can differ from the design by several centimeters, so we need to account for adjustability in the design.

RP   How are the nets manufactured and finally built up on site?

AB   The net parts of the sculpture are machine-loomed. The sculpture is produced in panels that are assembled to create the net shape. In order to hang these pieces, you need a sister line, which is a smaller rope that is attached to the structural rope. In the fabrication facility, everything is joined, so when the sculpture gets to the site it consists of a single piece. The net is spread on the ground and lifted with one or more cranes. It's as simple as that.

TOP *Dream Catcher,* West Hollywood, California, USA, 2017. As architects and engineers, SOM could detail the building at the connection point around the sculpture. So they were able to integrate the net structure into the building: It disappears in the exposed slab edge and is connected to a steel plate that is cast inside the slab.

RIGHT PAGE *Skies Painted with Unnumbered Sparks,* Vancouver, Canada, 2014. In the fabrication facility, everything is joined, so when the sculpture gets to the site it consists of a single piece. The net is spread on the ground and lifted with one or more cranes.

NEXT PAGE *Earthtime 1.26,* Munich, Germany, 2021. In Munich, we could not connect to any buildings since they were all historical. Instead, very large concrete blocks were used to anchor the sculpture. The blocks were hardly noticed by pedestrians because they focused primarily on the sculpture floating above them.

ALEJANDRO BERNABEU LARENA

FIVE THOUGHTS ON THE RELATIONSHIP BETWEEN STRUCTURE AND ARCHITECTURE

Structure is a key element of any construction, assuring its stability and resistance. Furthermore, it also contributes to its design and configuration. Starting from this principle, this essay elaborates on five ideas relating to the relationship between structure and architecture and its design process, as points of reflection and design strategies. Each idea is introduced with an artistic reference point, relating architectural and structural design to artistic creative thinking and processes, and presented alongside projects in which the author has participated, as reference and application.

LEFT PAGE Chapel in Sierra la Villa. Villaescusa de Haro, Spain, 2021. Architecture: Sancho Madridejos Architecture Office; Structural design and engineering: Bernabeu Ingenieros

Structure as opportunity

Spanish abstract artist Antoni Tàpies once said he started a painting by drawing a line, tracing a gesture. The painting was then the attempt to correct that first line[1] **[PAGE 44]**. To create or to design something, a starting point, a requirement, a challenge is necessary.

Structural requirements related to resistance and stability function can be understood as obstacles and impediments that may affect or distort the initial design idea, but they can also be considered as starting points, opportunities to improve the design: structure as an opportunity to develop and to improve design, instead of a problem requiring a solution.[2,3] Structure has not to be an annoying requirement of the project, but a motivation for developing it further.

National Museum of Science and Technology. A Coruña, Spain. The National Museum of Science and Technology in A Coruña (Spain), designed by architects Victoria Acebo and Angel Alonso, was one of the first projects I was involved in, and the first time that I realized a structural requirement can turn into a design opportunity.[4]

The building's structure and its architectural spaces are jointly developed to give shape to its three main elements: the structural façade, the interior communication core eccentrically located within the plan, and a set of large box-like volumes, supported both at the interior core and at the perimeter façade **[PAGE 45, TOP/BOTTOM]**. The roof level, which closes off the volume of the building, is formed by a set of steel trusses. The internal volumes, made of reinforced concrete, grow from the concrete core and are supported at the façade perimeter by a delicate steel structure in a double skin. This perimeter façade takes the gravity loads and horizontal wind loads, which are transferred to the roof level and to the concrete box-like volumes.

The structural façade is formed by a set of battened steel columns – placed within the double skin façade – that assure lateral stability in the direction perpendicular to the façade. In the direction of the façade, however, they are required to be connected to the concrete volumes to assure lateral stability, and in some parts additional bracing was required. Instead of a traditional X-bracing, which would have broken the continuity and uniformity of the façade, single bracing elements were distributed throughout the façade, leading to an irregular and aleatory disposition **[PAGE 45, CENTER]**. These elements solve the structural bracing requirements and lend a surprising appearance to both the inside and the outside. Besides, the roof trusses were divided into two levels, alternatively deploying the diagonal elements either in the upper or in the bottom level, following a similar process of disarrangement.

[1] "I'm a person so full of doubts and so insecure in front of a blank canvas that when I make the first brushstroke, I have the impression that I've already made a mistake. And all the rest of the painting really consists of corrections that I make to put that first mistake right." Lamazares, A.: (1993) "Antoni Tàpies" – Interview, Ronda Iberia, Madrid.

[2] Bernabeu Larena, A.: (2008) "Estrategias de diseño estructural en la arquitectura contemporánea. El trabajo de Cecil Balmond," PhD Thesis, Universidad Politécnica de Madrid. https://oa.upm.es/910; Accessed 2 October 2023

[3] Bernabeu Larena, A.: (2013) "La estructura alterada," Tectónica (40), Madrid.

[4] Rinke, M. (ed.): (2019) *The Bones of Architecture: Structure and Design Practices.* Triest-Verlag, pp. 108–115.

TOP Antoni Tàpies, *Pintora malvats*, 1988

RIGHT PAGE National Museum of Science and Technology. A Coruña, Spain, 2012
Interior view and bracing arrangement
Architecture: acebo x alonso (Victoria Acebo, Angel Alonso); Structural design and engineering: NB35 Ingeniería

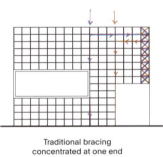

Traditional bracing
concentrated at one end

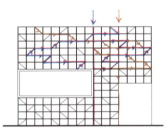

Muncyt bracing
distributed throughout the facade

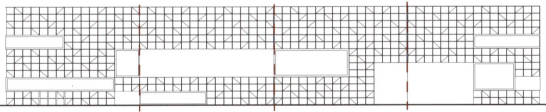

North Facade   West Facade   South Facade   East Facade

CHALLENGING GRAVITY

45

46 — FIVE THOUGHTS ON THE RELATIONSHIP BETWEEN STRUCTURE AND ARCHITECTURE

5 Merin, G.: (2014) "David Chipperfield's 'Sticks and Stones,' Toys with Van Der Rohe's Bones in Berlin," https://www.archdaily.com/552553/david-chipperfield-s-sticksand-stones-toys-with-van-der-rohe-s-bonesin-berlin. Accessed 2 October 2023.

6 Bernabeu Larena, A., Saéz Alonso, I., Gómez Mateo, J.: (2022) Facultad de Psicología de Málaga. Estructura mixta de grandes luces con apoyos a tresbolillo, VIII Congreso Internacional de Estructuras de la Asociación Española de Ingeniería Estructural (ACHE). Santander. Hormigón y Acero, volume 73.

Capacity of the structure to transform the space

Before starting the renovation of the Mies Van der Rohe Nationalgalerie in Berlin, the architect David Chipperfield presented the intervention *Sticks and Stones,* which involved deploying 144 tree trunks within the interior space, eight meters tall and perfectly aligned with the structural grid of the roof **[PAGE 46, TOP]**. A paradoxical intervention of introducing columns into a celebrated column-free open space, it reveals and highlights the capacity of the structure (columns in this case) to transform the space:

"There is nothing more complex or more simple than to arrange 144 columns in the most beautiful room in Berlin, and wait to see what it does, spatially [...] you see different symmetries, different spaces; you create rooms and vistas, and in a way that's what architecture is: it's nothing more than the arrangement of structure, walls, enclosure, view, shelter and material."[5]

Indeed, every structural element has a specific physical reality, and this corporeity affects the space in which it is located. Structure is not a mute element of the project – it necessarily participates in its spatial configuration. Proceeding from this reality, structural elements can be deployed and handled so that they remain hidden or unnoticed, or they can have a relevant presence and acquire prominence in the space in which they stand, and transform it.

Faculty of Psychology. Malaga, Spain. The Faculty of Psychology building in the University of Málaga, Spain, designed by LLPS architects, comprises a massive and compact three-heights volume. The architectural and structural configuration is determined by the more than 30 interior courtyards, which measure 18 × 3 m and are deployed in a staggered arrangement to allow the entrance of natural light **[PAGE 46, CENTER]**.

It took us lots of time and several trials to decide on what was the more convenient structure for this building. The major difficulty came from the staggered arrangement of the interior courtyards, which envisioned deploying structural supports only alternately at either side of the courtyard, allowing cross views through the courtyards. Several structural configurations and arrangements were considered, including continuous post-tensioned concrete slabs. Finally, a solution of composite steel beams and concrete deck was selected, following a complex configuration in which beams are supported one by the others, while they are eccentrically supported on the concrete courtyards' walls. This structural arrangement relates to the general configuration of the building and the interior courtyards, contributing and enhancing its presence[6] **[PAGE 46, BOTTOM]**.

The steel beams are deployed longitudinally at both sides of the courtyard, while transverse steel beams are only deployed alternately at one side or the other, depending on the support position. This configuration follows the same principle as the courtyards and supports arrangement, providing for a staggered distribution of the transverse beams. Additionally, the supports, made in concrete, are located outside in the courtyard, while the beams must be located inside so they do not interrupt the courtyard, generating eccentric beam-to-support and beam-to-beam connections, in a kind of reciprocal arrangement.

LEFT PAGE, TOP Installation *Sticks and Stones.* Neue Nationalgalerie Berlin, Germany, 2014 Architect: David Chipperfield

LEFT PAGE, CENTER/ BOTTOM University of Málaga, Faculty of Psychology. Málaga, Spain, 2022. Architecture: LLPS Arquitectos (Eduardo Pérez Gómez, Miguel Angel Sánchez); Structural design and engineering: Bernabeu Ingenieros

Optimized structures. Relation form – structure

The Marsyas installation at the Tate Modern, by the Indian artist Anish Kapoor, integrates space, color, shape, and structure[7] **[PAGE 49, TOP]**. The piece, on which he collaborated with structural engineer Cecil Balmond, is defined by a continuous structural PVC membrane that spans over 140 meters, almost the full length of the Turbine Hall. Since membrane structures can only support tension strains, the piece must necessarily adopt a geometry that ensures that no compressions appear in the membrane.[8] This is achieved with the help of three big structural rings made of steel, located at both sides and in the middle, that give shape to the membrane. The middle one is deployed horizontally, and, together with several sandbags, acts as counterweight and tensions the membrane, ensuring its equilibrium.

The relationship between form and structure offers an interesting approach to design, with the form suggested or even determined by its structural behavior, with the purpose of optimizing it. The field of form-derived structures is very broad, and many different relationships between form and structure may be established, from concrete shells to membrane structures, branched structures, tensegrity, or spatial configurations.

CAT Segovia, Spain; Chapel in Sierra la Villa, Spain; Alburouj Culture Hub. Cairo, Egypt. For more than 20 years, Sancho-Madridejos Architecture Office has been developing a very interesting line of research regarding "folding" as a process to create forms and spaces that are structurally efficient because of their shape. Indeed, if one begins with a flat surface – a plane – and then folds it, its structural configuration and behavior radically changes.[9,10] The flat surface is transformed into a spatial configuration, which greatly reduces the internal bending forces that determine the sizing of the structure. A plane supported at its edges transfers bending-active loads, while a folded plane can adopt a funicular configuration, transferring loads through axial forces, either tension or compression. It is the same process by which a straight beam, bending-active, is transformed into an arch, working in compression, or a hanging chain, working in tension, both of them structurally efficient.

Furthermore, it is not only that the process of folding transforms a plane into a spatial configuration – the folds themselves constitute rigid edges that also contribute to control and reduce bending forces.

As a result, structurally efficient configurations mainly subject to axial forces with limited bending are obtained, offering multiple spatial possibilities, as Sancho Madridejos have shown – with great structural intuition – in several projects that explore the spatial potentialities of folds. In the course of this conceptual exploration, after working with straight folds, they introduced a new variable – curved folds, which transform a plane into a curved surface, increasing further the spatial and structural possibilities offered by folds.

The Innovation and Business Development Center (CAT) in Segovia **[PAGE 49, CENTER]** or the Chapel in Sierra la Villa, Spain **[PAGE 42]**, are interesting examples of folded configurations with thin-shell reinforced concrete structures, while the Alborouj Culture Hub in Cairo, Egypt **[PAGE 49, BOTTOM]**, applies this exploration of form and structure to a complex geometrical configuration of a spatial steel structure.[11,12]

[7] Kapoor, A.: (2002) Marsyas, Tate Publishing, London.

[8] Balmond, C.: (2013) Crossover, Prestel Verlag, Munich – London – New York.

[9] Arquitectura Viva (ed.): (2022) Sancho Madridejos. Placeres del pliegue, Arquitectura Viva, 241.

[10] a+u (ed.): (2021) S-MAO. Sancho-Madridejos Architecture Office, a+u, 608.

[11] Rinke, M. (ed.): (2019) The Bones of Architecture: Structure and Design Practices. Triest-Verlag, pp. 108–115.

[12] Bernabeu Larena, A., De la Cal Manteca, M.: (2022) Alborouj Cultural Hub en El Cairo. Una retícula sencilla para dar forma a una geometría compleja, VIII Congreso Internacional de Estructuras de la Asociación Española de Ingeniería Estructural (ACHE). Santander. Hormigón y Acero, volume 73.

RIGHT PAGE, TOP **Anish Kapoor, *Marsyas*. Tate Modern, London, Great Britain, 2002**

RIGHT PAGE, CENTER **CAT Innovation and business Development Center. Segovia, Spain, 2020. Architecture: Sancho Madridejos Architecture Office; Structural design and engineering: IDEE, IDI Ingenieros, Bernabeu Ingenieros**

RIGHT PAGE, BOTTOM **Alburouj Culture Hub. Cairo, Egypt, 2019. Architecture: Sancho Madridejos Architecture Office; Structural design and engineering: Bernabeu Ingenieros**

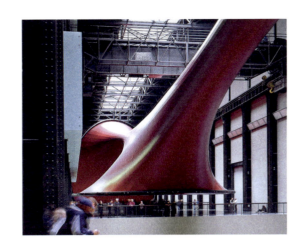

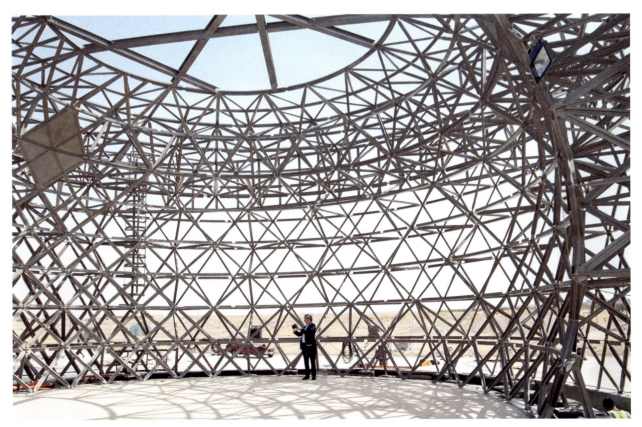

CHALLENGING GRAVITY

FIVE THOUGHTS ON THE RELATIONSHIP BETWEEN STRUCTURE AND ARCHITECTURE

13 Bernabeu, J.: (2017) "Estructuras en esculturas, los sueños de la materia," Cuadernos de diseño.

14 Bernabeu Larena, A., Carlson, J., Gómez Mateo, J., Olislager, B., Saéz Alonso, I., Verbraken, H.: (2021) "Mohamed VI Tower in Rabat," Proceedings of the fib Symposium on the Conceptual Design of Structures. Attisholz.

15 Bernabeu Larena, A., Gómez Mateo, J., Saéz Alonso, I., Arcones Torrejón, A.: (2022) Torre Mohamed VI en Rabat (Marruecos). Cimentación singular mediante pantallas de gran profundidad, VIII Congreso Internacional de Estructuras de la Asociación Española de Ingeniería Estructural (ACHE). Santander. Hormigón y Acero, volume 73.

Major structural requirements: high-rise buildings and large spans

The ambition to rise ever higher is a constant aspiration in sculpture and construction. One of the sculptures that best symbolizes this ambition is Brâncuși's *Endless Column*.[13] In 1918, Brâncuși began to make multiple versions of the endless column, consisting in the repetition of the same module which is formed by truncated pyramids symmetrically joined by the base. The repetition of an abstract module emphasizes the potential for endless vertical expansion. Most of Brâncuși's endless columns were built in oak wood. The highest column was built in 1937 in the Romanian city of Târgu Jiu and is a reference of sculptural installation on landscape **[PAGE 50, TOP]**. Brâncuși collaborated with Romanian engineer Stefan Georgescu-Gorjan to erect a very slender 30-meters-tall column, with its modules in cast iron, an interior steel column, and a concrete footing that stabilizes the piece.

To erect taller constructions and to span wider distances have always been ambitious challenges, forcing structural design to evolve and innovate. In these cases, the structural requirements are so important that they almost determine the configuration of the project. This is the case with high-rise buildings, large-span structures, or constructions in areas of great seismicity. The significance of these major structural requirements conditions the development of the project – but rather than limiting it, they can suggest the exploration and development of new and innovative structural types and configurations. Indeed, high-rise buildings led to the development of diagrid structures and of the interest in structural façades in the 20th century, and they have also furthered knowledge on dynamic wind forces effect and damping devices, while large-span roof structures inspired structural types such as stress ribbons, suspended structures, or spatial trusses. Facing unprecedented challenges is favorable to innovative design.

Mohamed VI Tower. Rabat, Morocco. With a total height of 250 meters, the Mohamed VI Tower in Rabat (Morocco), designed by architect Rafael de la Hoz in collaboration with Hakim Benjelloun, is one of the tallest skyscrapers in Africa **[PAGE 51]**.

The floor plan of the tower is organized by providing for an eccentric deployment of the inner communication core oriented towards the south façade, generating a large open space at the north side that contains the main uses of the tower (offices, residential, and hotel), while the south side houses the technical spaces and services. This approach avoids the existence of intermediate technical floors, a singular configuration that preserves the continuity of the façade and enhances its verticality and slenderness.

A tube-in-tube structural configuration was adopted, taking account of the contribution of both the inner concrete core and the structural façade in supporting lateral wind loads and seismic loads. The attention of the design team then moved on to the structural and architectural configuration and composition of the façade. Several alternatives, including diagrid configurations, were considered, before it was developed as a rigid Vierendeel frame that enhances the verticality of the tower **[PAGE 50, BOTTOM]**.

High-rise buildings imply robust structural configurations and particular construction systems. Every project has its own particularities, and the different structural solutions, although well stablished nowadays, may adopt diverse configurations. In the Mohamed VI Tower these were related to its location in a seismic area, with very poor soil conditions, its singular architectural configuration with an eccentrical inner core, and the intention to enhance the verticality of the tower.[14,15]

LEFT PAGE, TOP Constantin Brâncuși, *Endless Column*. Târgu Jiu, Romania, 1937

TOP; LEFT PAGE, TOP Mohamed VI Tower. Rabat, Morocco, 2023. Architecture: Rafael de la Hoz, Cabinet Hakim Benjelloun; Structural design and engineering: Bernabeu Ingenieros, Besix, Ney & Partners

Importance of the design process

In the 1980s, artist Luis Gordillo first began to take pictures that trace the different stages of the creative process behind his paintings, following their evolution and transformation. These pictures of the process, which have sometimes been exhibited together with the final painting, document the process and constitute a "record of lost and discarded ideas" [16,17] **[PAGE 53, BOTTOM]**:

> "Gordillo painting doesn't stop, it is continually rethought, the process is, more than ever, part of the piece. The observation of the process lets us know how the different elements evolve, and lets us study the interstices containing the ideas that will be repositioned during the construction process of the painting, de-hierarchizing it."[16]

In a context in which immediacy prevails, in which projects are required to be completed in less and less time, and in which the development of advanced modeling and construction techniques points the way straightforwardly to the result, it is necessary to stake a claim for the importance of the design and construction processes in themselves. Not only in terms of the final result, but as a process – a journey – in which the design moves forward but also takes steps back, and during which the project matures and evolves.

Extension of Euskalduna conference center and concert hall. Bilbao, Spain The Euskalduna Conference Center and Concert Hall was designed in 1994 by the architects Federico Soriano and Dolores Palacios. In 2010 an extension was added, increasing the exhibition area. The key element in the extension building was the roof structure, covering an irregular open-plan space of about 50 × 80 m with maximum spans of 45 m.

The initial architectural proposal provided for a set of curved lines crossing one upon another and covering the total surface, a configuration that moved away from the traditional systems of main beams and perpendicular secondary structure to respond to the irregularity of the floor plan **[PAGE 52]**. This configuration was structurally evaluated, proving to be a flexible system that could be naturally adapted according to its structural behavior.

At this stage, changed circumstances necessitated the reconsideration of the whole project, and put development on hold. When it resumed, starting from the previous experience and analysis, it was decided that new formal and structural configurations should be explored.

The initial idea of defining an irregular structural configuration was retained, but instead of providing for a set of clearly identified main structural lines, it was proposed that the surface should be covered by the repetition and superposition of multiple circular, rectangular, or curved shapes. These configurations, however, had a difficult structural behavior, requiring elements with high rigidity both in bending and in torsion. However, they also suggested the possibility of defining the structure by applying classical systems of reciprocal frame structures. Reciprocal frame structures are formed by a set of load-bearing elements arranged to mutually support one another in a closed circuit, having each element acting both as span and support. This naturally provided a great irregularity and flexibility, easily adapting to the geometry of the plan and contributing to the desired image of discontinuity and irregularity.

The singular application of a classical structural system – reciprocal frame structures – responded to the architectural intention, offering both flexibility and strong structural logic, concluding an interesting and creative design process **[PAGE 53, TOP]**.[18,19,20]

16 IVAM (ed.): (1994) Luis Gordillo. Exhibition catalogue, IVAM Centro Julio González, Valencia, Centro Andaluz de Arte Contemporáneo, Sevilla.

17 Caja de Burgos (ed.): (1998) Luis Gordillo (1983–1996). Caja de Burgos.

18 Bernabeu Larena, A., García Menéndez, D.: (2014) "Extension of Euskalduna Conference Center and Concert Hall: a contemporary application of irregular reciprocal frames," Structural Engineering International, 1/2014, pp. 63–67.

19 Bernabeu Larena, A.: (2015) "Sobre el proceso de diseño: estructura de la ampliación del Palacio Euskalduna," Revista de Obras Públicas, no. 3564, pp. 89–94.

20 Rinke, M. (ed.): (2019) The Bones of Architecture: Structure and Design Practices. Triest-Verlag, pp. 148–153.

TOP; RIGHT PAGE, TOP Extension of Euskalduna conference center and concert hall. Bilbao, Spain, 2012. Architectural proposal (Soriano y Asociados) and interior view. Architecture: Soriano y Asociados (Federico Soriano, Dolores Palacios); Structural design and engineering: IDOM

RIGHT PAGE, BOTTOM Luis Gordillo, *Corazón de Jesús en vos confío*, creative process, 1992

CHALLENGING GRAVITY

THE SIMPLE, ELEGANT FLOW OF FORCES

CHRISTIAN MENN AND STEFAN POLÓNYI IN CONVERSATION WITH JOSEPH SCHWARTZ AND HIS TEAM

On December 7, 2010, Prof. Joseph Schwartz and his team invited the two engineers Christian Menn and Stefan Polónyi to ETH Zurich to take part in a joint discussion. In February 2007, Schwartz had taken up the chair for structural design at the Department of Architecture and had developed a radical new foundation course based on the methods of graphical statics, which aimed to achieve an understanding of structural design based on geometry and proportions, instead of structural typologies. This new, core teaching philosophy was intended to impart an intuitive, but nevertheless precise understanding of forces that went beyond calculation, which explicitly brought structural and architectural issues together. Three years since the start of this new course, this talk was an opportunity to interrogate the requirements and possibilities of an interdisciplinary structural design.

This interview has been abridged and edited for legibility by Mario Rinke.

JS First of all, I would like to thank you both for coming here today. Today we want to talk about what the teaching of structural design can mean in the teaching of architecture. Here at the department, we were convinced from the beginning that this shouldn't be about teaching architecture students how civil engineers work, but rather imparting to them a feeling for structures in the context of the building in general. We want to teach them how to visualize forces and thus make it possible to reconcile form and internal forces. As a result, decisions can be made as early as the concept stage that guide the further course of the design. There is then actually no need for precise calculations to prove something that already did not work in their basic assumptions. To enter the discussion, I would like to ask you both: What comes to your mind about the engineer-architect collaboration, what can it mean?

CM I would like to start with a question. Are your backgrounds more in architecture or engineering?

JS We're from both sides. Most of us come from architecture, some of us have backgrounds in both. We try to have a certain balance.

CM I would perhaps like to say something. In my view, we have a kind of axis: one side is science, and the other is art. And I have the impression that the engineers want to become ever closer to science and the architects to art. This means they are drifting apart, and that is basically wrong. The two approaches should be brought together.

It's wrong to assume that in science we should become ever more exact. A bridge, for instance, is to be placed in an environment. This primary condition is topography and geology. And there, you have to ask yourself how to arrive at a load-bearing system which could fit in that place and would have great potential with respect to its appearance and cost. Once you have that, then you can begin with the bridge. I think it's different in architecture. Architects want to make something that comes from their minds. In other words, to create something. But I have the impression that engineers aren't in fact authors but translators. When we make invisible forces visible through their efficiency, then that leads to a good solution. And then you go from a load-bearing system to a load-bearing structure, in which these forces are visualized. Equilibrium simply means balance, harmony, etc., that is what appeals to us.

SP There is a very important phrase that we should return to. And that is "making the invisible visible." I would also like to set out a brief history of our profession. Building statics truly began with the lectures of Navier in 1823.[1] Before then, we had built very beautiful things through direct experience. From this point on, we had a theory which allowed us to go beyond direct experience. This meant that structures could be built for which calculations could be made. We engineers then had a repertoire of structural systems, and we later tried our best to adapt them in architecture.

Now, with the finite-element method and computers, we can calculate everything. Architects make the

---

[1] Claude-Louis Navier (1785–1836) was a French mechanical engineer. He directed the construction of several bridges and was professor at both the École Nationale des Ponts et Chaussées and the École Polytechnique. Navier developed the general theory of elasticity in a mathematically usable form and connected it, for the first time, to the field of construction. In 1826 he established the elastic modulus as a property of materials independent of geometry. Navier is, therefore, considered to be the founder of modern structural analysis.

most of this, tending to start with geometric order and then exceeding the limits of statics before going into dynamics, where we have to deal with vibrations. This is the big picture. And then, there is the other question of how a design process unfolds today. First comes the question of use, then that of architectural expression, and then the engineers get to work. How will this architectural expression be achieved – through the structure, or with the help of the structure? And if that is the situation, then how could the education of architects be oriented towards this? In any case, close collaboration between architects and engineers is necessary. It is the task of education to prepare architects for the kinds of conversations and collaborations they will have with engineers. I would always support something like what they do in Dortmund, where architects and engineers do three projects together over the course of their studies.[2] One project is housing, the next is something like a sports hall or a museum, and the third one is an engineering structure like a bridge or a water tower. The other various subjects are brought to the projects as and when required. Thus, the teaching input takes place at the very moment it is needed, rather than simply being delivered at an arbitrary time.

JS In my view, it is more a question of why it is so difficult for the kinds of people who are drawn to study engineering to open themselves to things that are beyond the technical, to see this wider spectrum of what is being produced in the field of architecture. The problem lies partly with the students, but also with those in charge of engineering courses. When you try to build something like this within the framework of existing educational structures, you have the problem that so many prejudices have to be overcome before the aim and purpose of this exercise is even recognized by those responsible for implementing it.

CM For structures above ground, like buildings, you can of course calculate anything with computers. But I would say it is more important that somebody understands what they are doing – for instance, knowing where there is compression, where you might have to be careful, as something could buckle or twist. For a student, it is certainly interesting to determine the path of forces. I would prioritize this in any case.

JS I would simply like to go in the direction of visualizing internal forces, which is just as relevant for engineering students as it is for architecture students. If we were to say: well, with today's computational methods we can calculate practically anything, that is in fact, for all sorts of reasons, rather useless. With the certainty of being able to calculate everything, you can't develop concepts. And to be able to develop structural concepts, one has to make certain of quite simple considerations at the beginning of a project. This also affects the ability to envisage architectural space, which naturally depends on the architect's attitude towards design. When they want to create something sculptural, then the set of requirements is different when they really want to involve the structure meaningfully as a topic in the design of the building. And when, as an engineer, you are asked to work on a project that has already been fully developed by an architect, you have to ask yourself whether you want to begin at all.

CM But aren't we in a kind of dichotomy? There are these "starchitects." I have the impression that many architecture students imagine themselves being such an architect one day. But for such an architect, the engineer is irrelevant. In the end, they'll say, "let's put a load-bearing structure in this, however you like." The bridge in Abu Dhabi by Zaha Hadid is a good example. She clearly had not thought about speaking with an engineer beforehand. If the engineer had come along and said, the arch should be like this instead, she wouldn't have wanted that. And for whom do we train the ordinary, or star, architect? And where does the engineer's assistance come in?

JS Of course, there are also designs that possess great qualities, both architectural and also in terms of their structure, in which the structure nevertheless plays a very subordinate role. And that is absolutely legitimate. There are also designs by "starchitects" where structure plays an important role. I don't think we can generalize so much.

CM I think education should serve all kinds of architects. It's important to train them on how to have an orderly and beautiful distribution of forces.

JS And to be able to positively influence architecture with it. For the past three years, we have been asking ourselves what structural design is, and what it could be.

CM Designing buildings is certainly different from designing bridges. With bridges, we have the possibility of designing something. That's not the same as a drainage system.

JS The design is the decisive factor, the concept.

---

[2] The Dortmund Model represents the unique combined education program for architecture and civil engineering at TU Dortmund University that has been in place since the Faculty of Architecture and Civil Engineering was founded in 1974. The architect Harald Deilmann (1920–2008) and Stefan Polónyi were instrumental in this endeavor. Its aim was to put an end to the separate educational pathways for architects and civil engineers that had existed since the end of the 19th century.

PREVIOUS PAGE Reinforcement work on the ceramic gallery Keramion.
Frechen, Germany, 1971. Architecture: Peter Neufert; Structural design and engineering: Stefan Polónyi

TOP Construction site of the Ceramic gallery Keramion. Frechen, Germany, 1971
Architecture: Peter Neufert; Structural design and engineering: Stefan Polónyi

BOTTOM Ponte Nanin and Ponte Cascella. Mesocco, Switzerland, 1968
Structural design and engineering: Christian Menn

CHALLENGING GRAVITY

TOP **Viamala-Brücke. Zillis-Reischen, Switzerland, 1967**
Structural design and engineering: Christian Menn

BOTTOM **Ganterbrücke. Ried-Brig, Switzerland, 1980**
Structural design and engineering: Christian Menn

CM Yes, you can't build a suspension bridge with pylons over a small stream. Scale is a fundamental principle.

JS But the design, these first conceptual ideas, where does it come from?

CM Of course, that has already been considered. One wants to make a structural system that has a high potential, both in appearance and economy. And this balance is, once again, dependent on the surroundings. Will you see the structure, or is it hidden somewhere, or is it a site with historical significance? All of that has to be taken into account.

JS Fundamentally, it is always a process, one which involves decisions. At the outset, there's the basic question of what type of bridge it should be: a beam, cable-stayed, suspension, or an arch. That is surely the main question that has to be answered at the beginning, more intuitively rather than scientifically, don't you think?

CM Well, when I think now of the Sunniberg bridge, for instance, the proposals that we had at the outset were essentially completely normal designs: pillars with a beam on top. And it couldn't be too expensive. A balance always has to be struck between appearance and economy. The bridge that stands there now was a good 15% more expensive than the cheapest possible solution.

JS But the choice of a cable-stayed bridge was decisive.

CM Yes, the decision in favor of such a bridge came from the fact that such a design would result in a more transparent bridge across the valley, blocking less of the view. This choice was a little more expensive. The rest came naturally – for that, we were simply translators.

JS The rest of the chain of decisions concerned constructional and technical aspects.

CM Yes, absolutely. We always chose the simplest way possible. If the towers are splayed a little, it was because straight towers would cause the cables to clash with the structural clearance of the curved bridge. It doesn't have any joints or bearings, so it doesn't have to expand along its length, but instead expands laterally. But then you can't use full-width solid piers, because they are too stiff. So you make a kind of Vierendeel truss instead.

JS How do you see the possibilities of imparting this feeling for structural form to students?

CM I just think that being able to develop a simple, elegant distribution of forces in a building is something that is in itself beautiful. Like in your school building [in Leutschenbach], where it goes back and forth until it reaches the ground.[3] Not everyone would see that flow of forces as simple, but it is very elegant.

JS One has to say that the load-bearing structure as it was ultimately built came from the fundamental consideration of stacking, which emerged from the first concept sketches we made together. The structural idea was only made sharper in the course of the project.

SP I might also bring up a particular example, from one of my many collaborations with Ungers.[4] When I worked with architects, I never spoke about structural problems, only about architecture, about their architecture. With the project for the Baden State Library, for instance, there were many functions arranged on top of one another. When the architects wanted to have a downstand beam to transfer the loads, I tried to talk them out of it. But I didn't tell them that I didn't want a downstand beam. Instead I talked about their architecture. Underneath was the parking area, and so I began to talk about the arrangement of parking. And in the end, the columns were aligned neatly on top of each other. It's something you can teach students early on: to develop floor plans which don't require transfer beams.

JS Why do you object to transfer beams so strongly?

SP Such beams don't belong in slab and column structures. All you should have there is columns and horizontal or vertical slabs, that should be enough. You shouldn't need a downstand except in an emergency. The downstand belongs to timber frame construction.

JS It's a question of appropriateness.

SP With an architect-designed building, you should be able to insist that something like that shouldn't really be possible.

JS What remains difficult are the different ways of thinking, the different language present in the two disciplines. We are always asking ourselves how we could make progress in that respect.

---

[3] Leutschenbach school building in Zurich (2009) by the architect Christian Kerez and engineer Joseph Schwartz.

[4] Oswald Mathias Ungers (1926–2007) was one of the most important German architects of the postwar period.

Architekt und Ingenieur | St. Paulus, Neuss

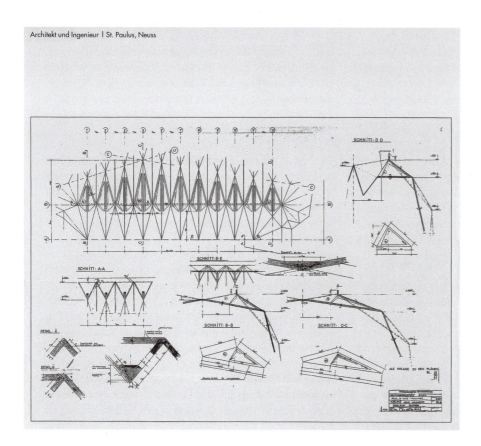

TOP/BOTTOM **Church St. Paulus. Neuss, Germany, 1968**
Architecture: Fritz Schaller; Structural design and engineering: Stefan Polónyi

SP In Berlin, I said to the design professors that we could supervise the designs of the students in terms of construction. I did this with Ungers, for instance. It was fun. In the process, the students also got a feeling for the elements of buildings. Some design professors enjoy that kind of collaboration, others find it an interference.

JS We're already doing that here at our department. But it's more about the general coupling required to overcome these different ways of thinking.

CM Isn't that extremely difficult? To have architects and engineers collaborating during their studies, while the engineering students might not yet have a feeling for structures and structural systems.

JS I think it's a shame that we don't manage to give the civil engineering students the requisite means within the first two semesters to make such communication possible.

SP The education of engineers needs to be completely rethought. But you aren't in a position to influence that.

CM Sometimes I receive the results of Austrian student engineer design competitions. A few years ago, one of these involved a pedestrian bridge over a stream. There were, of course, the most unbelievable inventions being proposed. I had the impression that it would have been much more fruitful if the engineers had got to know some architects instead – who work completely differently, iteratively revising their designs. The engineers, on the other hand, want simply the "given," the "task," and then results. The kind of statics that architects require is a statics of understanding. And engineers should develop a better understanding of architecture.

MR What would we need to change to make this possible?

CM I don't know. For the engineering students, it's not acceptable, of course, that they don't hear anything about architecture.

MR It's quite self-evident that architecture students are taught about structures, but for engineers there isn't a reciprocal branch of study.

SP Perhaps the bachelor curriculum should be rethought, its content reordered in terms of its sequence. The question of what belongs in the bachelor course, and what can be moved to the master course. It would then be possible to make the bachelor's course more related to practice, rather than, as is usually the case, students being taught almost pure theory in the first semesters. That's like trying to teach someone a language without forming any sentences, focusing only on teaching grammar. In the first four years of engineering, they only speak about grammar, without a single sentence being spoken.

JS Yes, things have really gone in the wrong direction. It used to be the case that one had to be able to calculate by hand. You had to have understood the foundations of statics to be able to dimension a beam, or some kind of frame. Otherwise, you didn't stand a chance.

CM Why do we always focus on problems in calculation, where they often lie elsewhere? That's difficult to understand. Take construction details in bridges, such as when chloride-laden salt water is allowed to run along the slab. These are the kind of mistakes that wreck everything.

GD How can we teach students to better understand these sorts of things? What methods would you suggest?

CM The simplest and most beautiful way is the truss. The truss is a wonderful thing. And it's something that can be quickly grasped. Slabs also behave like a truss. Well, I've talked enough now… I have to go catch my train. Mr. Polónyi, it was my pleasure. I hope you have a nice time in Zurich.

SP Thank you!

CM And Mr. Schwartz, thank you for the invitation.

JS Thank you so much for coming. We wish you a safe journey home!

Translation from German: Philip Shelley

Mario Rinke [MR] and Gabriela Dimitrova [GD] were part of the team around Joseph Schwartz [JS].

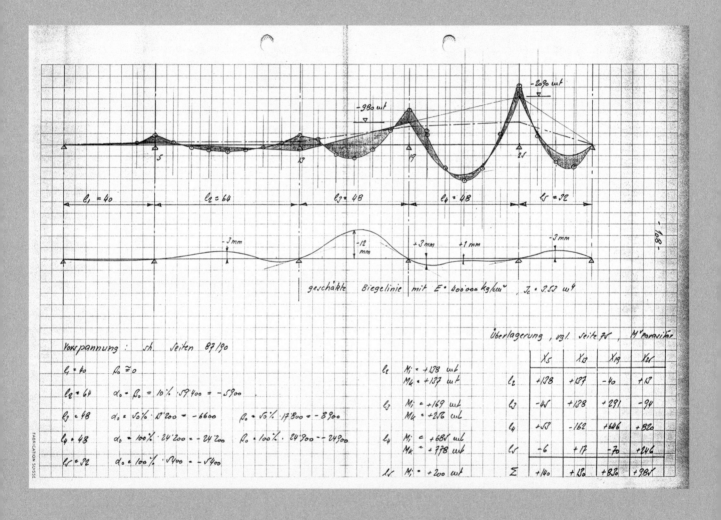

PAUL GAUVREAU

DESIGNING BY HAND IN AN ERA OF UBIQUITOUS COMPUTING POWER

Methods of precise design work

The structural design process brings together two essential activities: drawing and calculating. Designers draw to make their ideas visible in the crucial initial stages of the creative process, to demonstrate that their designs satisfy specific functional requirements (such as compliance with geometrical constraints), and to describe their completed designs to those who will build them. Designers calculate primarily to demonstrate that their designs satisfy requirements pertaining to safety and serviceability. They do so by predicting the response of a given design to specified actions through the application of scientific principles. As shown on **PAGE 62**, drawings are often incorporated into calculations.

Drawings and calculations used in structural design require a degree of precision appropriate to their intended use. Drawings used to verify that specified geometric constraints are satisfied, for example, need to be highly precise. The drawing on **PAGE 66** is highly precise. Although it is possible to design structures that will not collapse on the basis of fairly rough calculations, guaranteeing safety on this basis usually results in a degree of conservatism that cannot be quantified. By working with calculations that provide a suitable degree of precision, the degree of conservatism can be determined with reasonable accuracy and hence controlled by designers, thus making it possible to design works that are more suited to satisfy applicable practical design requirements and be economical.

Prior to 1960, all drawings required in the design of structures were made with pencil or pen on paper or some similar medium. Calculations were done using slide rules and graphic statics. Intermediate and final results were recorded in numerical or graphical form using pencil on paper. It is common to refer to working in this way as working "by hand," in recognition of the fact that it always involves the human hand making marks of some kind on paper.

Working by hand was deemed to be a perfectly suitable means of producing the precise drawings and precise calculations needed in the design of structures of all sizes and types, including works of considerable geometrical and statical complexity such as the Bridge over the Landquart at Klosters-Serneus and the George Washington Bridge **[PAGE 66, CENTER/BOTTOM]**. The body of structures designed before 1960 demonstrates that working by hand did not impede the ability of competent engineers to design good structures, or of brilliant engineers to design works that continue to inspire admiration and awe.

This situation began to change in the 1960s with the introduction of electronic digital computers into design practice. Engineers quickly recognized that computer-based technology could be applied in the production of precise drawings and precise calculations. The transformation from "by hand" to "by computer" as the preferred means for doing precise design work was slow at first but accelerated rapidly as computers became more powerful, compact, and affordable.

LEFT PAGE Hand calculation incorporating drawings for the Bridge over the Reuss at Wassen (Switzerland, 1978) by the Swiss engineer Christian Menn.

This transition was largely driven by perceived gains in ease and efficiency in the design process. Computers made it much less onerous to make significant changes to designs in progress and drastically reduced the time required to design geometrically and/or statically complex structures. The effect of this transition on the product of the design process, however, is more difficult to characterize. The advent of computers in designers' offices did in fact coincide with the development of some new and important structural systems, such as cable-stayed bridges. During the same period, however, there has been an apparent reluctance to innovate and instead to favor tried and true systems for many important applications, such as freeway overpasses.

Precise hand-drawn work is now rare in structural design. Drafting tables have disappeared, and even relatively simple calculations that could be done easily and well by hand are performed by computer. Going forward, the power and ease of computer-based methods for precise work is almost certain to increase further, as a result of further advances in computing technology.

When computers were first introduced into design practice, engineers chose to work by hand or by computer based on reasonable knowledge of both methods. Over the years, however, schools of engineering have stopped teaching precise drawing by hand, and although hand calculation is still taught, its effective use in the design process is not. In addition, many offices now contain no engineers who have done precise hand work of any significance. We have thus almost reached a point of no return, at which neither the academic nor the practical sector will have the capacity to transfer to young engineers the knowledge and skills required for an effective use of precise hand methods. This will make engineers incapable of making an informed choice of which method to use. It is therefore timely to consider whether or not there are aspects of precise hand work that are worth keeping.

This question must ultimately be answered according to whether or not the use of precise hand methods can enable designers to create better structures than the structures that would have been produced if all precise work were done by computer. It is difficult, however, to create two designs that satisfy identical practical requirements for comparison purposes, one done by hand and the other done by computer, with all other conditions being equal. For this reason, the question will be approached indirectly, by examining aspects of precise hand work that are likely to enhance the ability of engineers to design better structures. This article will examine two such aspects, namely: (1) working with limited means, and (2) the link between visual fine motor skills and high-level cognitive function.

The benefits of working with limited means

Doing precise work by computer imposes few limits on the choices available to designers, in the sense that we can draw and calculate practically anything that can be imagined. A full range of drawing types is possible, including hyper-realistic three-dimensional renderings. The degree of statical indeterminacy likewise poses no impediment when calculations are done by computer. In contrast, the types of drawing and calculation that can be done by hand are limited by available time and effort, as well as by the level of skill normally encountered in design offices. Precise hand drawings are normally limited to two-dimensional orthographic views made up from straight line segments and circular arcs only. Although precise hand

[1] Ærbo, K.: (1997) "Speech at the opening of the Arne Jacobsen exhibition in Aarhus," 2G, no. 4, pp. 138–142.

[2] Williams, T. and Tsien, B.: (1999) "On Slowness," 2G, no. 9, pp. 129–137.

calculations for the analysis of statically indeterminate systems are theoretically straightforward, the time and effort required to perform a comprehensive analysis of such systems increases dramatically with the degree of indeterminacy. These limitations on what can be drawn and calculated limit the scope of possible solutions when we design by hand.

It is common to regard any restriction on the scope of creative endeavors as a negative factor, since limiting the range of available solutions might well eliminate optimal designs. Thus, it is taken as an axiom that designers must "think outside the box." In fact, suitable limitations on scope can provide a useful framework for the design process, effectively focusing creative activity on what is most important. This was recognized by Danish architect Knud Ærbo, for example, in his comments on the extremely limited tools for hand drawing at his disposal when he entered practice: "If you looked at it today, you would have to say: it could not be done. But luckily we did not know then."[1] We can infer from this statement that Ærbo did indeed consider that the limited means available to him had a positive effect on his ability to design well.

When we restrict the scope of possible solutions at the outset of the design process, the possibility of eliminating good solutions does indeed exist, and for this reason any boundaries imposed on the scope must be given careful consideration. Precise hand drawing restricts designs to those that are simple enough to be represented using two-dimensional orthographic views made up from straight line segments and circular arcs. Precise hand calculation likewise restricts designs to structural systems that are simple and which embody a straightforward flow of forces. The use of precise hand methods thus favors designs that have no unnecessary complexity, which is an attribute that is generally consistent with low construction cost. So any restrictions on the scope of creative choice resulting from the use of precise hand work have the potential to guide the design process towards work that is economical.

Another beneficial consequence of the limitations inherent in precise hand work is what American architects Tod Williams and Billie Tsien call "slowness."[2] It is obvious that drawing and calculating take longer by hand than by computer. According to Williams and Tsien, however, the additional time required when working by hand is not wasted: "As our hands move, we have the time to think and to observe our actions." Designers can use this opportunity to reflect on their work as it is performed, and hence to gain deeper understanding and insight that, in the opinion of Williams and Tsien, provides a solid basis for good designs. When working by hand, therefore, designers can make a virtue out of the necessity of slowness.

It is of course possible to work slowly when computer-based methods are used. There is no longer, however, a compelling necessity to do so. Indeed, the promise of faster production in the design office provided the primary impetus for the transformation of precise design work from hand to computer. In the absence of any constraint to work slowly, many designers choose to work quickly, and in so doing sacrifice the opportunities for reflection provided by slow work as it is performed. This can lead to a more haphazard approach to design, in which trial and error takes precedence over understanding and insight.

When applied to precise hand calculation, the deeper understanding and insight gained through slowness is often transformed from an opportunity into a necessity. The only feasible way to calculate the structural behavior of even moderately complex systems using hand methods is to use *rational simplification*, which consists of the following steps: (1) distinguish between the essential and nonessential aspects of structural behav-

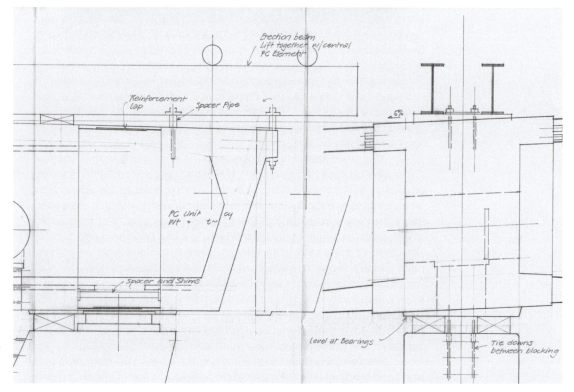

66 DESIGNING BY HAND IN AN ERA OF UBIQUITOUS COMPUTING POWER

3   Billington, D. P.: (1973) "Deck-Stiffened Arch Bridges of Robert Maillart," Journal of the Structural Division ASCE 99, pp. 1527–1539.

ior, (2) create a mathematical model of the structural system that considers only the essential aspects of behavior, and (3) perform a precise hand calculation of structural behavior using the model thus created. Rational simplification thus makes precise hand calculation feasible through the use of a simplified mathematical model, which in turn is created on the basis of a rational understanding of structural behavior gained before any precise calculations have been performed. This understanding can only be gained through careful reflection on the design in its early stages of production, and in this sense we can say that the understanding and insight gained from the slowness imposed by hand work is a crucial means of overcoming the limitations associated with precise hand calculation.

In all cases, the systems for which we calculate structural behavior are systems of our own creation. Whether or not a given aspect of behavior is essential or nonessential thus depends to a large extent on prior design decisions we have made. In other words, it is we who determine whether or not a given aspect of behavior is essential. It follows that an effective use of rational simplification always involves an intimate link between design and analysis. This link is often expressed in terms of dimensionless ratios relating geometric design parameters (such as member length, cross-sectional area, or moment of inertia) and quantities describing structural behavior such as bending moment or stress. For example, the Swiss engineer Robert Maillart developed a rational simplification for the design of his girder-stiffened arch bridges **[PAGE 66, CENTER]** based on his understanding of the effect of the ratio of the moments of inertia of girder and arch (I_g/I_a) on the distribution of bending moments in these two components.[3]

Precise hand calculations that use rational simplification require that the designer make an a priori distinction between the essential and nonessential aspects of structural behavior. In contrast, calculations done by computer normally use general-purpose methods of structural analysis and hence do not require us to make this distinction. When computer-based tools are used, one may proceed on the basis that everything is essential. When structural response is calculated on this basis, there is no immediate need to consider simple parametric relationships such as those described previously for girder/arch systems in developing a given structural system, as the method of analysis is intrinsically numeric. This effectively decouples analysis from design, making it more difficult to come up with optimal solutions because the effect of important parameters is hidden in a large set of numerical data.

It should be emphasized that there is nothing rough or approximate about rational simplification. Calculations done on this basis are not estimates that need to be refined or confirmed by other means, but are in fact sufficiently precise to be used in formal checks of safety and serviceability. The vast number of structures of all sizes and of all levels of complexity designed on this basis in the pre-1960 era provide compelling evidence of the validity of designing on this basis.

LEFT PAGE, TOP Photo and portion of a precise hand drawing for the new Jamestown Verrazzano Bridge (Rhode Island, USA, 1992) by the American engineer Charles M. Redfield.

LEFT PAGE, CENTER Bridge over the Landquart at Klosters-Serneus (Switzerland, 1930) by the Swiss engineer Robert Maillart.

LEFT PAGE, BOTTOM George Washington Bridge (New York City, USA, 1931 [upper level], 1962 [lower level]) by the Swiss-American engineer Othmar Ammann.

Precise hand work as an enabler of creativity

Doing precise hand work brings together hands, eyes, and brain in an intricately coordinated manner to create drawings and to record text and mathematics as required in the design process. In the seemingly simple task of positioning a straightedge to span between two given points, for example, the eyes determine how far the straightedge is from the points and the brain then gives instructions to the muscles of the hands to move the straightedge accordingly. This establishes a loop of information flowing from eyes to brain to hands, which is repeated many times during even the simplest of operations. Moving hands and fingers in this way, under precise control of the brain on the basis of information obtained from eyes and hands, will be referred to as "visual fine motor skills."

The demand made on visual fine motor skills varies according to the geometric precision required of the drawings and symbols to be created. It thus follows that, even though we normally associate a high demand for visual fine motor skills with precise hand drawing, it can also be found in hand calculations depending on the quality of penmanship required. (High-quality penmanship is present, for example, in the drawing on **PAGE 66**). By the same reasoning, the level of visual fine motor skills required in computer work is relatively low. The primary means of producing text and numerals is the keyboard, the use of which requires a manipulation of the fingers that is much coarser than that required in making the same symbols with a pencil. Drawing by computer can be done using several means, none of which involves highly precise geometric positioning of physical objects with the fingers guided by the eyes.

Engineers who have extensive experience in doing precise design work by hand are familiar with a particular state of mind that is induced by working in this way. The mind appears to be simultaneously stimulated and relaxed, and able to focus on the smallest of details while maintaining a broad, holistic perspective. These engineers have described how they do their best creative work while engaged in precise hand drawing. On the basis of this admittedly anecdotal evidence, the following hypothesis is put forth: doing precise hand work can enhance creativity.

A link between precise hand drawing and creative thought was claimed by American visual artist and art educator Betty Edwards.[4,5] She is known mainly for her novel method for teaching people to draw realistically from life. Her results were impressive, especially with students who had never been able to draw prior to instruction and were adamant that they had no talent for drawing. The foundation of her method is to stimulate within students a specific state of mind, characterized by intense focus on the purely geometric aspects of both the object to be drawn and its representation they create on paper. Edwards did not mention visual fine motor skills specifically, but neither did she make any reference to drawing by computer. It is evident from her method that for her, all drawing is precise hand drawing, and that cognitive faculties related to spatial perception are required both for observation of the object to be drawn and in manipulating the drawing implement on the paper, which places a high demand on visual fine motor skills.

Edwards observed from her own experience as well as accounts from her students that the state of mind thus produced consistently brought forth what she called "gleams from within," i.e., creative insights of one kind or another, often unrelated to the subject matter of the drawing in progress. On this basis, Edwards likewise posited that the act of precise drawing is an important means of enabling creative thought.

Although the arguments made by Edwards in support of this claim are compelling, her evidence is primarily anecdotal. If there is indeed a link between precise hand work and creativity, it is reasonable to expect that it would be reflected within the activity of the brain, i.e., that the cognitive functions which are mobilized in the control of visual fine motor skills in some way stimulate those areas of the brain involved in creative thought. Brain imaging offers a potential means of examining this hypothesis in a more rigorous manner.

Recent neurological studies, for example, have sought to identify the specific areas of the brain that are active when visual fine motor skills are

[4] Edwards, B.: (1999) The New Drawing on the Right Side of the Brain, rev. and exp. ed., Jeremy P. Tarcher/Putnam, New York.

[5] Edwards, B.: (1987) Drawing on the Artist Within, Simon & Schuster, Fireside Books, New York.

[6] Vinci-Booher, S., Cheng, H. and James, K.H.: (2019) "An Analysis of the Brain Systems Involved with Producing Letters by Hand," Journal of Cognitive Neuroscience 31(1), pp. 138–154.

[7] Fan et al.: (2020) "Relating Visual Production and Recognition of Objects in Human Visual Cortex," The Journal of Neuroscience 40(8), pp. 1710–1721.

used. One such study monitored brain activity using magnetic resonance imaging (MRI) as test subjects were given a handwriting task.[6] Another monitored brain activity by MRI as subjects were given a drawing task.[7] In both cases, the experimental setup did not closely replicate the conditions that would normally prevail in actual precise hand work. Current MRI technology requires test subjects to lie on their back during monitoring of brain activity, which constrains them to write or draw in an unrealistic and awkward position. Notwithstanding this, however, these studies did demonstrate that doing precise hand work similar to that performed in design activated areas of the brain associated with higher-level cognitive function. This of course does not constitute a definitive validation of the hypothesis that precise hand work stimulates creative thought in design, but neither does it refute it. Rather, it can be regarded as a small first step towards understanding the significance of precise hand work as a means of enabling better design thinking.

Summary

The buildings and bridges constructed before the 1960s provide incontestable evidence in support of the proposition that precise hand methods of drawing and calculating are sufficient for the design of structures of all types and all degrees of complexity. It follows that the vast majority of structures we currently build could also be designed in the same way.

Design is a creative activity, and, as such, engineers should be free to choose the tools and methods they use for their work. It is reasonable, however, to expect that they make this choice on an informed basis, i.e., based on correct knowledge of the advantages and disadvantages of the tools and methods under consideration.

Precise hand methods of drawing and calculating enhance the ability of engineers to design well. The economy of means imposed by precise hand work favors the design of works with no unnecessary complexity. Simplicity is consistent with low construction cost, which remains a primary design requirement for practical structures. This economy of means also promotes a discipline of slowness which enables designers to reflect on their work as it is produced. The understanding and insight thus gained is valuable in itself, and is essential for enabling precise hand calculation through rational simplification. Precise hand drawing is likely to enhance creativity. Although definitive proof of this hypothesis is not yet available, recent neurological studies have clearly demonstrated a link between the visual fine motor skills required in precise hand work and higher-level cognitive function.

On this basis, therefore, it makes sense for engineers to be aware of the benefits of precise hand work when they choose between hand work and computer work. Given that there are few designers remaining in practice who have done significant precise hand work, it is incumbent on schools of engineering to restore precise hand drawing and calculation to the curriculum.

This is not to say that it is impossible to design good structures without precise hand work. Although designs done completely by hand are still feasible for relatively simple structures, it is unlikely that engineers will be willing to give up the real and significant benefits offered by computers. Computers in the design office are here to stay, and the significance of precise hand work needs to be viewed as pro-hand rather than anti-computer. The challenge to engineers going forward will be to find the right balance between hand and computer for precise work that enables them to design the best possible structures.

KAI-UWE BLETZINGER
ANN-KATHRIN GOLDBACH
REZA NAJIAN

FORM FINDING BY SHAPE OPTIMIZATION WITH IMPLICIT SPLINES AND VERTEX MORPHING

There is no doubt that the procedure of form finding of mechanically loaded structures is an art. The resulting shape is the goal, and the paths to that goal are numerous, as are the tools applied. Everything is possible. The handles that control the process are plenty in number: many are rationally explained, others are heuristic in nature, intuitively chosen or even hidden in the complexity of procedures, tools, and their interaction. Even when principally using the same method, the final structural and aesthetic result of the form finding still tells us much about the mind behind it. Tools such as computational methods should be designed to support the individual's understanding of form finding and the design's aesthetics, allowing the largest possible space for design while keeping it efficient and controllable by a minimum of effort. Here, we present numerical shape optimization with vertex morphing as the solution: numerical optimization as a rational technique to guide the process and vertex morphing as a maximally flexible and easy-to-apply method of shape control with arbitrarily large numbers of degrees of freedom. The methodological kernel is provided by so-called implicit splines that don't need the fixed control meshes required by standard splines. Together with so-called filters – which, once again, may be defined explicitly or implicitly – they are related to variants of subdivision splines, allowing for a great variety of possible solutions for the form finding of structures. This paper gives an illustrative demonstration of the method together with various examples of optimal shell design and some other applications.

Form finding for shells: Design noise and the infinity of design space

The principal challenge in form finding can briefly be explained by an illustrative example. The task is to design the stiffest possible structure that can act as a bridge carrying load using a piece of paper. The solution is well known. As the piece of paper is unable to act to resist bending stresses, stiffeners have to be introduced by folding the paper. However, an infinite number of solutions exist, all of which do the job of creating stiffening solutions of at least similar quality that offer far better quality than the initially flat piece of paper. Surprisingly enough, even an arbitrary pattern of random folds appears to be a possible solution [PAGE 73, TOP]. The figure of the randomly crinkled paper is an ideal paradigm for the infinity of the design space or, more ostensibly, the "design noise." As for the actual example, the crinkled paper can be understood to be the weighted combination of all possible stiffening patterns. One can easily think of a procedure to derive any of the individual, basic solutions of distinct stiffening patterns by applying suitable "filters" to the design noise. It is clear that, as well as its size, the nature of the "filter"– i.e., the filter radius – can be freely chosen. This is a most important design decision which guides the form finding process and the final solution.

LEFT PAGE Optimized shell. Magnitude of displacement [PAGE 74]

Regularization of the "design noise" by implicit splines and vertex morphing

Following the above example, we take the crinkled paper as what we call the control field s of our procedure. From the control field s we derive the geometry x by applying a low pass filter A **[PAGE 72, TOP]**. The formula reflects the convolution of s with the material surface coordinates ξ and the filter function A of radius r which is centered at ξ_0 generating the geometry x from the control field s:

(1) $$x = \int A s \, d\Gamma = \int_{\xi_0-r}^{\xi_0+r} A(\xi, \xi_0, r) s(\xi) d\xi$$

As may be anticipated from the discretized version of the filter process **[PAGE 72, TOP]**, the control field s is the continuous equivalent of the control polygon s as it is known from standard splines. As an example, a cubic B-spline is created by filtering a linear hat function by a linear hat filter **[PAGE 72]**. This explains the well-known definition of subdivision splines.[1] Its generalization we call vertex morphing.[2-7] The vertices of the discretized control field s are the nodes of the underlying finite element mesh which has been created in advance by any standard pre-processor. When implementing vertex morphing, the discrete control handles s can be condensed out if the control field is discretized on the same mesh as the geometry x, which is the standard case. Then the discrete values of the control field must not be determined, although they are the crucial part of the formulation. The nice consequence for this application is that the control field must not be displayed at any stage of the form-finding procedure. The designer directly deals with the generated shape only, which is the subject of interest.

Still, the nature of filter function A may be freely chosen. The simplest variant is the linear hat function as introduced above along a line. On a surface it may be extended to a cone. Filter functions may be defined on a limited support: i.e., they are zero outside of r. Alternatively, they may span the complete structure. Most important is the filter radius r which controls the "waviness" of the generated shape. The radius defines the size of limited supports or a characteristic length of unlimited filters. With respect to numerical shape optimization, the chosen radius typically steers the optimization to local minima of the shape whose waviness is characterized by that radius r. As a consequence, the choice of the filter radius is an important design parameter. For many practical applications, the input of one filter radius value is sufficient. Also, different values of the filter radius can be applied to different regions of the structure. In all cases, even the most challenging design problems, the application of filter radii is effortless and intuitive.

[PAGE 73, BOTTOM] displays a characteristic example. The optimal shape of an initially flat shell with circular plan due to distributed vertical load is determined for maximal stiffness. Left: without applying filters, an algorithm determines the crinkled "design noise," while on the right we have the well-known dome that is obtained if a simple hat filter with the radius of the circular boundary is applied. From a numerical point of view, there is an additional argument for filters, as distorted meshes – as seen on the left – are artificially stiff. This must be avoided, and it can easily be done by, at the least, taking the smallest allowable filter radius to be some multiple of the element size, typically 2 to 4. For smaller filter radii, the mesh must be refined.

Last but not least, we distinguish explicit and implicit filtering. This is best explained by the discrete version of filtering – please refer to equation (1). Then the filter function A is replaced by a filter matrix **A** which filters the discrete control field values collected in vector s to the discrete shape

1 Catmull, E., Clark, J.: (1978) "Recursively generated B-spline surfaces on arbitrary topological meshes," CAD Computer Aided Design, 10(6), pp. 350–355.

2 Bletzinger, K.-U.: (2011) "Form Finding and Morphogenesis" in: Fifty Years of Progress for Shell and Spatial Structures, International Association for Shell and Spatial Structures (IASS), Madrid, p. 500.

3 Hojjat, M., Stavropoulou, E., Bletzinger, K.-U.: (2014) "The Vertex Morphing method for node-based shape optimization," Computer Methods in Applied Mechanics and Engineering, 268, pp. 494–513.

4 Bletzinger, K.-U.: (2017) "Shape Optimization," in Erwin Stein, René de Borst, T. J. R. Hughes (Eds.) Encyclopedia of Computational Mechanics, John Wiley & Sons, Ltd.

5 Najian Asl, R., Shayegan, S., Geiser, A., Hojjat, M., Bletzinger, K.-U.: (2017) "A consistent formulation for imposing packaging constraints in shape optimization using Vertex Morphing parametrization," Structural and Multidisciplinary Optimization, 56, pp. 1507–1519.

6 Antonau, I., Warnakulasuriya, S., Bletzinger, K.-U., Bluhm, F. M., Hojjat, M., Wüchner, R.: (2022) "Latest developments in node-based shape optimization using Vertex Morphing parameterization," Structural and Multidisciplinary Optimization, 65.

7 Najian Asl, R., Bletzinger, K.-U.: (2022) "Implicit bulk-surface filtering method for node-based shape optimization and comparison of explicit and implicit filtering techniques," Structural and Multidisciplinary Optimization, 66.

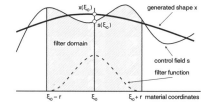

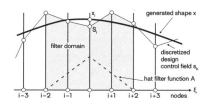

TOP Applying filter A to generate shape x from control field s, continuous (above), discretized (below)

RIGHT PAGE, TOP Stiffened shell structures made from folded paper. Clockwise from top left – a piece of paper used as a "bridge"; coarse stiffening pattern; random stiffening pattern; fine stiffening pattern.

RIGHT PAGE, BOTTOM Direct numerical stiffness optimization and filtering of a plate subjected to vertical distributed load

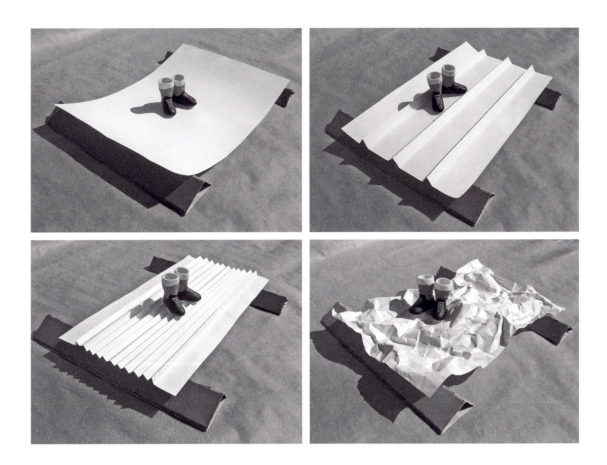

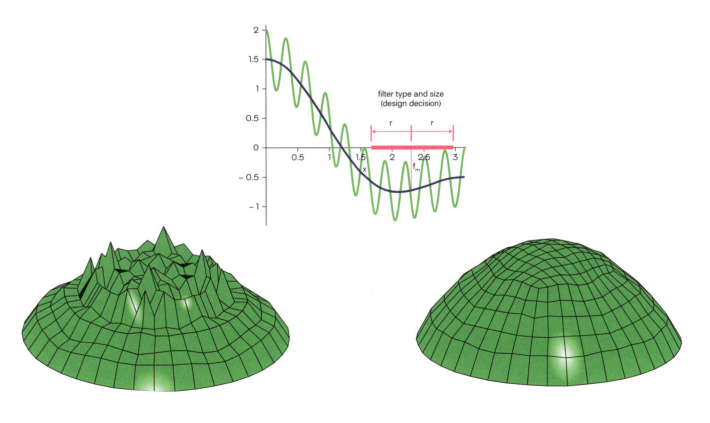

CHALLENGING GRAVITY 73

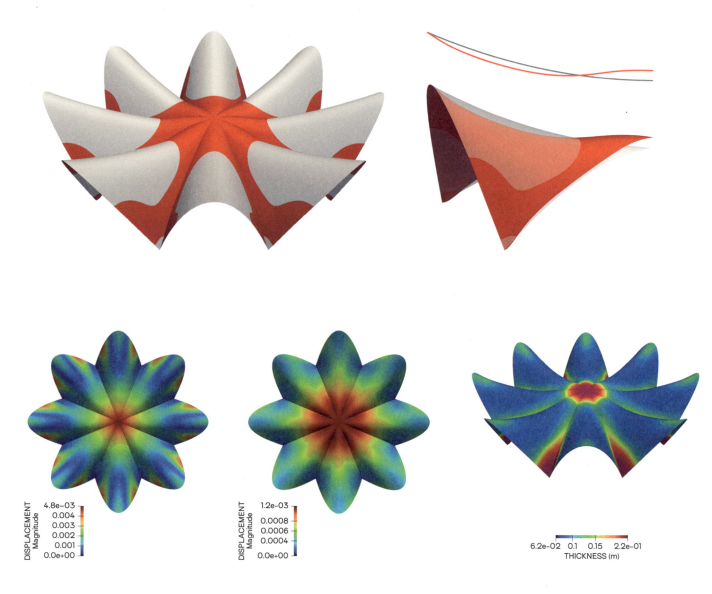

FORM FINDING BY SHAPE OPTIMIZATION WITH IMPLICIT SPLINES AND VERTEX MORPHING

[8] Mohammadi, B., Pironneau, O.: (2010) Applied Shape Optimization for Fluids, Oxford University Press.

[9] Jameson, A.: (2003) "Aerodynamic shape optimization using the adjoint method," in B. Von Karman Institute (ed.), Lecture at the Von Karman Institute, Brussels, Belgium.

coordinates collected in x, (2, left). In the case of equal numbers of control and coordinate numbers the operation may be inverted (2, right) with implicit filter matrix $\tilde{A}$:

(2) explicit filtering: $\mathbf{x} = \mathbf{A}\mathbf{s}$ implicit filtering: $\mathbf{s} = \mathbf{A}^{-1}\mathbf{x} = \tilde{\mathbf{A}}\mathbf{x}$

As an example, the implicit filter matrix $\tilde{A}$ may be defined as:

(3) $\tilde{\mathbf{A}} = \mathbf{I} - \varepsilon\Delta$

with the unit matrix $\mathbf{I}$, the Laplace operator Δ and some scalar ε which is equivalent to the filter radius, all together defining what is known as Helmholtz filtering or Sobolev smoothing.[8,9] The Laplace operator Δ applied to the geometry in terms of $\mathbf{x}$ represents the surface curvature properties. The result is the smoothing of the (unwanted) geometric "waviness" and ε, equivalent to r, as a measure of the wavelength. The convincing property of the implicit version of filtering is that boundary conditions of the generated shape $\mathbf{x}$ can be directly controlled compared to the explicit one. Without further explanation, one can imagine that there also exists a continuous equivalent filter function $\tilde{A}$ to correspond to the implicit filter matrix $\tilde{A}$.

The following examples are created by using explicit and implicit filtering — in the case of implicit filtering, eventually together with filter functions spanning the complete structure, thus controlling the overall continuity of the shape together with the boundaries. The choice of ε or, equivalently, the filter radius r is the design handle for form finding, steering the result to its respective solution.

Aside from the tremendous amount of mathematics in the background of the method, it is the simplest and most straightforward method to apply. All it needs is a finite element model of the structure as output of common CAD pre-processors. It must be fine enough to be undistorted and able to resolve the smallest expected curvature radii of shape. Pragmatically, it is better to choose a finer mesh than the minimum necessary. Every node of the mesh may move during form finding. This defines problem sizes with the number of optimization parameters as the number of mesh nodes multiplied by the number of coordinates at every node. Obviously, this gives very large numbers, which, however, can easily be treated as a consequence of the indirect control of geometry by the control field s and the filter idea. Refer to **[PAGE 73, BOTTOM]** and estimate the size of the relevant problem. What remains are the choice of filter functions (typically either explicit or implicit) and the size of the filter radii as control handles. For the following examples, very fine meshes are used. Typically, they are not shown because they do not give additional information. The filter sizes are not reported in absolute numbers. They are chosen to be large enough to give the displayed results. Since shell structures are most effective in transferring loading by an infinite number of alternative load paths, a related and also infinite number of optimal shapes exists. Consequently, the choice of a filter radius or, eventually, a certain distribution of filter radii (e.g., smaller at the edges, larger in the interior to allow stiffened edges with locally larger curvature) decide the result of the form-finding process.

The idea of this paper is to demonstrate stages of a typical design procedure: (i) Take any filter and filter radius, set up the optimization problem and receive a first optimal shape; (ii) discuss the quality of that shape with respect to its properties (e.g., its load-carrying principle, geometric properties, aesthetics, manufacturability, etc.); (iii) repeat the first steps as often as necessary to explore the design space to find alternative solutions;

LEFT PAGE, TOP Models of the original shell (grey) and the optimized one (red)

LEFT PAGE, CENTER Magnitudes of displacement, original (left) and optimized (center); filter technique applied to find the optimized thickness distribution (right).

LEFT PAGE, BOTTOM L'Oceanogràfic, Valencia, Spain, 2002. Architecture: Félix Candela The Valencia "Candela" shell was the last structure Félix Candela was involved in creating.

(iv) take your final choice from among the intermediate solutions found. The examples do not represent more than one of these. Since we could show any other as the result of a varied filter, the specific value of the filter radius is not important information. Typically, finding the shape of shells is a process. There are no optimal solutions without alternatives. A form-finding method, such as vertex morphing, must help identify them.

Explicit filtering and varying filter radii The shape of a three-point supported shell is to be optimized for stiffness subjected to self-weight [PAGE 76]. The ground plan is fixed. The shell thickness is kept constant – in particular, it does not allow for thicker edge beams. The size of the filter radius is varied, with smaller filter radii selected at the edges and larger ones in the interior shell domain, as given in the figure. By playing with filters, a large variety of shapes can be generated which represents well-known classes of optimized shell structures, all of which do not require extra edge beams: (a) the positive curved shell with special edges treatment, perhaps similar to Frei Otto's "Segelschalen," (b) the negative curved edge well known from many of Isler's shells, and (c) the "Candela type" hypar-like solution.[10] Of course, the aesthetic quality is far from satisfactory due to the comparatively small number of degrees of freedom in the design, but this example shows very nicely how different solutions can be found, in principle, by extracting them from the "design noise" of the chosen discretization. Nevertheless, the shapes are generalized splines as the result of applying explicit hat filters to the control field s. This field cannot be displayed, although it is the methodological nucleus.

The Valencia "Candela" shell Felix Candela is known as the master of hypar shells. He developed a principle of form based on negative curved hyper-paraboloids that were both aesthetically impressive and efficient to design and build. He even developed his own approach to the structural analysis of hypar shells.[11] The community agrees that structures such as his are optimal. The example that follows is a further analysis of the structural properties of the "Candela" shell in Valencia with the aim of identifying further improvement by applying vertex morphing. The implicit filter has been applied with a filter radius large enough to maintain a smooth overall shape. This example also demonstrates nicely that the filter works on the shape modification rather than on the resulting shape as the sum of initial shape and modification. As a consequence, the sharp gorges of the shape and the "Candela" characteristic are maintained. The existing shell in Valencia was the last structure Candela was involved in creating. It was designed and created by local engineers applying new technologies such as fiber-reinforced concrete.[12]

[PAGE 74, BOTTOM] shows the built structure. On [PAGE 74, TOP], one can see the models of the original shell (grey) and the optimized one (red). The stiffness is maximized due to distributed surface load, while the mass is held constant. As a consequence, the center of the shell is lifted and the outer regions of the vaults are lowered. The cross section and detailed focus on a vault show the high quality of geometry of the optimized shell in terms of curvature and waviness. The finite element mesh is very fine and not shown. The optimized shell deforms significantly better than the original one [PAGE 74, CENTER]. The maximum deformation is concentrated to the center and is reduced by a factor of 4. Very impressively, the deformation at the free edges is simultaneously reduced and homogenized. The localized large deflections at the edge have disappeared.

This example demonstrates how vertex morphing may be applied in order to study and to develop shells in line with accepted design principles, exploring the infinity of design space while also finding aesthetically

10 Mungan, I., Abel, J. F. (eds.): (2011) Fifty Years of Progress for Shell and Spatial Structures, International Association for Shell and Spatial Structures (IASS), Madrid.

11 Garlock, M. E. M., Billington D. P.: (2008) Felix Candela: Engineer, Builder, Structural Artist, Yale University Press, New Haven.

12 Domingo L. C., Lázaro C., Serna P.: (1999) "Design of a thin shell steel fibre reinforced concrete hypar roof," in Proceedings of the IASS Symposium 1999, International Association for Shell and spatial Structures, Madrid.

a) radius size 11:3 (interior : edge)

b) radius size 7:3

c) radius size 5:3

TOP **Different optimal shapes of shells extracted from the design space by varying the filter size.**

RIGHT PAGE, TOP **Market Hall in Algeciras, Spain, 1934. Structural design and engineering: Eduardo Torroja.**

RIGHT PAGE, CENTER RIGHT **Models of the original (grey) and optimized (red) shell**

RIGHT PAGE, CENTER LEFT **Cross sections (left); comparison of original (grey) and optimized (red) shell (right)**

RIGHT PAGE, BOTTOM **Vertical deflections – the original shell (left), the optimized shell (right)**

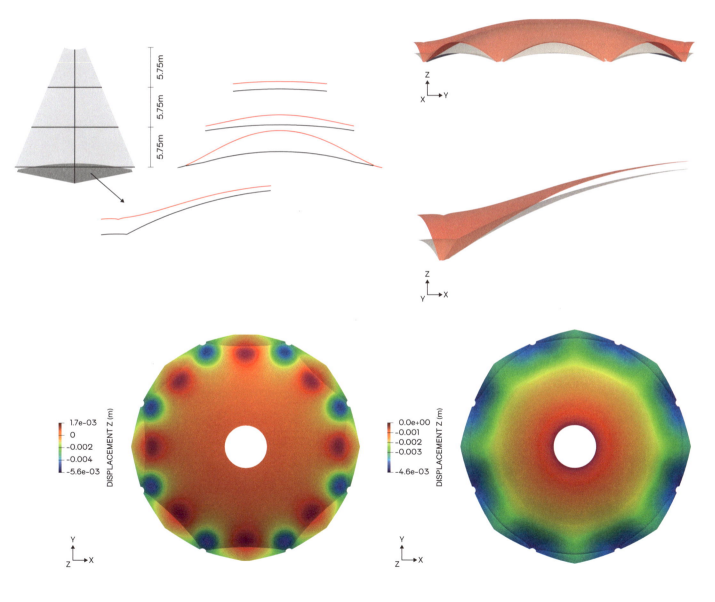

CHALLENGING GRAVITY

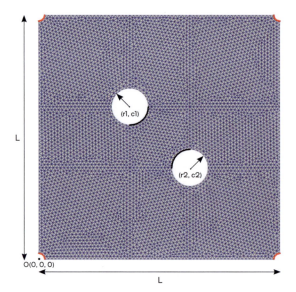

E = 30GPa, v = 0.2
l = 20m, t = 0.1m
c_1 = (7.5, 12.5, 0)m, r_1 = 1.5m
c_2 = (12.5, 7.5, 0)m, r_2 = 1.5m
── non-design (fully fixed)
── structure support (fully-fixed) & non-design (fully-fixed)
a fillet radius of 0.5m is applied at the corners
loading: (0,0, −3.5)kN/m² & uniform

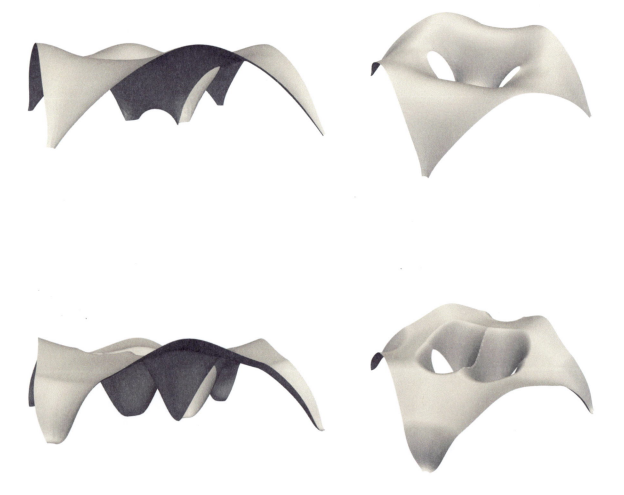

impressive solutions in engineering. It is, of course, still left up to everyone to search for further variants by varying the filters or modifying the optimization problem by adding constraints or simultaneously optimizing shape and thickness [PAGE 74, CENTER RIGHT].

The "Torroja" shell Another icon of concrete shells is Torroja's shell for the market hall in Algeciras [PAGE 77, TOP]. Again, the shape has been further optimized for stiffness due to distributed surface load and the constraints on mass. The implicit filter with a large radius has been applied. This technique allows one to maintain the characteristic kink between the "caps" of the shell and the interior region. Obviously, it would appear to be a good idea to raise the apex of the arches of the edge caps. Consequently, the originally positive double-curved interior dome is now transferred into a negative curved, "wavy" surface. The specific properties of vertex morphing allow one to generate another aesthetically pleasing solution. Again, further alternatives may easily be generated with varying filters and setups of the optimization problem.

[PAGE 77, CENTER LEFT] displays several cross sections in the radial and tangential direction through the original and the optimized shells from which the geometry of the newly form-found vaults becomes obvious. Again, the load-carrying behavior of the optimized shell is improved and made much more homogeneous than before – this can be anticipated from [PAGE 77, BOTTOM], which shows the vertical deflections.

Free-form "hanging model" shell This example is another academic case of a completely free-form shell. Over a quadratic plan, this shape is optimized for maximum stiffness due to vertically acting uniform load [PAGE 78, TOP]. Vertex morphing is applied with implicit [PAGE 78, CENTER], and explicit filters [PAGE 78, BOTTOM] together with large and small radii, respectively. The four corners and parts of the interior, initially circular holes, are held on the ground to be the supports of the shell. Refer to the figures for further information on the model definitions. Note the fine finite element mesh. Besides the supports, each of the nodes are allowed to move freely. Again, the number of optimization variables is very large but not of importance. In particular, this example nicely demonstrates the effect of the filter radius size. With large filters, one obtains a very smooth and continuous surface. The properties of an implicitly defined spline surface become obvious. As can be seen from the result of [PAGE 78, BOTTOM], small filters drive the shape to one with localized curvature. This may be useful if shapes with strong stiffeners need to be designed. Again, the possible range of form finding is demonstrated. Optimization is used as a tool of form finding. All shapes found are optimal solutions in equilibrium as a consequence of the chosen filter strategy.

Conclusions

The development and application of form-finding methods have a long tradition in architecture and civil engineering. Initially focused on form finding for shells, interest in this has been extended to form finding for tensile structures, the application of numerical techniques, and, on this basis, to structural optimization in general and shape optimization in particular. In any event, a magic tool box does not exist. Form finding techniques only help to find new solutions; they have to be guided with care through use of the remaining procedural parameters. Form finding remains an art, but methods, opportunities, and challenges evolve with the acceptance of computational methods as modern tools.

Free-form shell on quadratic plan
LEFT PAGE, TOP FEM mesh and model setup

LEFT PAGE, CENTER Optimization results with implicit filter and large radius

LEFT PAGE, BOTTOM Result with explicit filtering and small radius

PATRICK OLE OHLBROCK
GIULIA BOLLER
PIERLUIGI D'ACUNTO

CONCEPTUAL DESIGN OF STRUCTURES IN THE DIGITAL AGE

Solving problems that cannot be explicitly formulated

[1] Cross, N.: (2006) Designerly Ways of Knowing, Springer.

[2] Schön, D.: (1983) The Reflective Practitioner: How Professionals Think in Action. Basic Books, New York.

[3] Kotnik, T.: (2008) "Design as Exploration of Computable Functions Digital Architectural Design as Exploration of Computable Functions," International Journal of Architectural Computing 8(1).

The conceptual design of structures is a collaborative process that combines architecture and engineering. Its main objective is to ensure that load-bearing structures not only meet functional, programmatic, and aesthetic prerequisites but also fulfill essential technical requirements, including safety, durability, and performance. To attain these goals, a holistic approach is essential, encompassing the entire workflow from conceiving the structure's topology and form to selecting appropriate materials and defining construction and deconstruction processes. The conceptual design of structures lies at the interface of architecture and engineering, presenting an inherently complex and ambiguous challenge. Many design objectives cannot be predetermined, rendering purely analytical solutions impractical. While a precise formalization or general definition of the conceptual structural design remains elusive, certain common characteristics can be identified, as highlighted by Nigel Cross.[1]

The impact of conceptual structural design extends beyond the early planning phase and influences subsequent design stages and decisions. Typically, it is an iterative process that demands multiple steps. The initial step involves gathering information about the design problem, identifying goals, specifying constraints, and pondering contextual factors. During this step, designers draw upon their past experiences and references, either consciously or unconsciously. Once the information has been filtered, a series of initial design proposals are produced using various conceptual models such as sketches, texts, preliminary calculations, or physical prototypes. These models serve to enhance the understanding of the problem and explore different design options. After evaluating these initial concepts, designers either refine and transform their proposal or start afresh, incorporating feedback and new insights into the process. This iterative process of generation and evaluation is essential for resolving ill-defined problems and engaging in a reflective conversation with the situation, as described by Donald Schön.[2]

The integration of computational tools into the conceptual design process is intended to facilitate the dialectic between the initial divergent and subsequent convergent phases of design. According to Toni Kotnik,[3] the aim of incorporating computers into the design process lies in consciously exploring the potential of computable functions as design tools. This exploration involves understanding the formal relationships between sets of entities, the quantifiable properties associated with these sets, and their algorithmic transformations and interactions. By leveraging computational capabilities, designers can expand their exploration of design possibilities and refine their concepts more effectively.

LEFT PAGE Conceptual design proposal for the Olympic Stadium for Tokyo 2020 by Pierluigi D'Acunto, Lukas Ingold, and Patrick Ole Ohlbrock.

The use of computers in structural engineering and design

Before the introduction of computers in engineering practice in the 1960s, traditional tools such as paper-based drawings [PAGE 83, TOP RIGHT], manual calculations, and physical models were considered the primary means of designing structures. These methods involved breaking down engineering questions into simple sub-problems, and were heavily dependent on the designers' experience and accuracy. However, in view of the increasing complexity of structures and the consequent difficulties in understanding their actual behavior, newly developed numerical methods provided an "effective tool with which to manipulate in an elegant manner large amounts of data."[4] One such breakthrough was the introduction of the Finite Element Method (FEM), which emerged as a crucial outcome of this technological shift. Following early studies on its mathematical foundations by R. Courant,[5] the introduction of continuum-based finite elements by J. Turner in the 1950s marked a significant milestone in the context of computational structural analysis. Subsequent advancements by J. H. Argyris, R. W. Clough, H. C. Martin, and O. C. Zienkiewicz made pivotal contributions to the discipline.[6] The rapid development of computing devices, coupled with the increasing refinement of computer programs, fostered the emergence of calculation centers [PAGE 83, TOP LEFT], providing data processing capabilities for structural engineering purposes. In the 1980s, thanks to the rise of personal computers, engineering firms gained the ability to analyze and refine design proposals more efficiently in-house. This transformative development resulted in the gradual replacement of manual calculations with Finite Element Analysis (FEA) for verifying the structural integrity of designs.

As computers helped speed up calculations for the analysis of structures, they also quickly became an attractive option for studying structural forms in equilibrium during the early design phase. In the context of form finding, before the rise of computational tools, achieving the integration of form and forces in structural design required iterative procedures with the use of multiple physical models. Within this framework, fundamental work was done by F. Otto, H. Isler, and S. Musmeci.[7] The efficiency of computers in performing iterative processes led to a progressive transition towards digital form-finding methods. In the late 1950s, Isler was one of the pioneers in using computational methods to relate physical and digital models for the generation and control of complex shapes.[8] By the late 1960s, researchers at the University of Stuttgart consistently began using a combination of analog and digital models to generate cable-net structures in a more consistent way.[9] In particular, the design of the roof structure of the Munich Olympic Stadium (1967–72) contributed to the development of new computational form-finding methods, such as the Force Density Method (FDM).[10] [PAGE 83, BOTTOM]. It is also during the 1960s that I. Sutherland made a groundbreaking impact by introducing Sketchpad[11] [PAGE 83, CENTER], an early digital drawing system that laid the foundation for modern computer-aided design (CAD), allowing designers to directly interact with a graphical interface.

Following these early experiments – and thanks to the newly developed visualization tools – the creative potential offered by the interaction between humans and machines was soon recognized both by architects and engineers. Over recent decades, the integration of computation into the conceptual structural design process has witnessed significant growth: two distinct computer modeling approaches, namely parametric modeling and rule-based generative approaches, have proven beneficial to the digital design community.[12] These approaches support the formalization of de-

4 Bathe K.J. and Wilson E.L.: (1976) Numerical Methods in Finite Element Analysis, Prentice-Hall, Englewood Cliffs, p. 3.

5 Courant, R.: (1943) "Variational methods for the solution of problems of equilibrium and vibrations," Bulletin of the American Mathematical Society, 49 (1), pp. 1–23.

6 Sabat, L., Kundu, C. K.: (2021) "History of Finite Element Method: A Review," Das, B., Barbhuiya, S., Gupta, R., Saha, P. (eds.), Recent Developments in Sustainable Infrastructure.

7 Boller, G. and D'Acunto, P.: (2021) "Structural design via form finding: comparing Frei Otto, Heinz Isler and Sergio Musmeci," in Proceedings of the ICCH, 431–438.

8 Boller, G.: (2022) "The model as a working method. Heinz Isler's experimental approach to shell design," PhD Thesis, ETH Zurich.

9 Otto, F.: (1990) Experiments, IL 25, Institut für Leichte Flächentragwerke, Stuttgart.

10 Linkwitz, K.: (1972) "New methods for the determination of cutting pattern of prestressed cable nets and their application to the Olympic roofs Munich," Proceedings of the Pacific Symposium on Tension Structures and Space Frames, pp. 13–26.

11 Sutherland, E.: (1963) "Sketchpad: A man-machine graphical communication system," AFIPS Conference Proceedings 23, pp. 323–328.

12 Harding, J. E. and Shepherd, P.: (2017) "Meta-Parametric Design," Design Studies 52, pp. 73–95.

RIGHT PAGE, TOP LEFT Female employees at the punch card puncher, Zurich, approx. 1960

RIGHT PAGE, TOP RIGHT Typical working atmosphere of engineers and architects at Inland Steel Building without the computer, 1958

RIGHT PAGE, CENTER Ivan Sutherland working on the Sketchpad, which he developed within his PhD thesis.[11] His work is considered the ancestor of modern computer-aided design (CAD) programs as well as a major breakthrough in the development of computer graphics in general.

RIGHT PAGE, BOTTOM Three cable-nets that were form found using the Force Density Method (FDM).[10] The variations show how the force density in the main cables influences the geometry.

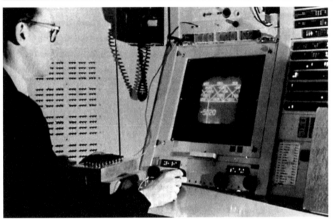
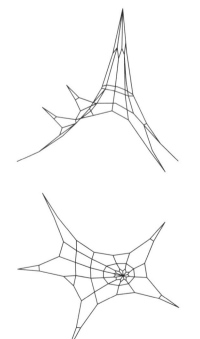
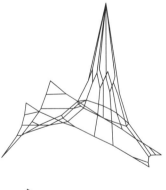
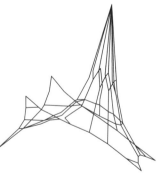
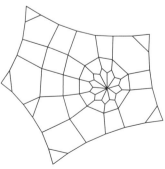
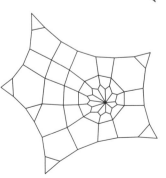

CHALLENGING GRAVITY

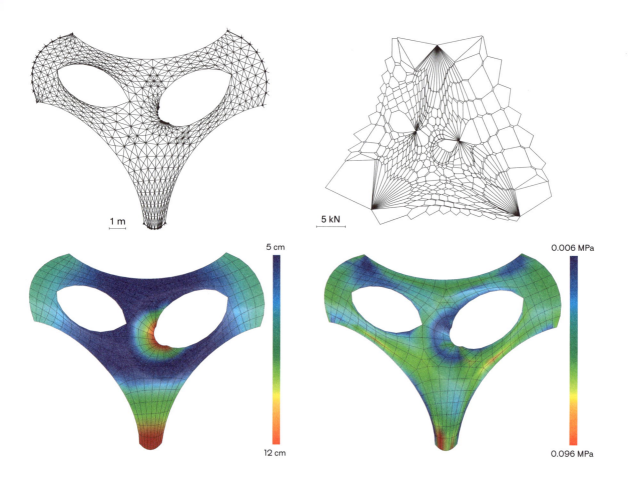

CONCEPTUAL DESIGN OF STRUCTURES IN THE DIGITAL AGE

13 Mueller, C. T.: (2014) "Structural Design Space Exploration," PhD thesis, MIT.

14 Oxman, R.: (2006) "Theory and design in the first digital age," Design Studies 27(3), pp. 229–265.

15 Gero, J. S. and Kumar, B.: (1993) "Expanding design spaces through new design variables," Design Studies 14(2), pp. 210–221.

16 Aish, R. and Woodbury, R.: (2005) "Multi-level interaction in parametric design," Smart Graphics, Springer, Berlin – Heidelberg, pp. 151–162.

17 Holzer, D., Hough, R. and Burry, M.: (2007) "Parametric design and structural optimization for early design exploration," International Journal of Architectural Computing 5(4), pp. 625–643.

18 Bentley, P. and Kumar, S.: (1999) "Three ways to grow designs: A comparison of embryogenies for an evolutionary design problem," Proceedings of the 1st Annual Conference on Genetic and Evolutionary Computation – Volume 1, Morgan Kaufmann Publishers Inc., San Francisco, pp. 35–43.

19 Shea, K.: (1997) "Essays of Discrete Structures: Purposeful Design of Grammatical Structures by Directed Stochastic Search," PhD thesis, Carnegie Mellon University.

20 van Buelow, P.: (2007) "An Intelligent Genetic Design Tool (IGDT): applied to the exploration of architectural trussed structural system," PhD thesis, Universität Stuttgart.

21 Konstantatou, M., D'Acunto, P. and McRobie, A.: (2018) "Polarities in Structural Analysis and Design: n-dimensional Graphic Statics and Structural Transformations," International Journal of Solids and Structures 152–153, pp. 272–293.

22 D'Acunto, P., Jasienski, J.-P., Ohlbrock, P. O., Fivet, C., Schwartz, J., and Zastavni, D.: (2019) "Vector-based 3D graphic statics: A framework for the design of spatial structures based on the relation between form and forces," International Journal of Solids and Structures 167, pp. 58–70.

LEFT PAGE, TOP **The Armadillo Vault by the Block Research Group at ETH Zurich. The projections in plan of the form diagram (left) and the force diagram (right) show the geometry of the structure and the forces acting in it respectively.**

LEFT PAGE, CENTER **The two diagrams show the distribution of the shell thickness (left) as well as the maximum stress (right) of the Armadillo Vault.**

LEFT PAGE, BOTTOM **The Armadillo Vault, which was exhibited in the Venice Biennale 2016, is an unreinforced stone structure comprising 399 cut limestone blocks assembled without structural connections or mortar. The vault, covering an area of 75 m² and spanning more than 15 m in various directions, has a minimum thickness of only 5 cm.**

sign processes for generation and transformation, providing valuable tools for designers. On the one hand, explicit parametric modeling approaches are primarily variable-based and generally operate in a top-down fashion.[12] On the other hand, implicit rule-based generative approaches usually operate bottom-up on a grammar-based level.[13]

Parametric modeling approaches

Recent advances in structural engineering software enabled the smooth integration of geometric design and structural performance analysis. In this context, parametric modeling has emerged as a highly influential approach that facilitates the establishment of logical connections and interdependencies between input design parameters, such as form, and corresponding performance outputs, such as forces and stresses.[14] In such an explicit modeling environment, the generation, evaluation, and transformation (optimization) of a design can be carried out almost simultaneously. Thanks to the rapid feedback loops between input and output, a structural designer now has the potential to explore and compare a wide range of design options and their performance more extensively than ever before.[12] Parametric modeling relies on explicit mathematical functions to convert input parameters into design outputs. The parameter space represents the range of possible inputs, while the design space, which encompasses variations in design, represents the collection of possible outputs.[13,14,15] In this design approach, the structure of the parametric model and its mathematical function dictate the properties and limitations of the design space.[16] While parametric models allow for variation, they can be limited to producing self-similar and predictable results within the design space. Relying solely on explicit parametric strategies may restrict the designer to a single topology or necessitate the simultaneous development of multiple parametric definitions.[17] The substantial effort involved in creating models with various topologies is a major reason why parametric modeling is not widely used in the very early conceptual stages.[12]

Rule-based generative approaches

Implicit bottom-up modeling approaches are inspired by the evolution of complex systems, where the generation process is driven by a concatenation of topological and metric formation rules that operate on a low-level primitive unit. An advantage of these combinatorial approaches is that they allow a broad design exploration,[18] which is enabled through the inherent topological flexibility of these approaches.[13,19,20] A common drawback of these approaches is that implicit generative processes often lead to design results that are difficult to control. This limitation, which hinders human designers from directly interacting with the design,[12] primarily arises from the presence of an indirect mapping from cause to effect. As a result, even a slight change in the initial configuration of rules or parameters can result in an unexpected and significantly different outcome.[12]

Computational graphic statics

In an attempt to bridge the gap between parametric modeling and rule-based generative approaches, the past decade has seen graphic statics integrated into computational methods and tools for structural design.[21,22] Graphic statics encompasses a collection of geometry-based constructions that enable the establishment of a reciprocal relationship between the form of a structure, represented through a form diagram, and the forces acting upon and within the structure, depicted in a force diagram.[23] Ideally, computational graphic statics can combine the advantages of an explicit parametric environment where form and forces are immediately coupled and can be interactively modified by the designer with the advantages of rule-based approaches to generate topologically varying instances of form and force diagrams, in which the static equilibrium is a prerequisite of the emerging structures **[PAGE 80 and PAGE 88]**. Controlling and visualizing the spatial force flow is essential during the conceptual design phase, as argued by Schwartz.[24] This visualization becomes crucial in finding a balance among numerous conflicting aspects that cannot be fully captured by numerical calculations alone. Thus, graphic statics and its computational implementations can greatly facilitate the conceptual design process, as exemplarily demonstrated by the Armadillo Vault project[25] **[PAGE 84]** and the Goián – Cerveira Footbridge over the Miño River project.[26] **[PAGE 87]**

Artificial Intelligence for the conceptual design of structures

Architects and structural engineers are increasingly recognizing the potential that Artificial Intelligence (AI), particularly Machine Learning (ML), holds for conceptual design.[27] Unlike traditional algorithms that rely on explicitly defined relationships between input and output, ML algorithms work differently. They learn these relationships directly from input and output data, uncovering complex patterns and correlations between them. This data-driven approach allows them to generalize and make accurate predictions or decisions based on previously unseen data, making them powerful and versatile tools for various applications.[28] In this way, computers are no longer just used for simulation and optimization but are increasingly becoming an integral part of the generative step in the design process. AI-driven generative design frameworks can autonomously create and explore design options based on given parameters and constraints, offering designers new insights and creative possibilities. Thanks to current unprecedented developments, Artificial Intelligence (AI) has started to be integrated into the standard workflows of architects and engineers. Real-world applications of ML in this context can be already found in the works of the Core Studio of Thornton Tomasseti and the Swedish start-up Finch 3D, to name a few.

One of the most promising aspects of AI integration into design is its potential to enable designers to navigate and manage complex, high-dimensional, multidisciplinary and topologically varied design spaces more effortlessly. In this context, ML-based methods like Self-Organizing Maps (SOM) have been used to capture the complexity of real-world environments by processing large streams of data.[29] **PAGE 89** shows an example of an SOM of thousands of structural design options for a stadium roof that have been automatically generated by a computational form-finding algorithm.[30] SOM serves as an unsupervised ML nonlinear data transformation technique that converts data from a high-dimensional space into a more manageable two-dimensional space. With the help of clustering techniques like these, it is possible to represent complex, high-dimensional data in a way that is easily understandable. This allows designers to obtain a clear overview of all available design options without experiencing eval-

23 Kurrer, K. E.: (2008) The History of the Theory of Structures, from Arch Analysis to Computational Mechanics, Ernst & Sohn, Berlin.

24 Schwartz, J.: (2011) "Teaching", in Co-operation: The Engineer and the Architect, Birkhäuser, pp. 243–249.

25 Block, P.: (2016) Beyond Bending: Reimagining Compression Shells, DETAIL Verlag.

26 Bernabeu, A., Mateo, J., Ruiz, F., Colmenero, G.: (2022) Goian – Cerveira Footbridge over the Miño River. Spain – Portugal, Proceedings of Footbridge 2022: Creating Experience, Madrid, Spain

27 Carta, S.: (2021) Self-Organizing Floor Plans, Harvard Data Science Review 3(3).

28 Málaga-Chuquitaype, C.: (2022) Machine Learning in Structural Design: An Opinionated Review, Frontiers in Built Environment.

29 Moosavi V.: (2015) "Pre-Specific Modelling Computational Machines in Coexistence with Urban Data Streams," PhD thesis, ETH Zurich.

30 Ohlbrock, P.O., D'Acunto P.: (2020) "A Computer-Aided Approach to Equilibrium Design Based on Graphic Statics and Combinatorial Variations," Computer-Aided Design, 121.

RIGHT PAGE Goián – Cerveira Footbridge over the Miño River (Architectural design: Burgos & Garrido, Structural design and engineering: Bernabeu Ingenieros).

TOP Form finding of the bridge with form diagram (left) and force diagram (right) using Vector-based Graphic Statics[22] and Combinatorial Equilibrium Modeling[30] (Ohlbrock and D'Acunto). Red and blue indicate tension and compression respectively.

BOTTOM The corresponding design of the curved suspension bridge won an international competition in 2017. It will connect the Espazo Fortaleza park in Goián-Tomiño, Spain, and the Castelinho Park in Vila Nova de Cerveira, Portugal. The proposed footbridge has a main span of around 250 m. The result is a very subtle and slender structure, a "line over the Miño River" that highly preserves the environmental values of the river and the landscape.

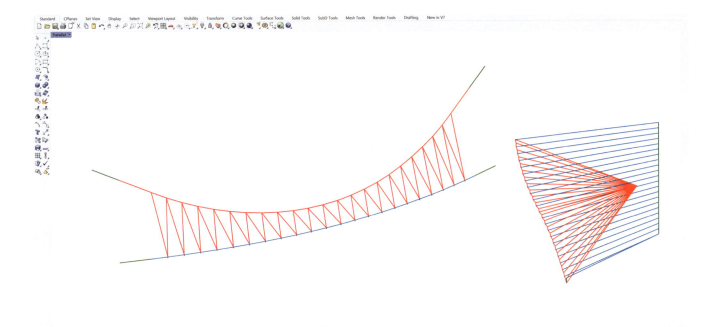

CHALLENGING GRAVITY

uation fatigue or getting stuck prematurely in the design process.[31] Thanks to recent developments in the field of ML, human designers can interact with a variety of design options simultaneously. Additionally, protocols of these human-machine interactions can reveal the individual and subjective decision patterns of designers.

In the future, AI-driven design frameworks will play a crucial role in simulating multidisciplinary design processes that address both quantitative and qualitative design aspects. However, a significant challenge in the field of AI-driven conceptual design will be to formulate precise questions, define an appropriate dataset in relation to the design task at hand, and gain a comprehensive understanding of the design space while maintaining control over the nonlinear processes involved in these data-driven approaches. As humans, we naturally seek consistency, rules, or patterns that can be universally applied and help us make predictions. Hence, striking a balance between leveraging AI capabilities and nurturing our intuitive understanding of complex relationships is crucial. To achieve this, full integration of machines within the conceptual structural design process is necessary. The machine will act as a collaborator and assistant to human designers, enabling a harmonious synergy between human creativity and AI's computational power. As structural engineer S. Musmeci foresaw in the early days of structural computation: "I believe that one day, perhaps in the not-too-distant future, this will be the way creative structural engineers design. Automatic calculation, far from limiting their imaginative possibilities, will represent efficient support for them, as well as a powerful means to amplify their impact on reality."[32]

31 Saldana Ochoa, K., Ohlbrock, P. O., D'Acunto, P., Moosavi, V.: (2021) "Beyond typologies, beyond optimization: Exploring novel structural forms at the interface of human and machine intelligence," International Journal of Architectural Computing 19(3), pp. 466–490.

32 Musmeci, S.: (1972) "Il calcolo elettronico e la creazione di nuove forme strutturali," Architettura & Computer, pp. 159–60.

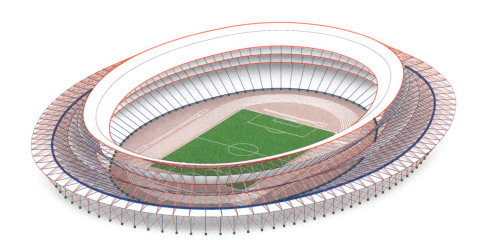

TOP Structural model of the Olympic Stadium for Tokyo 2020 by Pierluigi D'Acunto, Lukas Ingold, and Patrick Ole Ohlbrock. The design was developed with the help of the Combinatorial Equilibrium Modeling (CEM) form-finding tool based on graphic statics.[30] Red and blue indicate tension and compression respectively.

RIGHT PAGE A Self-Organizing Map (SOM) of many thousands of design options of roof structures[31] in the form of strut-and-tie models in equilibrium that have been generated using the Combinatorial Equilibrium Modeling (CEM).[30] Red and blue indicate tension and compression respectively.

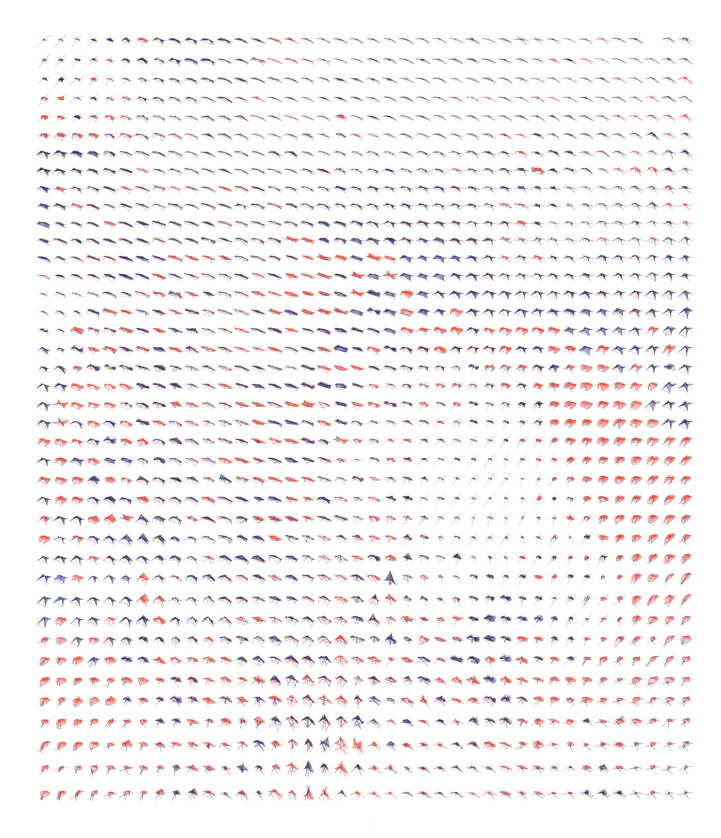

CHALLENGING GRAVITY

CHALLENGING
GRAVITY

**EXPOSED OR
CONCEALED**

LEARNING FROM
THE PAST

COMMON
RESPONSIBILITIES

If one were to assign the two terms *physical necessity* and *creative freedom* to engineers and architects, one gets answers that are as stereotypical as they are clichéd: the former is usually attributed to engineers, who are supposedly matter-of-factly sober, while the latter is regarded as a typical characteristic of architectural-artistic creativity. Why is this so? In reality, both have the same range of choices and limits that need to be explored in the course of a project. The key to this question lies in the fundamental understanding of architecture. Structures and architecture can never be considered separately in buildings. They always form a symbiotic unit, and this is the case regardless of whether a structure is in the spotlight or hidden from view. Sometimes the supporting structure is hardly recognizable as such, but can be felt. Elsewhere, however, it has a major impact on the spatial perception and appearance of a building. In the ideal project, it is not the architects alone who decide which path to take in this context, but engineers and architects working together in a team of equals.

The contributions presented on the following pages describe completely different approaches and projects, but they have one thing in common: close cooperations and exchanges between architects and engineers in order to realize unique concepts. A fundamental aspect here is an intensive interdisciplinary collaboration already present in the concept phase, in which all relevant influencing factors are collected and incorporated. Even if completely different strategies are chosen for this, it becomes clear that this is already a creative process. Looking back into history is also one of these influencing factors, because in dealing with it, important inspirations for design, construction, and architectural principles can be found. What also becomes visible in the contributions: There is not one right way, but always many possible ways. And in the end, one thing is true: the more intensive the collaboration between engineers and architects, the more consistent the project.

What architect Christian Kerez and engineer Joseph Schwartz have in common is their interest in understanding architecture as a system and developing a holistic spatial concept that encompasses everything. In the interview, they both explain how this attitude results in unique projects such as the House with One Wall in Zurich or the Pavilion for the Kingdom of Bahrain at the Expo in Dubai, and how the supporting structure can become an unusual architectural phenomenon.

In another contribution, architect Cecilia Puga presents two projects in which the boundaries between material, structural system, supporting structure, and architecture become blurred. The headquarters of Chile's Ministry of Cultures involves the restoration of a ruin and the implementation of a new office building. The second project – the headquarters for Arauco – shows a wooden building in which it was possible to define both the supporting structure and the entire interior with one single structural component.

The engineer Jürg Conzett describes the concept of conceptual design which means "meeting complex requirements with a system of measures based on simple principles." Conceptual design does not arise from a sequence or combination of individual problem solutions, but requires the "testing out of synthetic approaches." Conzett explains what these approaches look like, in particular with reference to some historical and contemporary bridge projects.

The starting point of Jeannette Kuo's article is a surprising comparison of two projects by Ludwig Mies van der Rohe and Antoni Gaudí. Her insight: "The abstraction of form with Mies and the structural form finding of Gaudí are in fact not so distinct from each other." Afterward, the architect explains, based on some projects of her office KARAMUK KUO, that load-bearing structures do not only have the task to hold up the building, but rather shape the spatial experience and the identity of the project.

Roland Pawlitschko

WE ARE THE ONES WHO TELL THE STRUCTURE HOW IT SHOULD CARRY LOADS

CHRISTIAN KEREZ AND JOSEPH SCHWARTZ IN CONVERSATION WITH ROLAND PAWLITSCHKO

RP You have worked very closely together for many years. What was your first project and how did you happen to meet up there?

CK The first project we worked upon together was the Liechtenstein Museum of Fine Arts, Vaduz, which I designed with architects Morger & Degelo [PAGE 96]. The building is special in that the outer load-bearing concrete wall has no movement joints, is as smooth as glass and blackish green in appearance. What I found fascinating about Joseph was that he always became intellectually involved with our questions and problems, and thought things through to the end. With him, it has never been a case of "No, that won't work." He is much more likely to give a clear assessment: we can certainly do that but the consequences are this or that.

JS We designed the concrete for the Museum of Fine Arts ourselves, which would be difficult today because it is now subject to far too many regulatory standards. Concrete is normally selected based on its properties. We focused on the ingredients – with all the consequences, for example, for the monolithic structure without expansion joints, for shrinkage, for the polished surface, and the aesthetics. We had to consider at an early stage the implications of abrading 5 mm from the concrete surface. We also had to define the minimum size of the aggregate and decide on the precise color. Christian and I first met more or less by chance through Morger & Degelo. He later approached me about an apartment building on Forsterstrasse in Zurich. As he explained the concept, I could immediately visualize it in three dimensions. That was the actual start of the very close working relationship we still enjoy today.

CK We had been in discussions with another engineer, who had told us that verifying whether our idea was capable of working structurally at all would take a great deal of time. Consequently, we asked Joseph and he came back to us after two days with hand-drawn sketches of the structural system on two pages of A4. The sheets showed the flow of forces, and he concluded that the project was not only possible, but could even be further refined in some areas.

RP What was the reason for the greatly differing assessments of the two engineers?

JS The problem is always the same. Structural engineers think too little about internal forces and are not able to work out the actual flow of forces, which is always by the simplest possible paths. Far too many students miss out on this part of their education – and the same applies to three-dimensional thinking. A structural wall standing on a floor provides the perfect example. Most engineers design the floor to carry the wall, which inevitably leads to a fairly thick floor construction. In reality, however, the wall is structural, which would allow the floor to be suspended from the wall, and thus be very thin. Anyone who considers the two elements in isolation and does not see the simple relationship between them has yet to find their way as a structural engineer. I see simplicity as: separating the wheat from the chaff and seeing what matters.

CK What binds us is our interest in understanding architecture as a system and developing a holistic spatial idea that includes everything. Specifically in the case of Forsterstrasse, for example, considering the wall and floor as one unit. In this respect the central question is: How do you introduce a space such as an underground car parking garage, which should not have intermediate walls, into a structural system based on shear walls? Unsurprisingly, the basement was the story we spent the longest time working on. Most architects would say that it is not really interesting because it just contains skis and a few suitcases. However, by thinking systematically, you can see precisely what and where the key issues are.

JS Finally, it is about arranging the elements so that as much architectural benefit as possible can be extracted while making complete structural sense. To be able to make this judgment requires a certain simplicity of thinking. Complicated calculations or a computer analysis will not take you to the objective because they can only check whether something works structurally or not. If the computer or some complicated manual calculations say "no," the engineer does not necessarily know why. It is not immediately apparent which parameters should be changed. We look at it from the other side: if you stick to some simple basic principles, then everything will work.

RP   Why can't computers do this as well?

JS   Computer programs are based on the theory of elasticity, which makes simple thinking difficult from the start. In addition, they are generally intended to provide verification of structural adequacy. In other words: you have to have something designed first in order to analyze it by computer. When you start changing an existing design with the intention of improving the final result, you can very quickly get into difficulties. For example: a column carries a large load, so you increase its cross-sectional area. This makes the column stiffer and attracts more force to it. The column ends up carrying an even higher load. Failure to grasp the principle that the load on a column can be reduced by making it thinner is an opportunity lost. Structural engineers have not sufficiently realized or have never heard that we tell the structure how it should carry loads.

RP   That brings us directly to your most recent collaboration: the Kingdom of Bahrain Pavilion for the World Expo in Dubai **[PAGES 101–103]**. The lesson, once again, was that less achieves more.

CK   In this project, we had also been working with another engineer to develop various solutions. We received feedback based on computer analyses, showing where the system as a whole was weak and would require additional support – without any clear statement about exactly what changes should take place. So we added some additional columns to brace these weak points and make them more capable of carrying load. This introduced more weight into the system, which led to new weak points. After three months, the weight of the structure had doubled. Suddenly, we had the idea of designing everything as they do in timber buildings – with primary, secondary, and tertiary structural elements that perform their own separate, different functions within the same structure. Joseph subsequently developed a primary system with us with intersecting member joints, each standing on three legs and arranged in a ring. He then extended this system over the whole space. Based on this idea, we explored how the arrangement would look inside the space. At this point, Joseph had not calculated anything. Instead, he intuitively judged some models as being more structurally viable than others, while we investigated their potential impacts: some of these intersecting member joints were too small and required additional columns to get the joints to work. In some places the columns were too

PREVIOUS PAGE Concrete Model of the House with One Wall. Zurich, Switzerland, 2007. Architecture: Christian Kerez; Structural design and engineering: Joseph Schwartz

LEFT PAGE Liechtenstein Museum of Fine Arts. Vaduz, Liechtenstein, 2000
Architecture: Morger und Degelo and Christian Kerez; Structural design and engineering: Joseph Schwartz

TOP House with One Wall. Zurich, Switzerland, 2007
Architecture: Christian Kerez; Structural design and engineering: Joseph Schwartz

TOP **House with the Missing Column. Zurich, Switzerland, 2014**
Architecture: Christian Kerez; Structural design and engineering:
Joseph Schwartz

close to the façade, in others they made the overall arrangement appear too uneven.

JS   While this was going on, of course, we were running through more calculations in the office. We next turned to the basic concept and the question of whether we could create the optimum structure using these thin columns with very few interconnected tripods if we eliminated any stability or buckling problems. In other words: the computer would not be needed to check for buckling. We could see straightaway that it worked flawlessly, and we even had a relatively wide scope of design freedom. Eventually we designed secondary and tertiary elements specifically to stabilize the other columns. What I found extremely fascinating was that the few rules we set up were a great help to Christian in developing and taking the design idea he had described as far as it would go.

CK   The columns create spaces like trees do in a forest. There are clearings where there are few or no columns, but also thickets where there are many. What is not easily communicated on the photographs – because the eye is drawn mainly to the members superimposed one upon the other – is that the space is very open, light, and extensive. This openness of the space was one of our primary considerations, as were the areas densely packed with columns acting as visual barrier in front of the empty, more secluded areas of the hall. We sought to create a rich range of spatial impressions within the same system. This change from open to dense was crucial for the spatial experience and was a direct result of the scarcely visible hierarchy of the basic structural system. We used a computer to design it, although it always gave us a physical model as well, which allowed us to discuss the columns and the spatial impact. Without a computer, the project would have hardly been possible, at least in the time we had available. Without the physical model, we would not have understood the drawings we created on the computer. And without the mock-ups, we would not have understood the actual scale of the effects of the space. In a nutshell: we did not leave it to the computer to generate the system. When you stand in a space, you see and feel certain densely concentrated or empty areas without having to understand them analytically or rationally.

RP   How would you describe your cooperation on this project? What is particularly important to you in this respect?

CK   We spoke about the project almost every day and discussed the members on the model. It was an iterative process in an almost informal atmosphere, which would not be guaranteed to work so smoothly with a large structural engineering consultancy.

JS   Even large offices may have one team able to develop a project like this. By and large, these teams consist of very few people. The problem in most large offices is their hierarchical structures, which can limit an engineer's scope for action. There is perhaps only a specific number of hours allocated within the budget and the team is expected to bring its involvement to a quick conclusion. It is not always appreciated by everyone that the more time invested at the concept phase, the less time is required for the detailed design. Developing an initial concept requires a small, effective team that approaches the task responsibly and in the right way. We speak too much about optimization today. There is no optimization. There is only the pursuance and sensible development of an idea, taking it as far as it will go towards achieving the shared goal. When Christian comes to us with a project that looks like a challenge, my mind immediately turns to the thought of how we could make the concept even better.

CK   An important participant is, of course, the client. We could never have completed the pavilion in Switzerland or Germany because we would have had to service and satisfy an edifice of doubters founded on unlimited pessimism. We always believed: the client liked it. So he wanted us to do it.

RP   Is the apartment block on Krönleinstrasse (the House with the Missing Column, **PAGE 98**), with its immense cantilevers, a project on which many structural engineers would quickly throw in the towel and question the whole basis for the proposal?

CK   Our projects are not just there to make an individual client happy with a tailor-made suit. They always contain generally applicable ideas. What properties can spaces have? How does it feel to stand in a very special space? There is always an existential dimension to the architecture, an experience. The buildings are not really homely in the sense that it is particularly comfortable and easy to live there. But they are unbelievably enriching. Spending time in these spaces offers a wealth of architectural experiences and therefore also attracts many people – and not only architects – who can imagine living there and are curious about what it would be like to live there or at least spend an hour in the space. That is the drive behind each of our projects – not the wish to walk a tightrope while everyone steps back in astonishment at how everything about it is complex or even dangerous. Projects always have an intrinsic character, which includes the choice of the means and the formulation of their implementation. In the case of the pavilion in Dubai, the load-bearing structure, which is often simply reduced to the necessities or concealed, becomes an unusual architectural phenomenon. It becomes a space-defining element that densifies, thins out, and comes together, lending this limited space a boundless wealth of experiences. It is about unifying architecture and structure and about providing the essential opportunities for experiencing the elements of the architecture. The last adventure has not yet been lived, the last innovation has not yet been created. Every commission is a unique challenge. In Dubai, we also had to ask ourselves: the pavilion will be there for just six months – is it really worthwhile putting so much effort into it? But if you think this way, you might as well never do anything more than the minimum. I believe that every commission offers a unique opportunity to make something new.

JS In architecture the end result has these qualities. In the discipline of structural engineering, the same does not quite apply. There, it is more about the application of principles. That is something we teach, something so important to us in the first year with our students. We show them the typology of currently fashionable structures and end with the quintessence: typology no longer has any role in the methodology they are taught, which is to analyze structures, to understand them and to design them. Instead, it is all about the arrangement of forces in space. In the end, everything can be reduced to compressive and tensile forces, which the engineer has to compose in such a way as to maintain equilibrium. That is the sole condition. Seen in this way, there is nothing left to discover in structural engineering in relation to the tectonics of loading. When you begin to direct forces through the space independently of a typology, you must immediately think about which material should be used to resist tension in this situation and what that means for the tectonics of jointing.

CK The principles are simple and predetermined. However, their interaction can lead to very complex results. In Dubai we used simple, trivial elements. There is only one basic load-bearing element: industrially manufactured, 5-inch-diameter standard steel tubes, straight out of the product list and welded together before being shown off with a brilliant varnish. However, something unique derives from their arrangement and that arrangement's complex diversity. The special part is not the element nor the principle, but the way they come together. And the same applies for the windows. The design is really trivial – simply a hole in the façade. There is a frame and there, where the columns punch through the skin, the penetration is simply left open. This creates a special effect: it looks as though these columns continue outside the building. However, outside the skin they ceased to have any meaning. That is spatially marvelous: infinitely long columns extending like light rays or lines into the distance.

RP Can it be said that a result is good if the preliminary and final design processes go well?

JS The process is a hard road. It is difficult to say whether that is good or bad. Many people decline taking this road because it is far from easy. You continually hear the nonsensical response: "That won't work," and in saying this I am thinking not least of the construction firms. In this respect we also need powers of persuasion and negotiation techniques to find competent specialists who not only are able but also have the motivation to realize the design. The motivation, in the end, is much more important than the actual process. To this can be added intuition. This feeling often has nothing at all to do with experience, despite it often being said to be so. It is, in fact, an annoyingly small number of premises that I keep in my head as guiding principles, which allow me to give an immediate answer around the table to every question. However, these are premises that you really must understand and make part of your mind-set; there are only forces in space.

CK Simple thoughts are often the most convincing. In the case of the House with One Wall on Burenweg in Zurich **[PAGES 94, 97]**, the clients asked us whether the house would fall down. At this point we took a sheet of paper, folded it and set it down on the table. It was immediately obvious that the building would remain standing. The clients would remember this gesture with the folded paper. In the end, it is these kinds of simple principles that are the easiest to grasp. Happily, at this early stage you do not know all the difficulties ahead that remain to be overcome.

JS The good idea makes up five percent of a good project; the rest is just down to hard work. But without that good idea, all that effort is not worthwhile. The interesting thing is that this comes up time and time again – for example, in the details – at a much smaller scale. Finally, as a structural engineer, you must be easily motivated at all levels and fascinated by the contributions you can make across a wide range of fields. An abundance of perseverance is also helpful.

Translation from German: Raymond Peat

RIGHT PAGE, NEXT PAGE Principle study, structure model and interior view of Kingdom of Bahrain Pavilion, World Expo 2020 in Dubai. Architecture: Christian Kerez; Structural design and engineering: Joseph Schwartz

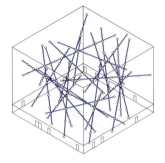 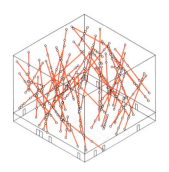 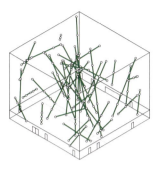

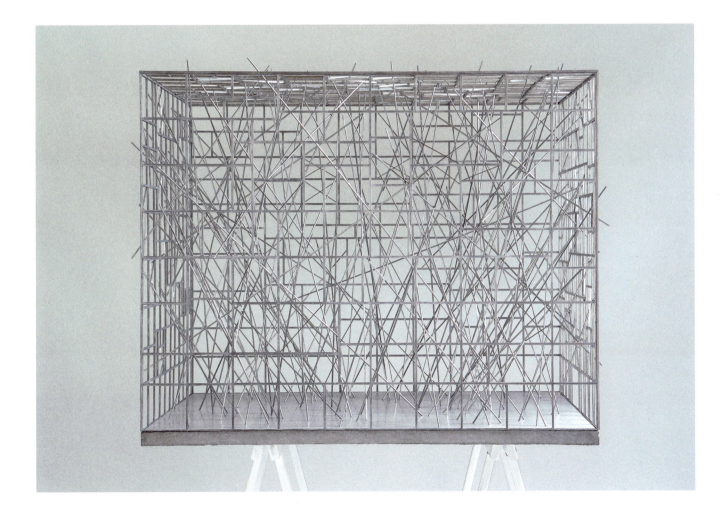

EXPOSED OR CONCEALED

CECILIA PUGA

A DIALOGUE BETWEEN AN ARCHITECT AND AN ENGINEER

1   Mostafavi, M.: (2006) Structure as Space, Engineering and Architecture in the Works of Jürg Conzett and His Partners, AA Publications, London, pp. 9, 17.

Architects do more than conceptualize and design buildings, just as structural engineers do more than merely calculate feasible specifications for those buildings, subordinating themselves to the formal gestures that architects propose. The integration between architecture and engineering should be understood as a pairing – or coupling – which creates a new entity that is assembled as the two disciplines merge. Architecture's impact "emerges from the creative mediation between the certainties of calculability and the uncertainties of spatial becoming."[1] It often acknowledges and highlights a clear synergy between the disciplinary fields and responsibilities. It arises from the collaboration and interaction with engineering in the early stages of conceptual and project discussions, as well as with the selection of the construction methods and processes that a particular solution could involve. As a requirement for structural design to leave room for innovation, in the book *Structures as Space*, a study of the work of Jürg Conzett, Moshen Mostafavi quotes a concept from Gianni Vattimo: "pensiero débole" (weak thinking). According to the author's approach, one must weaken the structures of objective thinking and suspend certainties – at least for a moment – to enter more speculative domains, where new creative possibilities may arise.[1] However, for architects who work in highly seismic countries, this "weak thinking" while developing building structures and the consequent possibility of innovation in engineering and architectural design is reserved for exceptional cases. Thus, it becomes a difficult goal to achieve: most engineers are inclined to avoid risk and prefer to adhere to the norm rather than participate in structural research and innovation processes. Unlike gravity-based load analysis – where the data is known and can be modeled – seismic action breaks everything down, adding unknown variables to the equation in terms of both magnitude and performance. This often contributes to the hardening of the structural engineer's position when faced with occasional invitations from architects to shift the limits beyond conventional solutions.

In the case of the building constructed together with Paula Velasco and Alberto Moletto in Santiago de Chile as the headquarters for the Ministry of Culture, Arts and Heritage, the structure traces (literally) the way it operates. The commission was for the restoration of a ruin and the designing of a new building on a site that had been subjected to successive demolitions and earthquakes. The former Pereira Palace is a simple two-story masonry structure built by French architect Lucien Henault in 1873 **[PAGES 106, 108 TOP]**. Following the footprint of the original typology, which connected the Palace's gallery with the courtyard and its side corridors in the form of a cross, we wanted the new project to be responsible for filling in the blanks resulting from the former demolitions and collapses, thereby giving the building its original space structure back in a contemporary way.

Now, the infilling of the structure gives shape to a new courtyard that stands in the area where the Pereira family had a garden **[PAGE 104]**. At the same time, the new structure embodies a negotiation between all

LEFT PAGE Palacio Pereira Courtyard, Ministry of Culture, Arts and Heritage's Headquarters. Santiago, Chile, 2019. Architecture: Cecilia Puga, Paula Velasco, Alberto Moletto; Structural design and engineering: Pedro Bartolomé, Cristian Sandoval; Restauration Consultants: Alan Chandler, Luis Cercós, Fernando Pérez

the historical eras collapsed into one space. The idea is one of the simultaneity and coexistence of different periods and époques, all overlapping. The conversation with engineering began at the competition stage, once we had a clear picture of the criteria for intervening in the preexisting factors and an idea for the new building that we were confident in (including its operation, decisions on the material, and the structural system).

Structure played a crucial role in the overall perception of space. Nevertheless, engineering's participation in the design process of the new structure was very limited: it operated as a way of mathematically verifying a proposal that arose entirely from architecture. In the operations to consolidate the structure of the ruin, on the other hand, engineering was a key actor in defining the strategy and the design of the surgical operations put in place to restore the monument. Early on, we understood heritage recovery as an operation that had to restore not only spatial and symbolic aspects but also technological aspects – and, fundamentally, the original structural performance of the building. This obliged us, together with the engineer and our advisors, to carefully delimit and define the operations for structural consolidation and the methodologies, processes, and materials to be used. We wanted everything to contribute to the building's structural performance as it was conceived. The aim was to have as few interventions as possible, just a small number of accurate operations to ensure the stability of the building in the face of future earthquakes. The construction of a rigid diaphragm in concrete over the existing wooden beams to hold all walls and façades together, the reinforcement of every existing opening with a 10 mm-thick embedded frame, and the repair of infinite cracks solved the stability issues suffered by the historical structure, all nonvisible operations that allowed the original structure to recover not only the necessary levels of safety and habitability but also the desired spatiality.

For the new structure, however, we used the image of scaffolding as a reference, emphasizing the temporary and dynamic condition of our concept of interventions in heritage structures, alluding to its nature as a work in progress, and simultaneously proposing a translucent lattice. It is a structure that allows light and air to get inside, and it reveals, without concealing, the view of the original structure associated with it. We used a noisy and dense isotropic concept for the structure involving finger-shaped concrete columns with a 25 × 25 cm cross section, in contrast to the continuity and bulkiness of the masonry walls. This created a high-density inner perimeter around the new courtyard. Those columns and their geometry allowed us to support the building on the sides adjacent to the heritage site, moving any vertical elements of the new construction away from its interior walls and façades. The "fingers" of the structure were moved according to the specific structural requirements of each area to ensure the structural autonomy of both pieces. The grid of columns and beams along the party walls provide the seismic structure of the building, creating a veil aimed to produce a particular vision of history and time by means of lights and shadows reflected onto the Palacio Pereira's remains and the visual overlaying of temporal layers, embracing coexistence. We are clearly dealing with an exposed structure. In this case, the building bears the history of its own construction and the forces at play in the form of traces that everyone can understand. As in most isotropic strategies, the building draws in space and flaunts the stresses of the structure, making managing these stresses – as well as the climate and ambience of the space – the subject of the project. In cases like this, the structural elements create episodes and rhythms that constitute the project's heartbeat. From the point of view of perception, the emphasis is on their function.

LEFT PAGE The architects' commission consisted of the recovery of a ruin and the design of a new building on a site that had been subjected to successive demolitions and earthquakes.

The proposal submitted in 2019 to the architectural competition for the design of the new Empresas Arauco's headquarters (Concepción, Chile) – developed with Paula Velasco, Joseph Schwartz, and Pierluigi D'Acunto, with technical support from the Swiss company Blumer Lehmann – allowed us to avoid the usual ground where the interaction between architects, engineers, and structural designers occurs only at the late design stage, thus opening up room for speculation and innovation that proved fruitful.

The competition promoted innovation and stimulated construction systems that could be industrialized and produced on a large scale. Although our project was a runner-up and will not be built, it presents interesting contributions in both constructive and structural terms associated with the technical and economic feasibility able to help us define a possible production and assembly process for multistory buildings using post-tensioned timber. The way to solve the structure emerged from a series of meetings and encounters at Schwartz's Zurich offices. Based on an initial concept (plans, cuts, scantlings, and references) developed in Santiago with Paula Velasco, Joseph Schwartz was able to take the proposal further. From the beginning, we liked the idea of achieving clean and calm surfaces using wood and a very transparent and lightweight building [PAGE 108, BOTTOM]. The vaulting systems seemed attractive, so we proposed to Joseph Schwartz that we use the structural vaults we had already used in other projects. The proposal was adjusted and radicalized through constant iteration between architecture and engineering until it reached a point of synthesis and efficiency that not only seemed appropriate but also excited us. Invited by Joseph Schwartz, Martin Bender from Blumer Lehman, a Swiss timber construction company, played a key role in the development process. Thus, this proposal, which is innovative in terms of timber construction for high-rise buildings, ensures the technical and economic viability of the system at the same time. Taken to more advanced stages of design, calculation, and testing, the development of this system would offer viable solutions to be applied in other programmatic and geographical contexts through prefabrication and industrial assembly processes.

The project conceived the office building as a structural skeleton capable of housing spaces engaged in an ongoing fluctuation, expressing its architectural and material qualities without depending on the presence of other layers. With its synthetic nature, this structure represents far more than a mere solution to load transmission or the building's stability. The architectural/structural component into which the system was decanted, the logistics associated with the transportation and installation of the prefabricated piece, the assembly requirements, the cost aspects, and other variables that were incorporated in our considerations led us to achieve greater precision in the design of the piece and the components that constitute the structural/constructive/spatial system. The supporting structure [PAGE 110] consists of a system of columns and timber slabs covering a span of 18 m, composed of unidirectional strips with a hollow cross section with an almost triangular shape, with a static height of 1.6 m and width of 8.0 m. These are supported by columns with a 300 × 700 mm cross section made of laminated wood. To avoid a strong transfer of tensile load at the joints, the slab elements would be assembled using post-tensioning cables linked to the wooden elements located at the top and bottom of the beams. The well-known post-tensioning technology of reinforced concrete structures would be adopted, using four 0.6" wires placed in steel ducts filled with injection mortar after post-tensioning. The change of direction of the beams by 90 degrees from one floor to the other allows each beam to be supported every 18 m. The beam has vertical traction cables

LEFT PAGE, TOP The former Pereira Palace is a simple two-story masonry structure built by French architect Lucien Henault in 1873.

LEFT PAGE, BOTTOM The project conceived the office building as a structural skeleton. The use of structural vaults offered the possibility of a very transparent and lightweight building with clean and calm surfaces using just wood. The change of direction of the beams by 90 degrees from one floor to the other allows each beam to be supported every 18 m. Two large and two smaller cores – built in reinforced concrete and with a circular floor plan – are activated to resist wind, earthquakes, and other sources of lateral load.

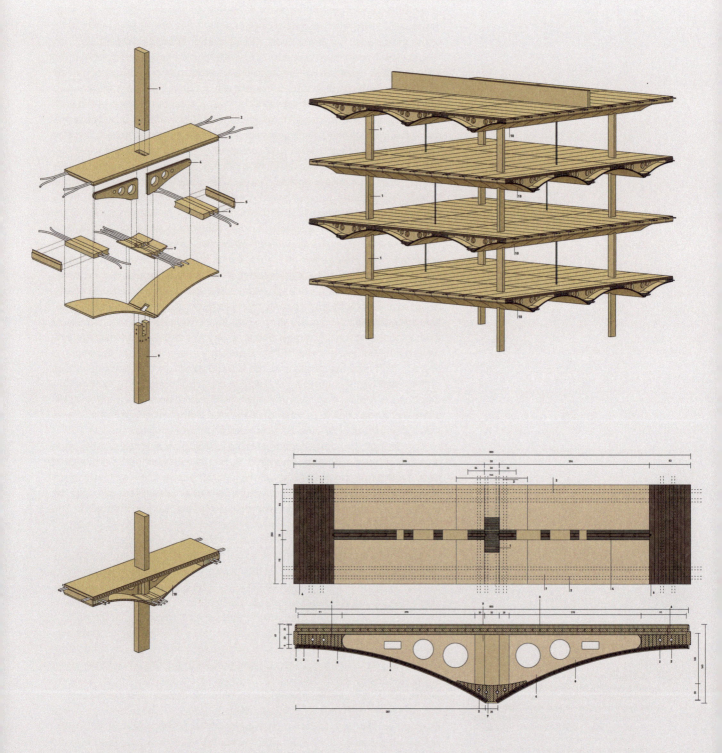

to the upper floor beam. Two large and two smaller cores – built in reinforced concrete and with a circular floor plan – are activated to resist wind, earthquakes, and other sources of lateral load.

The way this building works in structural terms is not self-evident. Architecture and structure merge into a single system, and the internal forces are camouflaged, becoming almost invisible to our trained eye for modern-structure reading **[PAGES 112-113]**. The structural/architectural component, the rotation of the bays, the alternating system of columns and tensors, and the post-tensioning that allows the construction of 18-meter span structural beams in wood are not immediately intelligible. At first glance, it appears to be a concealed structure. However, it is very much exposed: everything we see in the building is structure. Every surface that makes up the space is both architecture and structure: floors and ceilings are two sides of the same component, which is precisely designed and calculated to meet architectural and structural requirements simultaneously and as efficiently as possible. Nothing is surplus. Everything is "bones."

Both projects clearly show that most continuous or planar strategies are conducive to discretion or even concealment. They try to make us perceive or believe that things are sustained quite naturally, without stress. This means that we perform as illusionists, with our success and satisfaction residing in the "removal" of the structure, the articulations, and the expression of the constructive components. We stand astounded before them; their structural behavior is not easy to recognize. The underlying concept is not visible to our viewing habits. These "hidden" strategies offer calm and quiet spaces. Life is simple and flows without having to negotiate with the rhythms of the structure of such buildings.

But building traces change with technology. In a way, "understanding" or reading the structure is a cultural and cumulative experience. Thus, what we would have considered hidden in the past could today be readable and understood as "exposed" – perhaps because of comprehension. What we would once have considered shifting the limits beyond conventional solutions is a cultural and cumulative experience as well. Thus, what we could have considered an exceptional integration between architecture and structural engineering – perhaps due to iteration – could today be part of our regular practice as the result of pushing a little further this pairing – or coupling – as both disciplines merge, creating a new scenario.

LEFT PAGE The supporting structure consists of a system of columns and timber slabs covering a span of 18 m, composed of unidirectional strips with a hollow cross section with an almost triangular shape, with a static height of 1.6 m and width of 8.0 m. These are supported by columns with a 300 × 700 mm cross section made of laminated wood. To avoid a strong transfer of tensile load at the joints, the slab elements would be assembled using post-tensioning cables linked to the wooden elements located at the top and bottom of the beams.

TOP With its synthetic nature, this structure represents far more than a mere solution to load transmission or the building's stability. Architecture and structure merge into a single system, and the internal forces are camouflaged, becoming almost invisible. At first glance, it appears to be a concealed structure. However, it is very much exposed: everything we see in the building is structure.

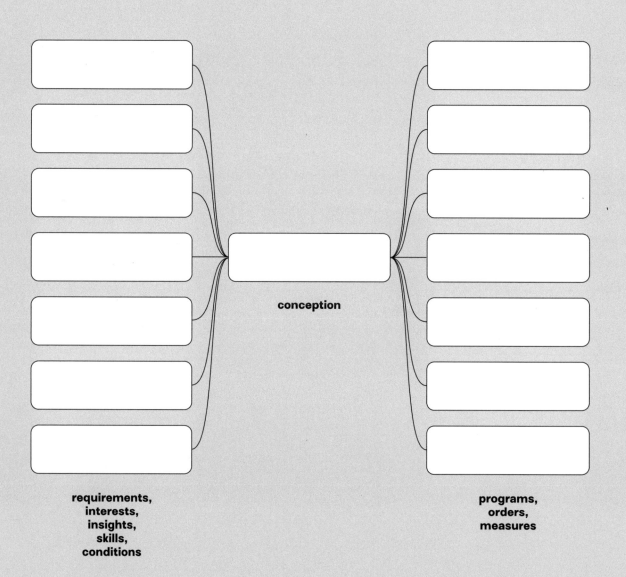

JÜRG CONZETT

CONCEPTUAL DESIGNING

Introduction – attempting a definition

Solving different problems with a single measure – that is the core of conceptual design. There is an element of economy in conceptual design, in both the intellectual and the material sense. This means that it stands in contrast to the division of functions in design and executed building on the one hand, and to the principle of collage on the other.

Conceptual design thus means meeting complex requirements with a system of measures based on simple principles. These principles are thoughts that can be put into words and drawings.

A conceptual construction is defined by a number of parameters and variables. The search for a conception is a creative task. Conceptions do not emerge from a sequence or combination of individual solutions to problems. Instead, they require the testing out of synthetic approaches.

I chose this butterfly figure many years ago to represent how the requirements and interests that can influence a concept are collected and brought together in the design process. This graphic gives an overview of essential influences from which one finally develops a "story" – a concept as the most important basis of the project.

The search for the manifold factors underlying a supposedly simple solution may enrich our knowledge. The following chapters illustrate the complexity of these considerations.

LEFT PAGE The conception as a butterfly figure

Design approaches

Concept

The waterfall bridge of the hiking trail "Trutg dil Flem" is based on the concept "externally post-tensioned arch in stone" [PAGE 117, TOP]. The few geometric dimensions of the bridge to be selected are the rise of the arch, the thickness of the arch, and the cross section of the post-tensioning strips. The bridge width and span, as well as the circular segment – the arch shape imposed by the fabrication – were predefined. The concept incorporating the prestressed ribbons lying on top of the stones increased the ultimate limit state of the stone structure compared with a traditional stone bridge, thereby saving material. At the same time, it made it possible to anchor the posts of the railing directly in the tautly prestressed steel ribbons, so that not a single stone in the entire bridge had to be provided with a drill hole.

Functional division

The Arenenberg Competence Center [PAGE 117, CENTER] by Staufer & Hasler Architects (CH-Frauenfeld) serves as an example of a load-bearing structure that is conceptually set up in opposition to the finishing (windows, interior walls). The columns as load-bearing elements stand freely and are not integrated into the system of non-load-bearing partition walls. Conceptually contrasting in a strict sense: the floor construction with floating floor coverings in polished reinforced concrete, which share the load-bearing function with the cross-laminated timber panels below. The floor, which is usually part of the interior finish, is part of the load-bearing structure in this case. There is a layer of solid impact sound insulation between the two layers that share the load-bearing function (without shear bond but transferring compression forces).

Collage

I would venture to call the Ebro Bridge [PAGE 117, BOTTOM] by José Antonio Fernández Ordóñez a collage. The differentiated division into different sections with clearly different materials (reinforced concrete piers and their capitals as well as Corten steel) appears here as a contrast to more conceptual approaches, such as "continuous girder with varying depth in weatherproof steel."

This example, as part of an examination of the work of José Antonio Fernández Ordóñez, who considers himself an artist, shows that the contrast between concept and collage is not meant to imply a judgment in every case.

RIGHT PAGE, TOP **Trutg dil Flem: waterfall bridge; Structural design and engineering: Conzett Bronzini Gartmann AG, Chur**

RIGHT PAGE, CENTER **Arenenberg Competence Center: interior view; Architecture: Staufer & Hasler; Structural design and engineering: Conzett Bronzini Gartmann AG, Chur**

RIGHT PAGE, BOTTOM **Bridge over the Ebro at Tortosa; Structural design and engineering: José Antonio Fernández Ordóñez**

EXPOSED OR CONCEALED

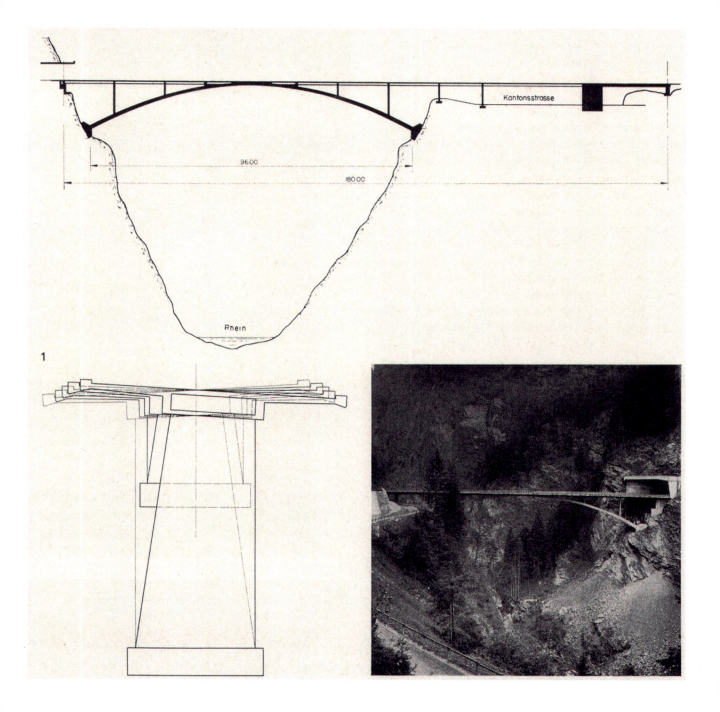

1

[1] Conzett, J.: (2019) "Alla ricerca di un'interpretazione / Il progetto del ponte Guayllabamba di Silvano Zorzi," Archi, no. 5.

[2] Menn, C.: (1969) "Viamala-Brücke der N13," werk, no. 9, p. 616.

A few geometric elements for a conceptual design

Stress ribbon

The design of Silvano Zorzi's stress ribbon bridge is determined solely by the choice of the slab thickness and the cross sections of the curbstones (span and sag are given by the traffic conditions). The prestressing cable cross sections and the reinforcement layout are determined as a consequence of these fundamental choices.[1] The concept appears simple to grasp. Nevertheless, there is a complex theory behind the dimensioning of these few parameters.

Arch with stiffening girder

The design of Christian Menn's Viamala Bridge is based on the principle of a stiffening girder above a shallow arch with spandrel columns advancing from the abutment towards the center of the bridge. The light arch spans shallowly between the load-bearing rocks on both sides of the valley. As a result, the abutment foundations are also easily accessible from above. The S-shaped routing of the roadway together with the arch, which is straight in plan, led to the positions of the spandrels in areas where the horizontal eccentricity between the arch and the roadway could still be easily handled. Menn comments: "The problem of designing an arch bridge with a horizontally curved deck in a statically, economically, and aesthetically expedient manner is thus reduced – after determining the interdependence of deck girder, spandrel columns, and arch – to the choice of very few initial elements."[2]

TOP **Design of a stress-ribbon bridge with 300 m span by Silvano Zorzi**

LEFT PAGE **Viamala bridge of the A13 national road by Christian Menn**

Analogies – related problem solutions in other disciplines

Integral calculus

The integral calculus is based on a simple principle: To determine the area under a function f(x) between a and b, search for another function F(x) whose derivative corresponds to f(x) and determine its difference between a and b. One could also approximate or solve the problem in another way, by adding the areas of numerous rectangles and triangles. But the solution via the integral calculus is more exact, time-saving, and elegant.

Now, the function F(x) can only be found by trial and error – there is no directly unambiguous procedure for this process. However, for a few hundred years now we have had a treasure trove of tables and rules that help in the search for F(x). Similarly, there is no method to develop a conception according to predefined rules. But it is possible to work with analogies to existing concepts. Often, though, what seems simple and obvious in retrospect is the result of a difficult search process.

Reciprocal systems

Culmann describes the simple principle of "reciprocally related systems" **[PAGE 121, TOP]** in Fig. 132 and 133 of his book *Die graphische Statik: 4:* The straight line "a" in the system "O" [Fig. 132] corresponds to the point "A1" in the system "O1" [Fig. 133]. This point with "O1" forms a parallel to "a." The distance between "A1" and "O1" can be freely chosen as a kind of scale. From now on, the relationships are clearly determined. The mapping of the straight line "b" to the point "B1" according to the same rule must at the same time follow the condition that the straight line ("A1""B1") corresponds to the intersection point ("a""b"), i.e., is parallel to ("O"-"a""b").[3]

Culmann uses this principle, the reciprocal dependence of point and straight line, for the construction of form and force polygons, which also behave "reciprocally" to each other. However, this is only valid for so-called central systems, where all forces pass through a common point. This point can also be infinitely distant, for example in a system of parallel forces. Here, a simple principle regulates a variety of possible applications.

However, this sophisticated concept of reciprocal figures remains limited to central systems: the universal application aimed at by Culmann remained unachieved. Analogously, conceptual constructing can also be generalized only in limited fields of application. The passionate pursuit of generality would be an unrealistic endeavor in the context of conceptual design, similar to Carl Culmann's work.

[3] Culmann, C.: (1875) Die graphische Statik, 2nd. ed., Verlag Meyer & Zeller, Zurich, p. 280.

RIGHT PAGE, TOP Carl Culmann: "reciprocally related systems"

RIGHT PAGE, BOTTOM Glenner bridge Peiden Bad, cross section and longitudinal. Structural design and engineering: Conzett Bronzini Gartmann AG, Chur

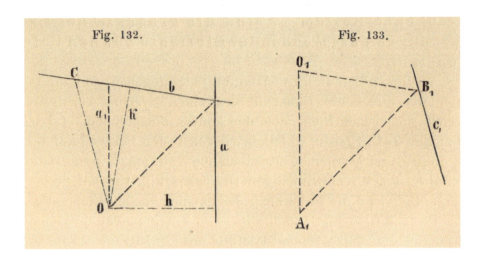

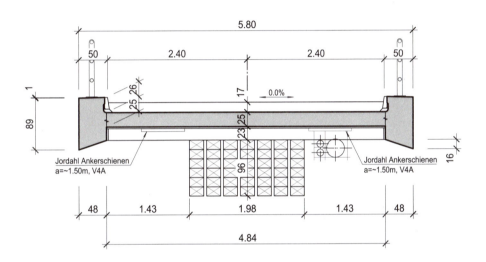

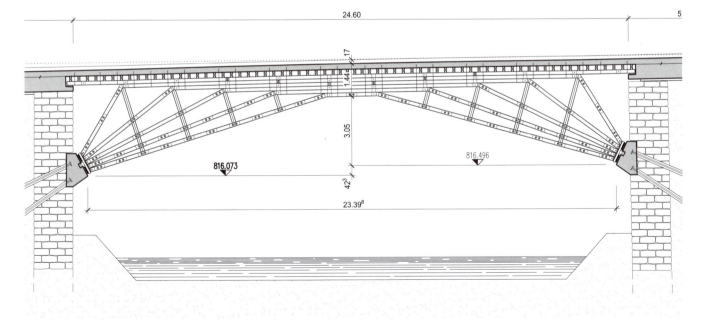

EXPOSED OR CONCEALED

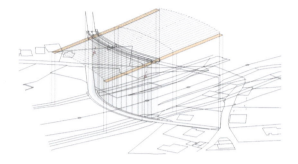

CONCEPTUAL DESIGNING

19th-century master detective as a role model.

The master detective analyzes and memorizes all the individual indications of his case. Then he leans back and invents a story. He checks to see if the story explains the details of the case. If not, he invents a new story and checks further. The stories are synthetic, they include the details.[4]

The engineer's stories are the conceptions. They can often be developed from modified ideas taken from existing constructions. However, more abstract thinking can also lead us to conceptions.

For the conception of the Glenner Bridge [PAGE 121, BOTTOM] in Peiden Bad, namely "strut frame made of solid wood with concrete nodes, protected from the weather by concrete decking," existing constructions were the godfathers. These include the Mur bridge in Murau (wooden central girder with roof) and Brunel's wooden bridges of the Cornish Railway (strut frame structures with cast nodes).

The bridge Punt, which connects the villages of Bondo and Promontogno following the destroyed old stone bridge in the landslide of 2017, follows the geometric-abstract conception "keeping the clearance profile with a trough bridge and accesses with a maximum inclination of 10%." The conception resulted in a linehaul of the bridge and its approaches extending far down the valley, with the bridge wrapping around the inclined cylinder of the given clearance profile [PAGE 122, TOP AND BOTTOM], so to speak. The tractrix curves for the practically right-angled connections to the existing roads provided for the widening of the road width towards these connections. The requirement for a low construction height (implicit in the conceptual design) resulted in a concrete frame whose asymmetric cross section at the frame corners – like the bridge as a whole – follows the clearance profile. This asymmetric cross section is well suited to bear the torsional effects of the bridge, which is strongly curved in plan.

Tribute to history – Albula railway

The bridges of the Albula railroad were built between 1899 and 1903, almost exclusively as stone semicircular arches.[5] Once again, we find a simple construction principle, standardized, and tabulated, which proves to be adaptable in many situations of the alpine landscape. The reasons that led to this conception are surprisingly manifold. The diagram on page 125 below lists 13 possible influences on this conception.

---

4   Rowe, C.: (1996) "Program versus Paradigm," in As I was saying. MIT Press, Cambridge, p. 7.

5   Hennings, F.: (1908) Projekt und Bau der Albulabahn, Denkschrift im Auftrage der Rhätischen Bahn, Chur.

LEFT PAGE, TOP Bridge Punt and clearing profile of the Bondasca torrent, before clearing the access roads

LEFT PAGE, BOTTOM The Punt as a physical model (model making: Lydia Conzett)

Summary

Conceptual designing is a multilayered task that cannot be formulated and solved in a purely analytical and straightforward manner. It appears impossible to capture a complex and often chaotic search process like conceptual design in categories and operative guidelines.

However, all the ways explained here share common ground: they are creative, they are inspiring, they are diverse, they offer latitude, they honor history, they are experimental. When they work together, they result in a comprehensive, holistic approach. This is reflected by the butterfly figure, which is an effort to bring together the different angles and perspectives of a project.

In this search, there is no one right way. Instead, a variety of possible ways usually exist. This will depend on how strongly the individual strands (on the left side of the butterfly figure) are weighted. The essence of the resulting concept, and thus the final project, depends on many decisions, some of them personal.

My experience with conceptual work suggests that the concept cannot be established at the beginning of a project with a subsequent deductive process, even if one may dream of this. Instead, the butterfly figure usually emerges in parallel with the project work, in an iterative dialogue – with oneself, with the project, and with others. This usually means long, and multiple revisions of a design to make it even more precise, even more suited to the peculiarities of the task and the context. Ultimately, it is an emotional decision to say that a design is now finished, coherent, accomplished. The concept as a butterfly figure forms a strong help in this consideration.

[6] Association for the Preservation of Swiss Scenery, Swiss Heritage Society

RIGHT PAGE **The conception of the stone viaducts of the Albula Railway**

Stone viaducts with semicircular vaults

Left branches (causes/context):
- Mostly deep valleys with steep slopes
- Resilient building ground
- Useful stone deposits near the construction sites
- Rising cost of steel bridges
- Little maintenance (at least for about 100 years)
- Insensitive to increasing traffic loads
- Collapse of the iron Münchenstein railway bridge in 1891
- The "national and solid construction" (Rob. Moser)
- The "inorganic iron structures of the Gotthard Railway"
- "Honour to the stone" – award-winning design for the Lorraine Bridge in Bern in 1897 (R. Moser/G. Mantel)
- tourist expectations
- Founding of Switzerland. "Schweizer Heimatschutz"[6] Movement 1905
- "National Romanticism" in Swiss Architecture 1895–1914

Right branches (characteristics):
- Standardization to certain openings
- quarry stone masonry
- pointed stone masonry
- layered stone masonry
- Hydraulic lime mortar for openings <= 25 m
- Cement mortar for openings > 25 m

EXPOSED OR CONCEALED

JEANNETTE KUO

STRUCTURING SPACE

[1] Saint, A.: (2005) "Architect and Engineer: A Study of Construction History," Construction History, 21, p. 24.

LEFT PAGE Project Rosental-Mitte Lab Building, House 6. Basel, Switzerland, 2029. Architecture: Karamuk Kuo Architects; Structural design and engineering: Schnetzer Puskas

For most of the history of construction, the question of concealing or exposing structure was never a concern. Material was load-bearing and architecture was an expression of that logic. What was structural was also for the most part architectural. The masonry construction that dominated the civic architecture of our Western built heritage and the timber construction of the Eastern heritage were equally direct in their application of material strengths and properties to the shaping of space. In fact, elements that appeared to be decorative or ornamental were often geometric efforts to structurally reinforce or optimize architectonic ambitions. Examples include the waffling of the Pantheon's concrete dome, the squinches in Islamic mosques, the buttresses of gothic cathedrals, or the dugong brackets of ancient Chinese timber construction. These elements negotiated structure, geometry, and expression while giving identity to an architecture that was grounded in a certain material constructive system. It was a system that made scant distinction between architecture and engineering. Today, the tectonic question is returning to the fore. In the face of pressing issues like climate change and resource consciousness, the role of structure in architecture can no longer be that of a sidekick. When we consider how to build sustainably and how to maximize the longevity and durability of our built resources, the primary structure of an architectural design cannot be ignored.

The separation of architecture and engineering is a modern invention, one that only took place during the final two hundred years of the thousands of years of our history of constructing objects. As new technologies forced increasing specialization during the Enlightenment and the subsequent Industrial Revolution, the bifurcation of the disciplines seemed both a matter of pragmatism and progress.[1] However, the unfortunate result of that disciplinary split is the rather oversimplified typecasting of architecture as an aesthetic discipline and engineering as a technical one, whereas we all know that it is far more complex than that.

If we look at two of the most misunderstood protagonists of our modern times – Mies van der Rohe and Antoni Gaudí [PAGE 128] – we will realize that things are not always what they seem: that elements that seem to expose are in fact concealing and elements that seem to conceal are in fact revealing. Mies is often considered a minimalist who works with structure to reveal its material honesty and performative truth, while Gaudí is considered excessive and flamboyant, his works dripping with seemingly frivolous ornamentation.

When we look closer, however, we would realize that both are in fact toying with us. Mies, with his penchant for using structural profiles, uses them even when they are in fact not necessarily needed. Instead, they are deployed to create a certain visual effect – an impression of thinness or weightlessness. This was the case with the structural profiles that articulate the curtain wall of the Seagram building. The technology of the curtain wall had evolved to the point that these structural profiles were in fact not

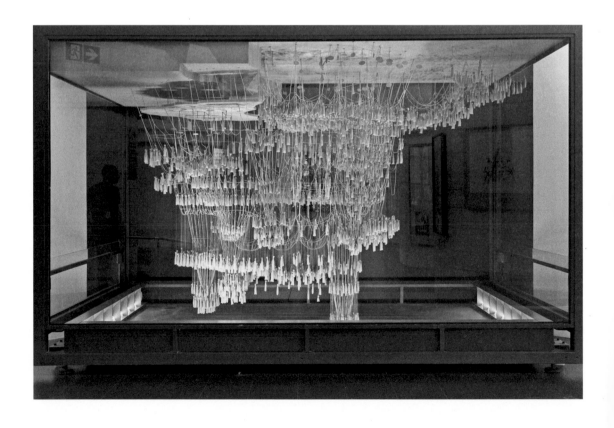

2   Scott, F.D.: (2011) "An Army of Men or a Meadow: The Seagram Building and the Art of Modern Architecture," Journal of the Society of Architectural Historians 70(3), pp. 330–353.

3   Collins, G.R.: (1963) "Antoni Gaudí: Structure and Form," Perspecta 8, pp. 63–90.

LEFT PAGE, TOP Seagram Building, New York City, USA, 1958. Architecture: Ludwig Mies van der Rohe, Philip Johnson; Structural design and engineering: Fred Severud

LEFT PAGE, BOTTOM Hanging Chain Model of Church of Colònia Güell, Barcelona, Spain, ca. 1900. Structural design and engineering / Architecture: Antoni Gaudí

necessary. There could have been simpler, more efficient ways to construct and even to stiffen the curtain wall should the wind loads pose a problem.[2] And yet the profiles were a conscious addition – an expensive, custom fabricated set of profiles – designed to elicit a certain effect. To Mies, the image of structure is just as important as the actual role of structure – he uses it to play with our perception of depth and of material lightness.

On the other hand, the flamboyance of Gaudí, which seems ornamental, is in fact a calibrated system in which each member is necessary for the overall equilibrium, a delicate network of structural optimization, itself a result of many years of experimentation with form-finding models. In fact, Gaudí's search for material optimization led to quite a few structural failures in his physical mock-ups and initial experiments.[3]

The abstraction of form we see with Mies and the structural form-finding of Gaudí are in fact not so distinct from each other if we understand that the relationship of architecture and engineering is always deeply entangled in a mutual search for visual and spatial effect. The role of structure in architecture is not merely one of technical problem-solving but one of spatial and organizational effect. Even when we choose to expose the structure, it is never really about structural efficiency or honesty of materials. Instead, it is about a play with perception. Whether we are architects or engineers, we're interested in things that are seemingly impossible. Rather than a display of structural might, we often go for the impossibly thin and delicate. Rather than stasis and stability, we are fascinated with the fragile equilibrium, the almost-chaos. In fact, the most thrilling structures often don't seem structural at all. The expressive synergy between structure and space is therefore ultimately that of illusion, of hiding or playing with a certain assumed truth. Every structural decision is therefore also a design choice.

We can also flip that equation and claim that every architectural decision is also a constructional choice and, in that regard, a structural choice. A successful collaboration is always a two-way conversation. While we expect engineers to talk to architects, architects also need to learn the language of engineers – enough to at least make the sparring productive. In the most ideal of situations, we become each other's critics, editors, and cheerleaders. In our own work and process at KARAMUK KUO, our collaboration with the structural engineer is a very close one – from the conceptual basis of the project until its construction. The role of structure is not only to hold up the building, but also to help to define the spatial experience and the identity of the project. Whether in the timber construction at the Weiden School in Rapperswil-Jona [PAGE 133, BOTTOM] or in the concrete construction at the University of Lausanne [PAGES 131-132], structure defines the relationships often implicit in the architectural program. In the Weiden School, the columns mark the threshold between the formal classrooms and the informal spaces, while the beams extend an experience of unity. In Lausanne, the sculptural concrete core serves as lateral bracing while at the same time housing the physical testing labs where environmental controls have to be maximized. Space, program, structure, material, are inextricably entangled. Invariably, the structure is always exposed, complicit in the architectural expression of the building's interior. It establishes the rhythms and cadences but also the textures and grains of the spaces, crafting the atmosphere through the way that it frames and guides movement, or brings character to an otherwise normative setting.

Sometimes the structure seems so natural that you might not even notice it, its integration so complete that it fades into the background despite being fully exposed. It's less a disruption of space than a reinforcement of space. At other times, its presence feels almost ornamental, the details or texture providing a certain specificity and definition to the space. What you don't realize are all the hours of discussion that took place between the architect, the engineer, and the contractor to get the joints looking so clean that all the exposed structure seems to just be part of the space, as was the case with the steel construction at the Archaeological Center in Basel-Land **[PAGE 133, TOP]** where the structure establishes a logic for inhabitation as well as possibilities for adaptation over time. This is a project whose competition brief already foresaw its future change and even its demise. Built atop ancient Roman ruins to house not only the administrative and research staff but also the collection of artifacts that is ever-growing, the structure not only had to be extendable but also eventually capable of disassembly. We chose a structural system not only for its performance and weight but also for its demountability and eventual recyclability. The filigree structure gave rhythm to the space, separating circulation from program in a continuous spatial language. This industrialized "nuts and bolts" system led to the exposure of joints and intersections.

Then there are the hybrid cases, like the structural solution at the Research Lab building in Basel **[PAGE 126]**, our most recent competition win, where the relationship between timber and concrete isn't only about material ecology but also about future flexibility and the expressive potentials of this marriage. Timber infills reduce a typical concrete slab to a horizontal frame – a grid that is stiff enough to function as a diaphragm but hollowed out to reduce the volume of concrete used. At the same time, the timber infill can be easily removed in the future to allow for vertical connections, giving the client agency over the life span of the building.

In all these cases, beyond the aesthetic choice, the structure and its architectural integration, there is also a question of sustainability. The life spans of the materials and the role that the primary structure plays in establishing a logic of durability or recyclability are among the main considerations behind each choice. The choice of timber, concrete, steel, or hybrid systems is therefore not only about an architectural willfulness but also about an understanding of the material ecology that we introduce into a very specific context. In each case, it was a conscious choice that served multiple purposes, reinforcing the architectural concept, and also providing an economy of means and an integrated thinking.

This forces us to not only revise the myth of structural engineering as a pragmatic and empirical discipline and architecture as the artistic one, but to question anew how these disciplines should be taught and transmitted. Collaborating with an engineer is like playing a jazz set. Sure, the architect takes the lead since we are also coordinating with the other consultants and maintaining the overall vision of the project, but it really is a jam session where the result emerges from a close, bantering exchange and productive synchrony. It's never really about the most efficient or the purest solution, nor is it always about the most flamboyant solution. The question of exposing or concealing is also always part of the game. But above all, it's almost always about a conceptual economy of means, about the way in which the architectural and the structural ideas align to produce a holistic solution.

RIGHT PAGE, PAGE 132 Structural model of the core and concept model. International Sports Sciences Institute, University of Lausanne. Lausanne, Switzerland, 2018. Architecture: Karamuk Kuo Architects; Structural design and engineering: Kartec Engineering with Weber+Brönnimann

PAGE 133, TOP Archaeological Center Augusta Raurica. Augst, Switzerland, 2022. Architecture: Karamuk Kuo Architects; Structural design and engineering: Weber+ Brönnimann with Kartec Engineering

PAGE 133, BOTTOM Weiden Secondary School & Gym. Rapperswil-Jona, Switzerland, 2017. Architecture: Karamuk Kuo Architects; Structural design and engineering: Kartec Engineering with Pirmin Jung Ingenieure

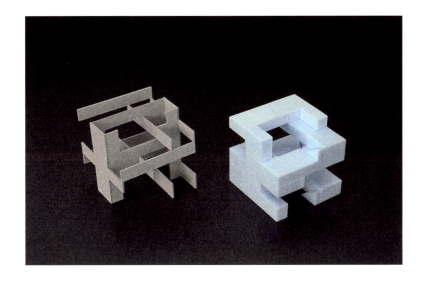

EXPOSED OR CONCEALED

EXPOSED OR CONCEALED

CHALLENGING
GRAVITY

EXPOSED OR
CONCEALED

LEARNING FROM
THE PAST

COMMON
RESPONSIBILITIES

The recent promises of digital technologies, new materials, and manufacturing methods concentrate the great optimism that has actually always characterized engineering. Engineering has traditionally stood for high levels of problem-solving, forward thinking, and new ground. Modern engineering is now a good 200 years old, if one places its beginning, as is usually done, at Navier's introduction of the theory of elasticity around 1819 at the École des Ponts et Chaussées in Paris. Much more concretely, he, together with other natural scientists, turned engineering education upside down there, and only a little later also at the École Polytechnique in Paris. Since then, engineering has stood for the transformation of our world, the promise of a better future through reasoned action and developed technology against formidable problems.

Interestingly, historical references are usually absent when appreciating latest technology. Historical retrospection has usually served to measure progress, in a sense using history as a reference point for the distance traveled. However, this is countered by the fact that many important technological figures place themselves quite naturally in a large context of existing historical ideas and concepts. Some have even gone so far as to claim that it is basically impossible to invent anything new. In any case, this historical awareness reveals the very notion that while concrete problems and circumstances change over the decades and centuries, there are still very basic technical ideas handling them. This awareness of the existing complex wealth of ideas has always been able to serve as an intellectual tool and can continue to do so in the future.

To tackle the challenges of our and future generations, it is therefore essential to formulate new visions: How do we shape our environment with technical means in a world that is changing rapidly? What can new manufacturing and design processes for new materials provide in this regard and how can the complex digital design and calculation tools be exploited? The role of technology is changing, but not so much because the technology itself is changing so much, but more importantly the changing problems we want to solve with it.

The following contributions stand for an approach of polychronic technical ideas, i.e., that technical contexts, principles, and thus also complex technical ideas exist in different temporal constellations and can therefore be made usable when considering new situations. In the broad resurgence of wood in construction, Thorsten Helbig and Florian Meier show how considerations of the play of forces and manufacturing can lead to a striking design process of load-bearing structures in timber construction. Tullia Iori, on the other hand, uses fictional contemporaries from different eras to recount the significance of technical developments, but also their links with politics and society, within the history of building over the last 200 years. Here, the use of technology as a cultural asset for national identities is also revealed. In a comparison between Switzerland and Norway, drawn in a discussion by Federico Bertagna and Patrick Ole Ohlbrock with Joseph Schwartz and Bjørn Normann Sandaker, the focus is on the culture of design. In the teaching of equilibrium to young students, the aim is not only to develop the competence of thinking in terms of forces and shaping load-bearing structures, but also to shape the young designers as intermediaries in an environment that is undergoing dynamic change. The section ends with an interview with Aurelio Muttoni and Roberto Gargiani about teaching conceptual design of structures to young engineers and architects.

Reference points are useful points of orientation in progressive thinking. And history is always inscribed in visions, because every challenge has its own history and culture. Old ideas are often themselves clever constructions that combined the unheard-of and the unattainable in their time.

Mario Rinke

THORSTEN HELBIG
FLORIAN MEIER

MATERIAL TECHNOLOGY AND SUSTAINABILITY – VISIBLE AND INVISIBLE INFLUENCES TO INNOVATIVE STRUCTURAL FORM

How material is shaping structures today

Structures are widely considered to be exemplary in their proper use of the material when they respond to the strengths and weaknesses of the material from a mechanical standpoint. For example, the high compressive strength (but low tensile strength) of concrete results in ideally compression-only structures such as thin concrete shells. Lightweight structures, such as cable nets, visualize the capacities of cables in tension (with no compressive capacity). Over the course of time, engineers followed the same trajectory, continuing to optimize form and minimize the use of material: the universal paradigm of structural engineering design. As a consequence, form follows forces: the load path is legible to the viewer.

We structural engineers consider a construction to be honest if the flow of forces can be read and the structure is designed appropriately for the material. Due to the perception of the inner "mechanical activities" (Theodor Lipps, 1897), based on an "unconscious mechanical knowledge," the viewer (even a viewer without pertinent knowledge) perceives well or correctly designed (honest) structures, as aesthetic structures.

More than anything else, material innovation may have provided the most impactful catalyst for structural innovation over the course of the past two centuries. An example is the emergence of iron – and later steel – construction in the 19th century. Wood and stone had previously been the primary building materials, and the significantly different mechanical properties of iron and steel, along with a completely different production and manufacturing process, forced engineers and architects to formulate entirely new structural designs. Borrowing largely from their pool of knowledge on timber construction, the structural systems, individual members, and especially the jointing of members in iron and steel construction resembled those of wooden predecessors. Only through intensive innovation across many decades could a material-specific design language be developed: Steel beams were first cast, then hot-rolled, into wide flange shapes. Riveting and then welding changed the way individual pieces were fastened. Iron and steel's high-performance mechanical properties, combined with innovation in structural form, allowed for wider-spanning and more delicate structures, such as Wilhelm Schwedler's domes in Germany or Vladimir Shukhov's towers in Russia.

Another, equally impactful development was the emergence of reinforced and then prestressed concrete design in the 20th century. In this case, engineers such as Robert Maillart and then Pier Luigi Nervi understood the material's strengths and weaknesses at an early stage and shaped structural forms that remain iconic until today.

On the other hand, the grey energy locked away during the structure's creation and the emissions caused are difficult to read, calling our traditional viewing habits into question. Lightweight construction is not sustainable a priori, and a mass-intensive "heavy construction" can be

LEFT PAGE Stuttgart timber bridge, a novel timber bridge typology. Weinstadt Birkelspitze, Germany, 2019
Structural design and engineering / Architecture: knippershelbig and Cheret Bozic Architekten

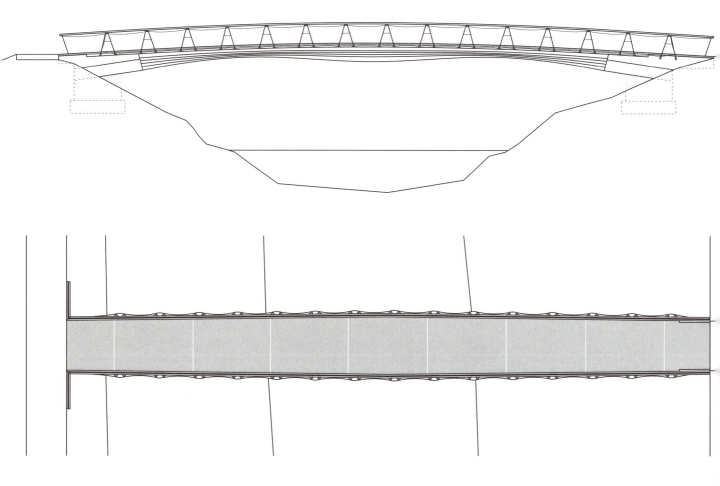

more resource-efficient. For a light, i.e., weight-reduced construction, we often use high-performance materials, the production of which requires immense amounts of (largely nonrenewable) energy. Lightweight constructions reduce the energy requirements of mobile objects (cars, airplanes) because less mass has to be moved. Given the immobile nature of our buildings, mass and energy often do not correlate directly. Higher masses are in some instances even an advantage, since thermal and acoustic requirements have to be taken into account in addition to the load-carrying capabilities. A mass timber or heavy rammed earth construction, on the other hand, can appear "light" in a sustainability context when the relatively low greenhouse gas emissions during production and even absorbtion and long-term storage of carbon dioxide offered by wood is considered.

We should also collect information about the conditions under which our building designs are manufactured, built, and used. Entirely invisible to the visitor's eye: the potential human (and environmental) cost or suffering that can occur from the extraction of raw materials or material processing to building erection and use. The supply chains and manufacturing processes in the construction industry are closely intertwined in our globalized world and require comprehensive data and research to be made fully transparent and traceable to the end user.

As a consequence, we can only succeed in creating the ideal construction if we also think about everything that is not visible when developing it.

Wood's re-entrance in the structural engineering world

Unlike its main competitors on the global construction materials market (concrete and steel), wood appears to provide answers to the main challenges of our time. As an organic material, wood was the most commonly-used bridge construction material up until the 19th century. It is readily available in many areas of the world and is easily workable by artisanal means. In Europe and Asia, some wooden bridges that were built more than 500 years ago still bear witness to the performance of the natural material and the craftsmanship passed down through generations required for the construction and maintenance of these bridge structures. In the 19th century, however, industrially produced iron followed by steel – and, in the 20th century, by reinforced and prestressed concrete – largely replaced wood and stone, the traditional bridge construction materials. The trend intensified further as the "new materials" were perceived to be more durable, requiring fewer replacements. Many of the wooden bridges built in the second half of the 20th century suffered moisture-related damage after a relatively short period of use, largely due to inadequate wood protection from rain exposure. This also reinforced the public's opinion that wooden bridges are not durable and are too expensive to maintain.

In parallel to this unfortunate development, and largely away from the gaze of the public and the larger engineering community, technological change in material development started to gain momentum. The transition from artisanal (manual) to industrial wood construction started at the beginning of the 20th century with the gluing of board lamellae to form glued laminated timber, and intensified enormously over the course of the last 20 years. Today, dimensionally stable beam or slab-like elements can be manufactured as components that can be precisely classified in terms of mechanical strength. They are easily mechanically workable, favoring modern CNC-based manufacturing processes, and are therefore suitable for construction processes involving a high degree of prefabrication. Modern gluing

LEFT PAGE **Stuttgart timber bridge, elevation view, elevation drawing and top view drawing. Weinstadt Birkelspitze, Germany, 2019 Structural design and engineering / Architecture: knippershelbig and Cheret Bozic Architekten**

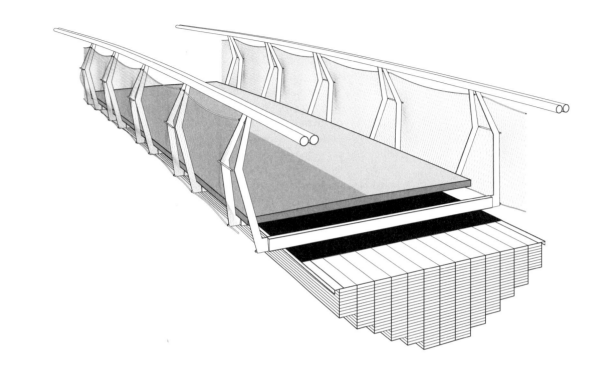
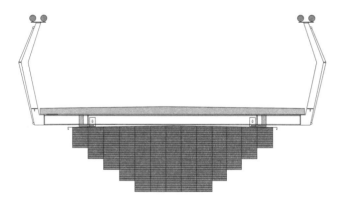
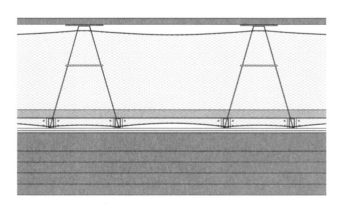

MATERIAL TECHNOLOGY AND SUSTAINABILITY

and screwing technologies enable efficient production and quick assembly. However, in spite of these technological developments, wood, the renewable bridge construction material, has remained of secondary importance only.

In 2012 only 62 out of the 9,200 bridges in the inventory of the state of Baden-Württemberg, Germany, were made of wood. A research and development project that started in 2013 attempted to take action and provide solutions to reverse this status quo. The project initially analyzed eleven old, still-used wooden bridges in the Stuttgart area to get a sense of the prevalent issues in wooden bridges. The MPA (material testing institute) of Stuttgart identified accumulating moisture in the support area and below leaking seals as the most common cause of damage. Wood is a capillary porous system: water can be stored in micro and macro pores. In the presence of increased amounts of moisture (with an equilibrium moisture content above approximately 20%), wood-destroying fungi can settle. The covered wooden bridges of the Middle Ages were therefore able to survive the centuries because the load-carrying wood was sheltered from moisture by paneling or sufficient roof overhang. This, combined with good ventilation of the construction, allows the structure to rapidly dry even if it is wetted by intensive rainstorms. Protection of the wood against moisture is therefore essential for its durability.

The Stuttgart Timber Bridge

The Stuttgart timber bridge, a novel timber bridge typology developed over the course of this research project, is designed to avoid the weaknesses of its recent, short-lived predecessors. It is also a covered bridge like its older, long-lived ancestors, although its assembly does not replicate their appearance in the traditional sense.

The massive beam made of block-glued laminated timber that forms the body of the bridge is located entirely underneath the walking surface, which shelters the wood from direct rain exposure **[PAGES 138, 142]**. Additionally, the sides of the wood element are inclined at a maximum angle of 60° – commonly used to avoid rain exposure from the sides. The horizontal gap between the timber construction and the walking surface ensures good ventilation, while a vapor-permeable membrane covers the solid wood body. Bearing areas and traditional roller supports at the ends of a bridge are known to be particularly prone to moisture damage and require frequent and costly maintenance efforts. Those issues can be avoided by applying the principle of the integral bridge. In order to realize an integral bridge – i.e., a bridge without roller supports and movement joints – the bridge girder and abutment must be monolithically connected to one another. When carrying out a structural analysis on a system of this type, it is essential to consider the soil-structure interaction, as the temperature/moisture-induced expansion or shrinkage of the bridge girder will not be compensated for by roller supports in a statically determinate system – the bearing stiffness therefore plays an important role in the overall development of internal forces as a consequence of expansion and shrinkage combined with externally applied loading. This was rigorously analyzed using a prototypical bridge design and varying bearing stiffness parameters. It can be demonstrated that glued laminated timber has very favorable properties for use in integral bridges: the thermal expansion coefficient is low (about a third of that of steel or concrete), the ratio of specific weight to high geometric rigidity is favorable, and the wood's inherent relaxation behavior reduces acting constraining forces.

LEFT PAGE Stuttgart timber bridge, axonometric view, section, partial elevation view. Weinstadt Birkelspitze, Germany, 2019. Structural design and engineering / Architecture: knippershelbig and Cheret Bozic Architekten

How forces and manufacturing processes inform the shape of the structure

When the bridge concept described here was used for the first time at the Remstal Garden Show 2019 (close to Stuttgart, Germany) the spans required for the crossing were of between 14 and 32 meters. In the case of the two longer bridges, the shape of the superstructure follows the bending moment diagram of a single-span girder transitionally and rotationally fixed on both sides under the effect of a uniform external load. The structural section viewed in a side elevation was configured to respond to this bending moment diagram: as a consequence of the high (negative) bending demand at the fixed supports, starting from its maximum section depth at the two ends of the bridge girder, the bridge cross section reduces its depth to a minimum at the moment zero point (approximately at the bridge's third points), and then increases again towards the mid-span of the bridge, where larger positive bending moments occur.

The characteristic stepping in the cross section of the two sides of the girder makes the production method legible [PAGE 145]: the individual glued laminated timber beams – thirteen in total, each 20 centimeters wide – are provided with an individual bending radius and are "stacked" on top of each other and glued to form a 2.60-meter wide, 30-meter-long bridge girder block up to 1.26 meters deep. Prior to gluing, the top-oriented sides of the individual beams are trimmed using a smooth-curve saw-cut, and will eventually support the upward-facing, gently curved walking surface. Due to the fact that the lower side of the beam remains unaltered (no cross-fiber cuts), the moisture-sensitive fiber cuts that have been mentioned only occur on the upper side, which is protected from moisture by a transverse and longitudinal gradient and a vapor-permeable membrane. As stated above, it is additionally ventilated by the 15-centimeter gap between the structure and the actual top-mounted walking surface panels made of fiber-reinforced concrete. After the block-gluing is finished and the rebar dowels were epoxied into the end grain on both ends of the bridge in the workshop, the bridge girder was transported to the construction site. The prefabricated bridge superstructure was lifted onto the previously completed abutments in just two hours; the shear cleats bolted to the superstructure served as a temporary bridge bearing until the cavities between end grain and abutment had been fully grouted and cured with concrete.

A novel bridge typology, shaped by sustainability and durability considerations

The world's first integral mass timber bridges shows the technical and design potential of the oldest and renewable bridge construction material and aims to address design objectives that were in recent history often overlooked: sustainability and durability. Such a monolithic structure without joints and bearings can be quickly assembled and is easy to maintain. Its high degree of prefabrication reduces time and cost on site. The mass use of wood and low-energy intensive processing results in a negative embodied carbon value when balancing the global warming potential for the superstructure with the sequestered carbon of the wood: more climate-damaging carbon dioxide is permanently sequestered in the wood body than was emitted during the manufacture, transport, and assembly of all superstructure components. The structure brings these design considerations to the viewers' attention by allowing them to shape its form, thus developing a novel, unique design language.

RIGHT PAGE Stuttgart timber bridge, fabrication at Schaffitzel Holzindustrie: positioning of the curved glulam layers (top left), force diagram of the bridge (top right), block-laminating the glulamlayers (image and diagram, second row from top), rebar epoxied to end grain (third row from top, image and section drawing), assembly at the site (bottom left), detail of grouted monolithic timber-concrete connection (bottom right). Weinstadt Birkelspitze, Germany, 2019. Structural design and engineering / Architecture: knippershelbig and Cheret Bozic Architekten

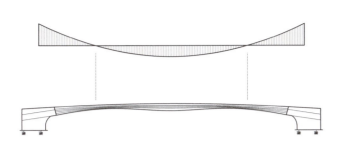

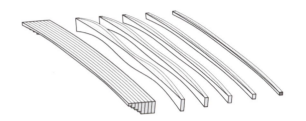

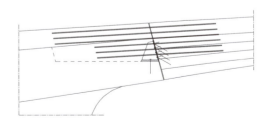

LEARNING FROM THE PAST

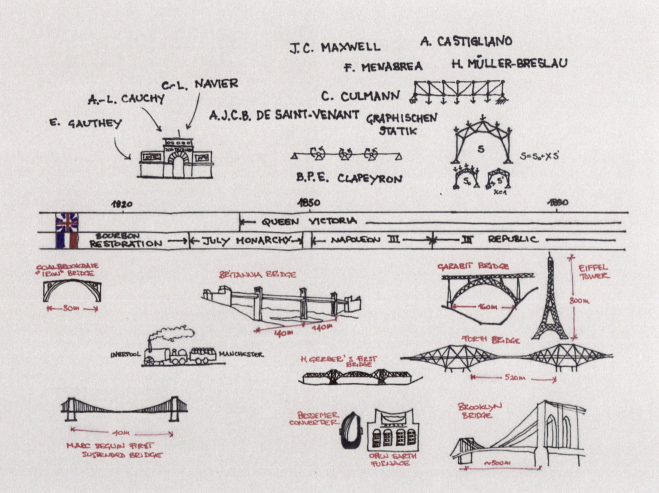

TULLIA IORI

TELL ME, PROF., WHAT IS THE USE OF THE HISTORY OF CIVIL ENGINEERING?

"Tell me, daddy. What is the use of history?" is the incipit of Marc Bloch's famous book *The Historian's Craft*. I invite you to read it for the general answer.

With regard to the history of civil engineering, I would like to simplify the problem by telling three stories, about three fictional engineers who lived in the nineteenth century, in the twentieth century and in the first century of the new millennium (predicting the future can only be a conjecture but, as a historian, I accepted one of the most popular lines in futurology research, predictive history, with constant speed, no acceleration and no technological singularity).

The first story is about Charles [PAGE 146]. According to his diary: "I was born in 1810, in France. My family was rich and in 1830 I attended the École Polytechnique, the best engineering school in the world at that time. My mathematical analysis professor was Augustin-Louis Cauchy and Claude-Louis Navier taught mechanics. At that time, teaching bridge construction meant teaching masonry bridge construction. The textbook was decades old, full of Ancient Roman bridges examples. Around 1820, Marc Seguin invented wire suspension bridges. In 1826 Navier tried to build one suspended bridge over the Seine but he failed. What an embarrassment for the École!

I wasn't interested in suspended bridges – they seemed to me medieval, like drawbridges. Instead, I preferred to design bridges for railroads, the new superfast way of connecting places. I admired George and Robert Stephenson, who completed the first railroad between Liverpool and Manchester in 1830. As soon as I graduated, I moved to England to join my uncle. Stephenson hired me and I managed many construction sites. Then, in 1846, he involved me in the design team for the Britannia Bridge, a continuous wrought-iron beam 140m span. What I had studied at the École was not enough. To understand the behavior of the continuous beam, we tested a scale model, and it worked fine. Then, a few years after the inauguration, a classmate of mine, Benoît Clapeyron, demonstrated the "three moment theorem." After him came many scholars devoted to understanding statically indeterminate structures – the big calculation dilemma of that period – and they fixed it: they just added a condition – the minimum work – and everything was solved. The solution to the big question was in plain sight, but only Maxwell understood it in 1856!

In the meantime, I decided to move back to France. For a few years, I designed compressed-air foundations for bridges, a new technique for bridge foundations in deep water. I designed the metal caissons, but I never went down into the caisson: the workers were sick after returning to the surface and many of them died. A few years later, a doctor figured out why workers were getting sick and how to prevent it – the compressed air technique spread throughout the world and completely transformed methods of building bridges.

Then, I met Gustave Eiffel. He was thirty-four when he founded his company and he hired me: I had a lot of experience in construction and he needed someone older to manage his team. He hired young engineers from

LEFT PAGE The fictional engineer Charles lived in the world of structural engineering in the nineteenth century.

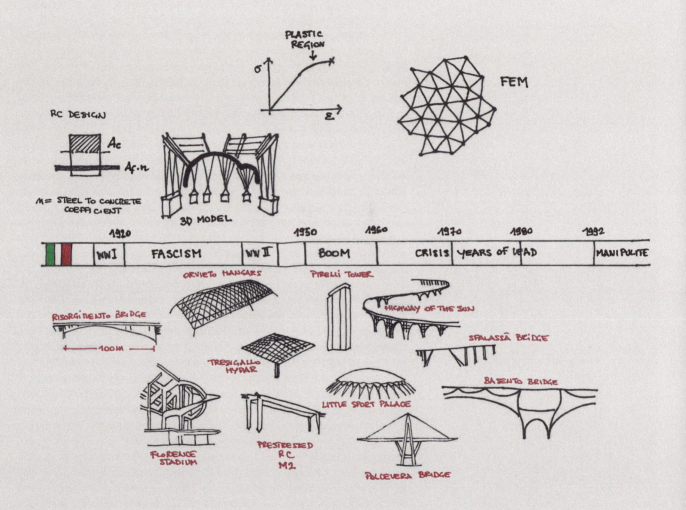

TELL ME, PROF., WHAT IS THE USE OF HISTORY OF CIVIL ENGINEERING?

Switzerland. They studied with Carl Culmann in Zurich, at the best university in the world at that time. They calculated faster than us, using a new technique: graphical statics. I didn't understand anything about the theory behind it, but the application was easy. Our company was the only one in France using this new method of calculation: Eiffel won all the bids. I managed the construction site of the Maria Pia bridge in Porto (1877), a gigantic arch spanning 160 m.

Meanwhile, new things were happening: in 1867 a German engineer, Heinrich Gerber, invented a new kind of beam bridge, the cantilever beam, named the Gerber beam in his honor. There was more to come: we started to use steel, the new material, produced with the Bessemer converter and the open-earth process. But Eiffel didn't trust steel: he said, "wrought iron was the perfect material for bridges." In 1883 I received a telegram from the United States (my first telegram, just invented!) from Emily Warren, the wife of Washington Roebling, who I met in France visiting a compressed air foundation site. She invited me to the inauguration of a suspension bridge spanning almost 500m in New York, the Brooklyn Bridge: the piers were neo-medieval, but it looked nothing like a drawbridge. I was wrong when I was young! When I retired, Gustave asked a last favor of me: to manage the construction site of a tower in Paris for the 1889 Expo: we changed the skyline of Paris! What a pity that the tower had to be demolished. The following year, we went to the inauguration of another stunning bridge: in Edinburgh, on the Firth of Forth: 520 meters of span. A steel bridge: looking at the bridge, Eiffel realized that he had underestimated that powerful material. Heinrich Gerber was there too, with us: he couldn't believe his eyes. His simple invention transformed into such a huge bridge!

Every now and then, I think of Navier's classes. Before his time, technological progress went very slowly. New things took decades, centuries to mature. Navier figured that the world would always go at the same speed. What an error! In our century, we knew of completely new, amazing materials, revolutionary ways of performing calculations, big, global new challenges like the railway. In the nineteenth century, the history of engineering changed completely."

The second story is about Giulio, an engineer of the 20th century **[PAGE 148]**. Again, according to his diary: "I was born in 1900 in Italy, in Rome. When I was ten years old, my father took me to see the construction site of the Risorgimento Bridge, over the Tiber. The company used a new material: reinforced concrete. Every now and then, on the banks of the river, I would see a gentleman in a white raincoat, who spoke French: his name was François Hennebique. He decided to design the bridge, with its 100-meter span, without following the rules of his patent. Thanks to him and the revolutionary bridge in Rome, reinforced concrete became a free material: no more royalties! After the bridge was inaugurated, no one believed that it would remain standing. Hennebique calculated it, refusing to use elasticity theory. A German engineer checked the calculations of the bridge and demonstrated that the bridge should collapse. But the bridge did not collapse. I still walk on it each Sunday!

I fell in love with that stubborn reinforced concrete: concrete and steel together, joined in a marriage. Each material takes the load it can bear best. It was so easy to think of this kind of mixed solution, but nobody did it before Monier and Hennebique. I graduated in engineering in Turin, in 1924. We studied mostly masonry and steel construction; reinforced concrete was given very little space in the books. But at my university the teacher was Camillo Guidi, a fan of reinforced concrete.

LEFT PAGE The fictional engineer Giulio was born in 1900 in Rome. He tells of the many technical changes linked to reinforced concrete in Italy and around the world.

2020 — COVID ♥ ———— 2050 ———— 2070 ———— 2090

I was hired by Pier Luigi Nervi's construction company: he founded his first company when he was thirty years old. He asked me to supervise the construction of a stadium in Florence. It was a success! Nervi never smiled: there was nothing to smile about, in those years in Italy. Mussolini had taken power: dictatorship and Fascism. Mussolini did not like reinforced concrete: he preferred the materials used by the ancient Romans, marble and bricks. In 1935 Mussolini invaded Ethiopia and the League of Nations imposed sanctions against Italy. Nobody sold us steel anymore. We could no longer find steel rebar on the market. In 1936 Mussolini said that to build with reinforced concrete was forbidden. The Fascists said we had to build with stone and brick, as the Romans had always done.

Fortunately, Nervi didn't listen to them. He obtained some work from the Air Force: hangars to protect aircraft. We could use reinforced concrete but we had to save steel. He invented a new way to build structures: he divided them into many pieces and our workers prepared them on the ground. Then they would put the pieces on a scaffold and connect the pieces with cast-in-place concrete: a jigsaw puzzle. Nervi got help from a professor at the Milan Polytechnic, Arturo Danusso, who made a scale model for him to understand the behavior of the structure without mathematical calculation. Nervi also invented a new material, *ferrocement* to build thin curved slabs.

Then in July 1943 Fascism fell in Italy. In September, after the armistice, Rome was occupied by the Nazis. Nervi closed the company for a year. He did not want to collaborate with the Nazis. He took the slabs home and spent time checking how they performed under the weather. After the war, putting the two inventions together, Nervi built his masterpieces: 100m diameter domes using *ferrocement* and structural prefabrication. He became the most famous engineer in the world: the Fascists had forbidden him to use his favorite material and, without complaint, he invented a new successful way of building.

In the meantime, I escaped to Switzerland. I was Jewish and I couldn't stay in Italy. In Switzerland I met Gustavo Colonnetti, he was my professor at the Turin Polytechnic. He also had to escape, he was an anti-Fascist militant. In Vevey, he organized a university camp where young exiled people could study, and I helped him. Colonnetti taught everyone a technique he learned in France: prestressed concrete. It seemed like an ingenious invention. Prestressing concrete with steel cables lends the concrete tensile strength. Again, it was so easy to think about this kind of coaction, but nobody could do it before Eugene Freyssinet.

In the university camp, I met Silvano Zorzi. When the war ended, I went to work with him. We designed dozens of prestressed concrete bridges together. In the meantime, the private car became popular. Italy built hundreds of kilometers of highways. In 1964, when the Highway of the Sun was opened, Italian engineers were a benchmark for the world. They did everything with concrete: skyscrapers, dams, highways, domes, even cable-stayed bridges like the Morandi bridge in Genoa: no other material could compete in our country. So much for the Fascists!

Later, things changed in Italy: the economic boom ended, workers began to strike, students began to protest. When workers began to cost too much, Zorzi invented machines to build beautiful bridges using fewer workers: self-launching formworks, "little by little" automatic systems.

I retired when a visionary engineer, Sergio Musmeci, built a fantastic bridge in southern Italy, in Potenza, using a soap bubble as a model. Musmeci tried to use finite elements methods (FEM), a method of calculation that four guys had invented in the United States in 1956, but he need-

LEFT PAGE The fictional engineer Sofia was born in Botswana in 2000. Her story of structures in the 21st century takes place in the future.

ed an automatic calculator. "Calculators will come soon," Musmeci said "and then everything will change. I can't wait!" He unluckily died young, and he didn't see the advent of calculators.

Every now and then, I thought about professors of my era: how much more of them I have seen! Everything changed in the 20th century: new materials, new way of building, new calculation methods, new social challenges. My teachers knew that everything would change: they had learned the lessons of the nineteenth century, but now the pace of change was much faster. The most important thing they taught me by their example is not to be afraid of crises. Crises are incredible opportunities for change, for growth. This is true on a personal level, too: after the persecutions, the war, the exile, a second life began for me. Crises propose new problems, new problems need new solutions.

We have walked the timeline of the nineteenth century; then that of the twentieth century; now it is the turn of the 21st century. This is the history of Neo Jane, a female engineer [PAGE 150]. According to her diary: "I was born in 2000, in Botswana. While I was attending university, the COVID-19 pandemic arrived. During the curfew, from my home, thanks to the Internet, I could attend university courses all over the world: a big opportunity amid the tragedy.

I took my PhD in Singapore. In the meantime, in the second half of the 20s, the world witnessed the birth of the United States of Africa. The peaceful revolution started from South Africa and from my rich Botswana. Africa did what the United States of America and Italy had done in the 19th century, and Europe in the 20th century (after a very bloody war). Africa was saturated with "rare earths," the lanthanide series of chemical elements, the new oil. Due to strong investments, Cape Town's university became the most important engineering university in the world.

In its laboratories, a new construction material was invented: starting with a rare metal, dysprosium, number 66 in the periodic table, and reinforced with thulium, another lanthanide with the atomic number 69. The combined material was stronger than steel and more beautiful than silver and titanium: thuliumed dysprosium, the material of the century.

After graduation, I was hired by a company investing in modern, high-speed transportation system across Africa: it was kind of a guided road. We would design the plan and then robots would assemble it on their own: the beams were all the same, so the robots were never wrong. And above all, they didn't get hurt (zero accidents at work) and there were no strikes.

Then, with thuliumed dysprosium, we designed and built a bridge over the Strait of Gibraltar spanning 13 kilometers to connect Africa to Europe (We did a little test before: the bridge over the Strait of Messina, in Italy, 3 kilometers span, a big dream for that backward country).

Then, in the middle of the century, a new calculation theory for structures arrived: trying to understand the behavior of rare-earth metal structures, scientists finally understood that elasticity does not exist, it is only an apparent effect of a more complex theory. Everything became much clearer, just as it did when Einstein explained that Newton's gravity force was only an apparent force due to the curvature of space-time. The new theory was under everyone's eyes, but only Sharbat, an Afghan professor, understood it in 2056 (56, what a special year: in 1856 the Maxwell paper, in 1956 the FEM paper, and now the Sharbat paper). She was in exile, in Switzerland, after the return of the Taliban dictatorship to Afghanistan: she was expelled from the university, like the Jews during Fascism. A second life began for her in Lausanne, near Vevey. And then …

What is the moral of my tales? Don't be afraid of innovations, new materials, new systems of calculations, new technologies, new challenges. Even if you don't accept these turnarounds, they will still come. Don't be afraid of crises: crises are always an opportunity for innovation. Be an engineer of your time. Always look around you. And do it quickly, because everything is faster now.

Let's study history! To make new things, you have to know everything that already happened in your world. History is a tool to imagine the future! Learn the path that your predecessors took. Put yourself in their path and continue their journey. You are leading a very large group, standing behind you, watching you and supporting you: Navier, Stephenson, Eiffel, Hennebique, Nervi, Musmeci… and so many others. Join the history of structural engineering!

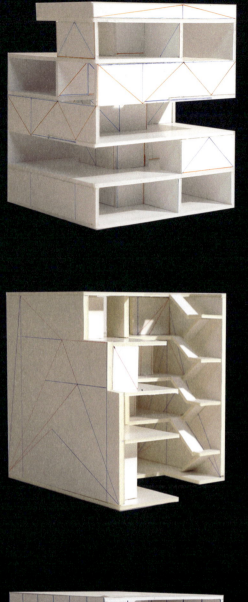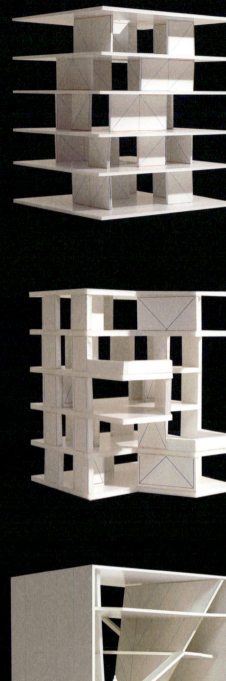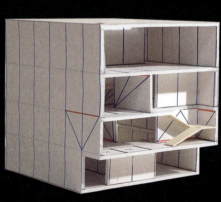

TOP Chair of Structural Design (Prof. Dr. Joseph Schwartz), ETH Zurich. Engineering Students' models for a multistory building combining walls and slabs. Autumn 2022.

A CONVERSATION ON STRUCTURAL ENGINEERING, ARCHITECTURE, AND EDUCATION BETWEEN SWITZERLAND AND NORWAY

BJØRN NORMANN SANDAKER AND JOSEPH SCHWARTZ IN CONVERSATION WITH FEDERICO BERTAGNA AND PATRICK OLE OHLBROCK

FB   The overarching topic of this conversation concerns the role of structural engineers within the design process and the role of education. Engineering schools play a key part in training young engineers in making a real contribution, along with architects and all the other professionals involved in the design process. As a first, general question, we would like to ask about the kind of contribution structural engineers should bring to the design process.

BNS   In Norway, some engineers are in fact very engaged in the design process, but I would say that most of them are quite far away from that. I agree that this might have a great deal to do with how they are educated. My first comment would be that the involvement of engineers should at least be more than it is now, and that engineers should be prepared and educated to take more responsibility for design choices. Their role is not that of sitting there waiting for something to calculate. That's how we were trained: we were given the system and we were asked to calculate the bending moments or shear forces within it. I started my engineering education nearly fifty years ago, but younger colleagues who graduated recently told me that it is not very different now. Perhaps it's even worse in a way…

JS   It is! I think one reason why it's worse is due to the fact that contemporary tools seem to be more comfortable, more efficient…better in any case. It is precisely these tools that are the problem. I think we should reflect on the tools we have as engineers before speaking about possible ways of working together. As Bjørn mentioned, the civil engineer is generally given something to calculate and the "right" solution can then be found relatively easily through powerful computer programs. However, "right" or "wrong" does not exist in our world. It's always a question of boundary conditions and of self-awareness: if I take a design decision, what are the consequences? That's the question.

As for working in cooperation, I think you can make a contribution only if you are very strong in your own discipline. For an engineer, being strong doesn't mean being able to calculate everything – although that may be a nice skill to have. Instead, it is about being able to have enough intuition to decide, on the spot, about questions that go beyond: "Does this work or not?" This has never been discussed by Christian Kerez and myself over the last twenty-five years, for instance. The discussion is always on the level of what the consequences will be of taking this design decision, and this opens up the possibility of cooperating.

BNS   My former colleague, Professor Kristoffer Apeland, was very good at that. He could see very quickly where you should actually spend your time in terms of calculation, irrespective of the regulations and standards. He used simple stress considerations, so he could quickly say: "Okay, this is 10 N/mm^2, you shouldn't be concerned about that," this kind of things. That's why he was so brilliant as a teacher in helping young aspiring architects who really wanted to do something extraordinary. He could give them the necessary confidence to bring their project forward.

FB   Architectural education might be a bit different, though. From their first year in university, architects are trained to deal with ill-defined design questions that are not amenable to unequivocal answers, but instead require the creation of a set of customized rules to tackle the design task. Conversely, engineering students mostly deal with closed problems, grounded on specific theories and methods that, if correctly applied by the student, will eventually lead to the right solution. However, as Joseph mentioned, no "right solution" exists for design scenarios. Could this be one reason why engineers are more comfortable analyzing structures rather than designing them?

JS   Until I was sixty years old, I believed that civil engineers and architects were different species. In recent years here at ETH, we have learned that this is not at all the case; it's a question of education. If you give engineering students suitable tools and the opportunity to think in terms of much more open categories, then you will see that they are eager to have tasks with more than one correct solution.

BNS   It's also interesting to reflect on the background of the people who generally educate structural engineers. To be an engineering professor in Norway, you obviously need research competence. Candidates have doctorates in concrete cracking and other extremely specific and technical topics. As a result, engineering schools are often full of people interested in quite narrow aspects of an otherwise very broad discipline. It's a mystery why engineering schools don't hire people from practice. In architecture it's almost the other way around: they hire practicing architects that are outstanding, conveying their competence, skills, and attitudes to architecture to young students.

JS Here at ETH it's a little different, perhaps. As in the German system, practice is traditionally considered very important, and I think this tradition is not totally lost. In fact, when I was asked to serve as professor at the Department of Architecture it was a must not to give up the private office.

BNS Does this apply to the Department of Architecture only? Or also to the Department of Engineering?

JS Engineering is different. It used to actually be forbidden to work in practice while being a professor. Now it is possible, but Christian Menn and others of his generation had to give up their firms. When I started at the Department of Architecture, we made an agreement that I could invest one day per week in my private office. Back then, I was often involved in competitions, and that was considered a major benefit for the school.

BNS I'm glad to hear what you say, but I'm not surprised. ETH has a tradition of strong designers within engineering, but in Norway I often see that faculty members within engineering have research interests and experiences within topics that don't necessarily qualify them to teach the design of structures...and when I use the expression "the design of structures" here, I am thinking of something that is a little different from what is usually meant by "structural design"; the analyses that verify the stability, strength, and stiffness of a system, and the consequences of these for the sizing of structural elements. I tend to talk about "the design of structures" as the design phase during which structural strategies and structural form are considered and decided upon, design choices that also take architectural ideas and the qualities of spaces into account.

JS Regardless of the topics you are interested in as an engineer, I personally think you must live the profession if you want to teach structures. It's not enough to just tell them something. You have to convince the students by being authentic...in the sense that what you are telling them is not only something that you have proved to work, but is also something that makes you really happy to do this kind of job.

I was myself very strongly interested in the calculation of tau stresses and in investigating the development of concrete cracks and so on. For several years, I have been really in love with all these small problems. However, when you're starting out in practice and you see that with this way of looking at things you're not able to do something intelligent, you must be honest with yourself and acknowledge that there must be another way.

FB This brings us back to the question of tools. Despite it not being appropriate to talk about "right solutions" in design scenarios, we can perhaps discuss what the "right tools" are that engineers need in order to design.

JS Once again, we should talk about "reasonable tools" rather than "right tools." From my point of view, the tools civil engineers are using are much too restricted and much too focused on analytical models and calculations... in this sense, finite elements programs are a disaster. Certainly they are useful if you have to quickly calculate something, but this is just an aid; the main decisions cannot be taken in this way. These tools cannot guarantee an understanding of the design space – of how different parameters affects the result – and that's the most important thing. It's a pity that it was so fascinating over the centuries to solve differential equations. The elegance of the underlying mathematical models has nothing to do with design or with the development of forms that make sense. However, these elegant mathematical methods in engineering fostered the idea that there must be right and wrong solutions when developing a structural system.

FB And it also fostered the idea that civil engineers can put everything on a clear scientific basis, while, from the perspective of some engineers, architects completely lack that basis. And vice versa, engineers are often seen as technicians without any sensitivity for the quality of space and for anything beyond technical aspects. This is also something that needs to be solved before starting to work in cooperation...

JS We had the feeling that it's possible to find a way out of this dilemma by showing that when you are speaking about statics, this may be dealt with both in a deductive and in an inductive way. If we are able to bring in more intuition and to show that all these mathematical calculations are ultimately based on something not so difficult...you know, the flow of forces is laminar and people don't understand that this makes the whole process very, very simple in some ways.

In this sense, graphic statics is a good tool because it allows a sort of communication that is on the same level as that undertaken by architects. On the other hand, this creative work of developing stress fields[1] also helped us a lot with gaining experience in making efficient sketches using different colors, and so on. This sketch about the Bahrain pavilion is a nice example. We had an online meeting with Christian Kerez in the afternoon, but I had many other things to do that day, and then five minutes before the meeting I had to produce something to start the discussion at least. I had made some reflections on it, so I could quickly sketch my idea. Eventually, you feel that this simple sketch was really the key to arriving at the solution. Other engineers involved in this project spent half a year calculating and simulating and were not able to find the solution. I think we should really train civil engineering students in this direction. We have seen in our Structural Design course[2] for civil engineers at ETH that if you give students the opportunity, they will produce very interesting things from the very start: you only have to stimulate them.

FB In addition to this class of methods and tools that, thanks to their visual nature, trigger the intuition Joseph mentioned before, another tool that might be worth discussing is the use of references. In the course "Architecture as a technological practice"[3] that Bjørn teaches at NTNU, students are taught to build up their own catalogue of references. That's perhaps another tool that engineering students should be trained to deal with. What's your experience with this?

BNS My experience is that this is a very good addition, and it's very much wished for and valued by the students who take this course. The engineering students react very positively to being exposed to historical, but also contemporary structures, buildings, and issues related to architecture. So I think we need to involve this aspect of the profession. Within the course, students are also asked to write essays on topics related to architecture and technology, for example on the achievements of personalities like Torroja and Nervi, or on particular buildings etc.

JS This is very personal, but for me references were never interesting. I have an internal wish to understand what I'm doing – from scratch, really. When you teach, sometimes you realize that things that seemed clear are not clear anymore right at the moment you have to explain them. People often told me that I was crazy taking responsibilities for certain projects, but if you're really developing things from the very beginning and trying to explain them as simply as possible, without any lack in the

1   Muttoni, A., Schwartz, J. and Thürlimann, B.: (1997) Design of Concrete Structures with Stress Fields, Birkhäuser.

2   https://www.schwartz.arch.ethz.ch/Vorlesungen/TE_D/index.php.

3   https://www.ntnu.edu/studies/courses/AAR4250#tab=omEmnet.

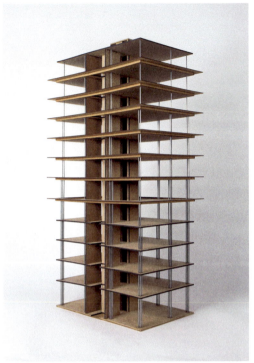

TOP/BOTTOM Student project. "Clustered Columns" – a multistory, mixed-use building by Henrikke Omre and Mie Aspelin, AHO 2022.

TOP Chair of Structural Design (Prof. Dr. Joseph Schwartz), ETH Zurich. Structural Design course, final reviews. December 2022.

BOTTOM Skarnsund Bridge (Inderøy, 1991). In 2008, the bridge was listed as a protected cultural heritage. Designer / structural engineer Johs Holt AS

argumentation, then it works. For me, this always counted a little bit against using references so much. This is my character. I played with materials as a child and I was convinced that with scrap material I could do very interesting things. This influenced my way of thinking very strongly, giving me a belief that I'm able to understand things in my field – not 100% perhaps, but at least 80%.

BNS   We might be talking about slightly different things. Let me give an example. Once, as part of a project for The Norwegian Public Roads Administration related to bridges, we asked Norwegian architects and engineers to name the most successful bridge in Norway. There was a clear winner: the Skarnsund bridge, which was designed by an engineer without the support of an architect. When the engineer in charge was interviewed, he said that the moment he realized he was to design that bridge, he started traveling around to look at other bridges of the same category. This is what architects usually do. He obviously knew all the theoretical aspects of cable-stayed bridges, but when he had to take the responsibility for actually designing the bridge, he wanted to understand what works and what does not work, visually. And that was very surprising – and also cause for relief in a way – that he, as a structural engineer, worked in that way. So, this is what I mean by having references.

JS   I think a very important aspect when looking at references is how you read them, because looking at things on its own is not very helpful. Christian Menn always stated that when building a bridge, equilibrium is the most important thing. He didn't mean the equilibrium of the forces, though. He was referring to the equilibrium between the bridge and the landscape. And if you're not able to read this when you look at a bridge, then you can look at a lot of bridges and it might even become confusing, eventually. That is to say, references are certainly helpful, but only if you're able to learn something from them. I agree that this should also be part of education, to show to the students how to see the strong and the weak aspects in these references. I'm not a good observer myself, but it's something you can learn. Architecture students are trained to do this, as we never were.

OO   I fully agree with you. You can say that you understand something truly to the end if you can break it down to simple principles and if you can explain it to somebody else. Could it be an interesting model for education to ask students to teach younger colleagues, somehow?

JS   Architecture students do this in the studios, they always have to explain and to defend their projects. The essays that Bjørn previously mentioned also go in this direction. Students are asked to explain what they have seen, and I think this is something that is missing right now. Civil engineering students are never asked to present what they have done, and that's also a pity.

BNS   I would like to bring up another aspect…When I observe engineers in dialogue with architects or even with architecture students, I detect a curious mix of hostility and servility. It seems that some engineers show resistance to architecture as such, while others merely make comments like: "Yes, this can be done." Seen from an educational perspective, the latter attitude is not very helpful either. "It can be done," sometimes implies that if you use enough concrete here and steel there, then we can make the structure stand up. Instead, the dialogue should be more like: "I'm trying to see what you wish to accomplish, but … if you move this element there over to here, you might achieve, firstly, a better, more rational structure, and also, importantly, a better architectural result." But this approach seems to be very hard to find.

JS   I was always convinced that the kind of hostile attitude some engineers show is no more than an effort at concealment. It's a problem of weakness – they probably feel overwhelmed and not able to participate in the discussion. One doctoral student at our Chair wrote a PhD on the cooperation between civil engineers and architects.[4] As an experiment, we assigned the same design task in two distinct courses, one for architecture students and the other for civil engineering students. We let these courses run until mid-semester, and then the doctoral student intervened, trying to bring the two groups together. Architecture students saw this as a big opportunity to ask structural questions and civil engineers wanted to know more about urbanistic aspects and so on. We learned a lot from this, because we had plenty of prejudices about the possible reaction ourselves. However, these prejudices break down immediately if you only try to work against this sort of attitude. I learned a lot over the last ten years – once, I was convinced that this is not possible.

BNS   The danger is that they take these prejudices against the other discipline, be it engineering or architecture, from the university out into practice. I think we are very fortunate at AHO and NTNU, in this sense. Architecture professors back us up in the sense that they encourage students to really talk with experts from other disciplines. We hope that this is something that they will bring with them into practice…they shouldn't see the engineers as people who try to make them stumble or kill the project, but quite the opposite. So we need to think carefully about what we say to these young students.

[4]   Hofmann, H.: (2021) "The Coprofessional Practice of Design," PhD thesis, ETH Zurich.

FB Going back to the experiment Joseph mentioned of giving engineering students and architecture students the very same task, as far as I remember, the architects immediately saw the opportunity, while engineers were quite skeptical in the beginning …

JS But they were interested, nevertheless. For sure, a lot of architecture students immediately saw the big chance to improve their projects, while it took engineering students a bit longer to react…

FB It's clear that there is a different attitude in these two groups of students. From the perspective of a teacher who's teaching both architects and engineers, what are the main differences between these two groups of students?

JS Well, you have to motivate architecture students a little bit more for technical things and show them that these technical things can be developed in a similar way to the way in which they are developing the project concerning proportions of space, light, and everything. You must show them that there is in some way the same logic behind it. Conversely, you can show the civil engineering students that at the end, developing an architectural project is something very similar to developing a technical project.

BNS It's a difficult question. I'd like to approach it from the position of the professor holding a lecture, and the reactions you get when you stand in front of 100 engineering students or architecture students. The engineering students are much more modest, often silent, but very focused, while the architecture students in general are much more free and blunt: "Hey, I didn't get that!" or "What do you mean by that?" It is certainly a different culture…

JS But is it like this in the first week? I've always had the feeling that when students start here at ETH, they are just like children. Then, after a few months, they are no longer children. They very soon develop their identity as students of this or that discipline. This is, once again, a question of education…we should be aware that from the very beginning of their studies we should try to bring architecture and engineering students much closer together. At HSLU in Lucerne, we used to organize a small trip during the first weeks of their studies. Both architecture and engineering students would participate, and they were asked to design and build a small footbridge. We gave them two-meter-long, thin timber bars and a little bit of cable and they had to build a four-meter-long bridge. It was interesting to observe that it was not possible to tell the difference between civil engineering students and architecture students in these groups.

OO Engineers and architects are generally trained in separate departments, and you have experienced both. In some countries, there are mixed programs that include both architecture and civil engineering. If you could shape the curriculum of architecture and engineering, would you put them together? Or would you let them run separately?

BNS In Scandinavia, there's a program at Chalmers Technical University in Gothenburg where you can study the traditional civil engineering curriculum, or you can apply for another program, which is indeed a mix of architecture and engineering. At some point in this program, students decide whether they want to become an architect or an engineer. And you can also become professional in both fields by adding a year or two to your studies. In Denmark, at the Technical University in Copenhagen, they have a program called "architectural engineering" where they set out to educate engineers who also study architecture-related subjects. The course that I'm involved in at the NTNU in Trondheim, Norway, is actually part of something called a "minor" in architecture offered to students of structural and civil engineering, which is another alternative model. I've been observing interdisciplinary curricula in Scandinavia for some years. They generally seem to be successful, considering that the graduates are very attractive in the job market. Myself, I tend towards a distinct architectural education and a distinct engineering education, but I am strongly in support of introducing into each curriculum adequate subjects that may act as touching points that are now too often missing. I think that would be perhaps the safest way to do it. Students from both disciplines will need deep insight into their own specialty, plus a knowledge of some of the other profession's core subjects.

JS This is a crucial question. On the one hand, there this question of being strong at least in one discipline. On the other hand, there is the question of the role of the architect. Are architects still able to control each and every design aspect today? What is the role of the other professionals involved in the process? How should we deal with this need for an ever-growing number of specialists? The result of this specialization is that in some cases the architect is only doing the first sketches for a competition: ultimately, all the others have to build it. This cannot be the solution, because in the end there is nobody who really has control over the process, meaning that nobody is able to see the consequences of design decisions within the different disciplines regarding the end result. And this is crucial, as the optimum of the project is never the optimum of the single disciplines. In fact, it's something totally different.

TOP/BOTTOM The Nordic Pavilion, Venice, Italy (1962). The double array of thin reinforced concrete beams on the roof integrates space-making, load-bearing, and light-diffusing functions, thus dissolving boundaries between disciplines. Architect: Sverre Fehn. Structural design and engineering: Arne Neegärd.

LEARNING FROM THE PAST

500-year Tower, TEN with Neven Kostic, 2021

TEACHING CONCEPTUAL DESIGN OF STRUCTURES TO YOUNG ENGINEERS AND ARCHITECTS

AURELIO MUTTONI AND ROBERTO GARGIANI IN CONVERSATION WITH PIERLUIGI D'ACUNTO

PD   Good afternoon, Aurelio and Roberto. I would like to ask you some questions on the role of the conceptual design of structures in the training of young engineers and architects, an area in which you have long been – and are still – very actively involved. In his book *Costruire Correttamente*, Pier Luigi Nervi emphasizes the significance of the university education of structural designers, considering it fundamental to ensuring correct design of architectural structures. In particular, Nervi states: "It is to be greatly regretted that the highest capacities of our mind, such as intuition and direct comprehension of the fundamental laws of the static-constructive world – those same capacities that have allowed, in the distant past, the realization of works in front of which the most modern methods of theoretical investigation must bow in an act of reverent and modest admiration – have been banished from our schools and overshadowed by abstract and impersonal mathematical formulas."[1] Nervi's text refers to the university education of young architecture and engineering students in the postwar Italian context. To what extent do you believe Nervi's words are still relevant today?

RG   Nervi's books and other writings should be contextualized within the moment of their publication if we are to understand their significance and value as models for a type of design that can articulate the principles of structure and technology, not only in engineering but also in architecture. Nervi wrote *Scienza o arte del costruire?*,[2] which was addressed to the students of the Faculty of Architecture in Rome, within this specific framework: an overall reform in architectural education, aiming to foster an awareness of the importance of new economic building materials against the backdrop of postwar reconstruction. During these years, Nervi was perfecting the *ferrocement* technique in order to offer it as an economically feasible system for reconstruction, suitable for a workforce that was immigrating from the countryside. The book, like other essays by Nervi, asserts a model of practical engineering, shaped by the historical context, the reasoning behind the construction site, the character of the labor force, the materials, and the implementation.

AM   One must acknowledge that Nervi, although he probably wasn't the only one during those years, was one of the first engineers to realize that the profession was moving away from the conception of structures and giving too much relevance to calculations.

RG   You are absolutely right. Right from the beginning, Nervi, like other engineers-entrepreneurs, did not base his research solely on mathematics. Perhaps he was aware that relying solely on calculations could lead one to conceive structures that would have been complicated to build given the constraints imposed by labor and the limitations of the construction site – such as those posed by wooden formwork for concrete, for instance.

AM   Nervi's words are certainly very relevant for any engineer. His work was intended as advice to young professionals to focus more on conceptual design and perhaps less on calculations. In connection with this, I would also like to mention Torroja, who, in the 1950s, echoed the same sentiments. These engineers have undoubtedly left a mark, and there are certainly talented engineers who have realized the fundamental importance of conceptualization. If we look at the Swiss engineering landscape over the last few decades, for example, the situation has greatly improved. How do you see it, Roberto?

RG   I will try to answer your question based on the theoretical position that I first adopted only a few years ago, after my teaching experience at the EPFL directing the Superstudio workshop, in which you also participated. I believe that the professional figure of the engineer, as defined since the mid-18th century by the French school (an issue which, of course, extends beyond the professional and cultural status of the engineer), is no longer relevant. For about two centuries, the main goal of engineering research seems to have been the optimization of materials within structures, driven by economic motives and guided by principles of abstraction and efficiency that today could be considered significant evidence of the production logic of capitalism and the rules of its market. The aim was to make the materials within a structure as effi-

---

[1] Nervi, P. L.: (1965) Costruire Correttamente, 2nd ed., Hoepli, p. 8.

[2] Nervi, P. L.: (1945) Scienza o arte del costruire ? Caratteristiche e possibilità del cemento armato, Edizioni della Bussola, Rome.

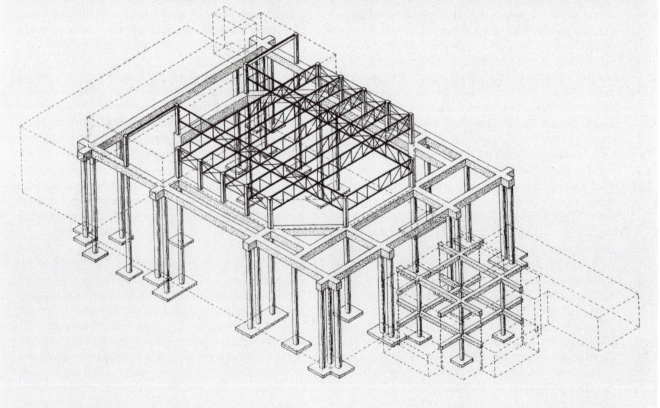

TOP Digital collage by Filip Dujardin

BOTTOM Temporary theater at the Exposition Internationale des Arts Décoratifs et Industriels Modernes by Auguste and Gustave Perret, Paris, 1925

cient as possible in order to achieve maximum economic savings. However, the price of this was the abandonment of the concept of the long-term persistence of a building, a concept that had guided the builders of outstanding structures in the past. It appears that even mathematical tools, if used – as I believe they have been in many cases – to exclude the parameter of the duration of a structure over time, have contributed to the dominance of an optimization principle that fits perfectly into the logic of economic savings in the pursuit of profit (of materials, time, labor, etc.). At present, it is urgently necessary to reconsider the design of any structure in light of the parameters of time – which means that the resistance of parts should no longer be considered to be purely static. The structure should probably be articulated once again into permanent and temporary parts, depending upon function over time. In short, it is in my opinion necessary to reconsider the so-called scientific foundations of the discipline and identify parameters that allow transforming the static concept of resistance into that of persistence, to define a new idea of sustainability.

AM I agree with you, but I am not fully in accord with the final part of your answer. The engineering we still conceive of today is a product of the Industrial Revolution. At that time, the goal was to optimize structures because steel, a new material, was being used for the first time. Steel was expensive and not easily available – unlike stone and wood, readily accessible back then. This tradition has persisted over time. You mentioned the French school – hence Eiffel, obviously – but I would also include the British and American schools. We are still the products of these schools. However, I do not wish to deny this tradition because I believe it is still relevant. In fact, it is becoming relevant once again due to the emergence of environmental problems. Instead, my criticism relates to the fact that starting from the 1970s, when everything was easily available and low-cost, and the material was no longer expensive, it was the labor force that began to become costly. During this time, we started to waste materials.

RG Certainly, dear Aurelio; yet it would appear to be essential today to continue questioning the foundations of scientific knowledge – and more, to verify whether it is possible to update its parameters based on contemporary conditions (at least, this is what is happening in my research). I believe that we should question the origins of the "theory of structure." How much have the rules of that science been derived from principles of abstraction that ended up being identified with the success of artificial materials from the 19th- and 20th-century industry? We should ask ourselves whether the foundations of those rules are still relevant, because the system we have produced using those rules may lead us to exclude more hybrid structures which could exhibit much more complex behaviors and are less controllable by the rules of a *mathematics* that, moreover, seems to have become increasingly used as the support for engineering learning, the reverse of what Nervi had hoped for. Perhaps what we need is a new Nervi, but one no longer bound by being the entrepreneur of his own, unique material.

AM However, a misconception leads to the belief that minimizing materials is merely the result of mathematical optimization. Instead, I believe that two more obvious counterexamples are Nervi and Maillart, both of whom were building entrepreneurs and both of whom focused their minimization of materials not so much on calculation but instead on intuition and structural conceptualization. In my opinion, the opposition between mathematics and intuition is wrong. I see them as two elements essential to engineering. In my view, engineering works best when one component does not outweigh the other.

PD It should be noted, however, that the education of civil engineers almost always focuses on structural analysis, not so much on structural design. How can young engineering students be better acquainted with the fundamental topic of the conceptual design of structures?

AM Structural analysis is an absolutely necessary but not sufficient component. Two other fundamental components are required in order to complete the training of an engineer. Firstly, a course on the history of construction is essential. This is crucial because it allows students to understand the extent to which the creative-intuitive aspect has contributed to producing remarkable works and to making the engineering profession beautiful, stimulating, and interesting. Secondly, there should be a significant increase in the quantity, number, and quality of projects that students work on during their course.

RG I have the impression that engineering schools are increasingly avoiding teaching design. The recent profiles of professors in engineering schools belong to a universe that is closely linked to the realm of mathematical abstraction, to experimentation that seems to be stuck down the blind alley of the academy, as Nervi feared. There is no doubt that we need to raise the question of design again, as you have argued, and take into account our knowledge of the origins and history of our discipline, as is your hope. Moreover, I believe it is necessary to reconsider what the engineer of the 21st century should be designing during their educational learning process.

AM I believe that what you design is not so important – it is crucial, first and foremost, to become aware of the importance of design and, secondly, to learn how to design. Here, I am sharing my personal experience. Joseph (Schwartz) and I were incredibly fortunate because we had Christian Menn as one of our professors. With Menn, we learned how to design bridges. As I have always told my students: what you design during your training is not so important. When you learn how to design a bridge, you also learn how to design a building structure and any other engineering project.

RG However, I insist that the current condition compels us to question which themes should be addressed in engineering design. In my opinion, it is necessary to initiate a collective discussion to identify the topics capable of triggering a critical reformulation of the foundations of design, to make it suitable for the challenges of the 21st century.

AM Then let's add a third essential component to the education of engineers. We need a course on the ethics of responsibility. I'm referring to the ethics of responsibility in the Hans Jonas sense, which involves the fundamentals of technological thinking and the need to compel engineering students to reason and question as to why and what they should design. These, along with the two previously mentioned components, are the three fundamental elements missing in engineering education. They should be added to the necessary – but not sufficient – technical-scientific component, to return to my initial idea.

PD We have extensively discussed young engineers. Now, let's focus on the education of young architects. Often, the teaching of structural engineering within architecture degree programs is presented as a simplified version of the structural engineering courses taught to civil engineers. As a result, many young architects end up considering structural engineering to be a purely technical subject, disconnected from the theme of design. How can we approach young architecture students and engage them in the topic of conceptual design of structures?

AM In this respect, I am going to be quite radical. While I am absolutely convinced that the technical/scientific component is fundamental to the education of engineers, I am equally convinced that all of this is not at all necessary, and is in fact a burden in the education of architects. This is a conclusion I reached in the spring of 1996 when Mario Botta and Aurelio Galfetti asked me to teach at the Accademia di Architettura in Mendrisio. I have always criticized the teaching of statics to architects, but this is partly because I had read with great passion the books by Mario Salvadori and James Gordon, which in my view were going in the right direction. So I said to myself: I'll try to develop something that is exactly the opposite of what is usually done. So, I developed a course on the statics of structures for architects without a single equation.

RG Today, we are experiencing a dramatic and fascinating phase that, paradoxically – for engineers – could be compared to what was happening in the last decades of the 19th century when engineers specializing in the construction of metallic bridges began to work alongside architects, providing them with consultations for the design of increasingly tall buildings. Given the current environmental and climatic challenges, there is now more than ever an urgent need for a new collaboration between architects and engineers to define formulas for a "resistance" that is entirely different from that which we defined between the 18th and 20th centuries. What should the scientific skills of the engineer be in relation to contemporary and future problems? This issue also applies to educational experimentation in engineering and architecture schools, where it is most urgently necessary to create the conditions for a collaboration that will later become professional – as you, Aurelio, have always advocated. We have come back to the question posed by Nervi's books and the need to adapt his didactic perspective to the emergencies of contemporary construction.

AM Regarding this, I also have a very radical vision. When, more than twenty years ago, we founded a faculty that brought together architects, civil engineers, and environmental engineers at EPFL, I came up with the slogan *projeter ensemble* (design together). I firmly believe that in engineering and architecture faculties, students must learn to design together. I see no other alternatives. This is essential to understanding how to do things and questioning what is right to do. Engineers must know how to work with architects, and architects must learn to collaborate with engineers. It is only by working together that problems can be solved.

RG I completely agree. Architecture and engineering schools cannot continue operating in parallel without meeting. It is essential – both for engineers and for architects – to introduce shared workshops into the educational curriculum where they can come together to discuss the future of design for the 21st century.

AM I would like to return to the second question and my mention of the lack of three fundamental components. The first component is the history of construction; in this context, both engineering and architecture students should be shown the quality of projects conceived by two professionals who know how to collaborate, for example, Joaquim Cardozo and Oscar Niemeyer or Matsuro Sasaki and Toyo Ito. The second component is the project: here engineering and architecture students should be taught to design together because once they graduate, they will be working together. Additionally, there should be a course on the ethics of responsibility as they apply to construction. Once again, the disciplines should be brought together, as the questions raised today are common to various construction professions.

PD Aurelio, let's go back to your personal experience. Your book *The Art of Structures*[3] is now available in several languages and has provided the foundation for structural design teaching for years at both the EPFL in Lausanne and the ETH in Zurich, as well as at various other universities. How did the idea for this book come about, and how has the book contributed to the education of young engineers and architects?

AM Well, this book was born when I was teaching in Mendrisio, and it was the answer to that question you asked me about teaching structures to architects. I said to myself: you must base it on something completely new. The book started out with the idea that you cannot do structural design if you do not understand how the structure works. Then I realized, while teaching architects, that this approach would also be useful for engineers. Because engineers have always been taught how to calculate and have never been taught how a structure works. And, above all, they have never been taught to start from the structure and then arrive at the calculation and not vice versa. Engineers must know how to calculate, but above all, they must understand how the structure works. On the other hand, it is sufficient for architects to understand how the structure works. This is based on the misconceptions of 20th-century education, and on its belief that knowing how to calculate was enough to understand how the structure works, whereas in reality this is completely wrong.

PD Now, a question for you, Roberto. Unfortunately, the curricula of engineering and architecture degree programs often do not include the study of the history of engineering and construction. How can this topic contribute to the education of young engineers and architects?

RG Today, as we witness the collapse of certainties, it becomes more urgent than ever to seek paths to which we have previously not paid enough attention. The historical perspective and the parameters of our truths have changed radically. We are no longer certain of the design criteria necessary to build a vision for the future. The intellectual pleasure of knowledge has given way to the urgencies of the contemporary condition. We must fundamentally reformulate the problems, and this requires a critical attitude cultivated through the stratification of knowledge. Engineers should nourish themselves with this stratification because the future is so fascinating and uncertain that the clear path we once had is no longer evident. We need to reinvent the statics of structures, reinvent the parameters of their calculation, reinvent the use of diverse materials to shape composite and hybrid constructions, reinvent a vision of the theory of structures that includes previously overlooked parameters, and reinvent a concept of the social economy of materials to contribute to the resolution of contemporary societal problems. There is no doubt that alternative schools and teaching methods are needed, and their definition requires collective intellectual energy and political foresight to revolutionize educational courses. I believe this direction should be contrary to the one certain engineering and architecture schools are heading towards.

AM That's clear. It is essential to understand that today's societal challenges require not only the invention of new tools but something much deeper. Simply replacing a tool from the 2000s with one from the 2020s makes no sense. We need to ask very different questions. Schools are undergoing a radical change, and only those that can adapt while maintaining quality will be able to shape competent professionals for the future.

PD Speaking of tools that help us to understand the functioning of structures, in the book *Form and Forces: Designing Efficient, Expressive Structures*, Allen and Zalewski wrote that: "[Graphical methods] contribute to intuitive understanding and visualization of behavior. They greatly facilitate all statical operations. In the early stages of design, they have significant advantages over numerical methods in their simplicity, speed, transparency, and ability to generate efficient forms for cables, arches, trusses, and other structural devices."[4] To what extent do you agree with this observation? Do you think that teaching graphic statics is effective in this context?

AM I believe that graphic statics is still very useful, provided that it remains at an intuitive level. In other words, hand-drawn graphic statics allowing one to visualize the forces efficiently is very helpful. However, when graphical statics becomes complex, it can become a cumbersome system that many students don't

---

[3] Muttoni, A.: (2011) The Art of Structures: Introduction to the Functioning of Structures in Architecture, Routledge.

[4] Allen, E. and Zalewski, W.: (2009) Form and Forces: Designing Efficient, Expressive Structures, Wiley.

understand and end up using mechanically, which can be counterproductive. Secondly, graphic statics only answers one structural engineering question: how loads are transmitted within a structure, from action to reaction at the supports. It does not, however, contribute to answering the question of how a structure deforms. If I were to teach architects again, I would briefly introduce freehand graphic statics and then complement it with other computational tools, such as parametric finite element models. These tools are very useful, but they should be accompanied by a critical interpretation of the results. A parametric digital model is almost like a physical model because it allows one to experiment, modify, and visualize the consequences of these changes in real time. However, if this empirical approach is limited to mere play, I believe that it becomes very restrictive. On the other hand, if this empiricism is connected to a quest for understanding and enables generalization, then playing with parameters exercises intuition and becomes extremely useful.

PD Parametric models are extremely useful in the field of graphic statics. For example, by adjusting the span of a structure in the form diagram, one can evaluate in real time how the internal forces change in the force diagram. Conversely, by modifying the magnitudes of the forces in the force diagram, one can immediately visualize how the shape of the structure changes using the form diagram. This approach can be used as an active tool for conceptual structural design and form finding. On the other hand, parametric models based on the finite element method can instantly provide an idea of how transformations in the structure's geometry influence deformations.

AM In reality, the analytical approach also allows for generalizing problems. However, when it is limited to the mechanical resolution of a problem, it becomes detrimental. When, instead, it offers great intellectual freedom for understanding and generalization, then the analytical approach also becomes a formidable tool.

PD And what is your point of view on graphic statics, Roberto?

RG Graphic statics appears to me like an architect's sketch, a sort of exercise of the hand that guides the eye and the mind in intuitively understanding the functioning of a structure. The fact that some fundamental principles of graphic statics can be traced back to diagrams published in treatises on stone cutting written by mathematicians during the 17th century would lead me to suppose the existence of some unexplored potential in that system of comprehending the logic of structures.

PD Aurelio, you have compared digital models to physical models. But what is the role of physical models in teaching structural design? Do you consider it important for architects and engineers to build physical models in the conceptual structural design phase and experiment with these models?

AM Being the son of a construction entrepreneur, I spent my adolescence working on construction sites. In my father's company, there was a blacksmith, a mason, and a carpenter. I learned a lot from these three figures, and this has been extremely beneficial for my profession as an engineer. I really enjoyed working with the blacksmith using the anvil and hammer; working with hot iron is an extremely formative experience. When you work with carpenters or engage in small joinery works, it is also highly formative. All these activities are extremely educational and would be very useful for students. So, it is not strictly necessary to build physical models. Instead, one can work with materials, learning about them firsthand and not just theoretically. For example, if you have never cut, screwed, glued, milled, or planed, you would find it challenging to design with wood. Thus, at the university level, I would suggest practical courses that promote the construction not only of physical models on a small scale but also of full-scale structures. Ideally, I would also combine the construction of these structures with their design.

PD To conclude: do you have any recommendations for young architects and engineers approaching the conceptual design of structures?

AM My recommendation is that one should be curious but also modest! I'll conclude with an anecdote about optimizing structures. When I started working in Ticino, one of the first projects I worked on was with Livio Vacchini. For this building, Vacchini had designed squared pillars with a width of 43 cm, based on Le Corbusier's *Modulor*. After seeing the drawings, I proudly said to him, "Livio, I did some quick calculations, and 25 by 25 is sufficient for me." He looked at me in great astonishment and said, "What are you saying? This must be *at least* 43 by 43!"

PD And with this very amusing anecdote about the relationship between architects and engineers, I would say that we can conclude the interview. Thank you very much, Aurelio and Roberto, for your time. You have certainly provided many insights for those reading the transcript of this interview to reflect upon.

TOP Portico Zamboni, Oratorio di Santa Cecilia, Bologna

BOTTOM Codic Design Factory (Creative Factory: Design for a New Worksphere) by Atelier Kempe Thill, Düsseldorf, 2020

LEARNING FROM THE PAST

CHALLENGING
GRAVITY

EXPOSED OR
CONCEALED

LEARNING FROM
THE PAST

COMMON
RESPONSIBILITIES

Drawing on my experience as a researcher, teacher, and practitioner in the fields of digital transformation for circular construction and regenerative built environments, I have always considered the role of ethics essential in the conceptual design of structures. While our education system and profession consider structural stability, material science, or (even) aesthetics essential, we often overlook the importance of teaching environmental sustainability to the upcoming generation of engineers, let alone teaching them how to consider the broader socioeconomic aspects of sustainability. Nevertheless, I firmly believe that it is vital to integrate ethical considerations into the fabric of our educational system and profession, as it is only by looking at design through this lens that we can truly embrace a regenerative perspective. By incorporating ethics into our approach to the conceptual design of structures, we not only foster sustainability but also lay the foundation for creating a better future. It is through this conscious and principled mind-set that we can ensure our built environment is not only environmentally sustainable but also socially and economically.

In today's world, it is paramount to incorporate ethical considerations into all facets of resource-saving construction. Within this section, we explore a range of perspectives from industry experts, academics, and professionals who provide valuable insights into sustainable planning, responsible resource use, and waste reduction in structural design. The chapters within this section shed light on innovative approaches, collaborative endeavors, and design philosophies that place environmental consciousness at the forefront. These perspectives strongly resonate with my own beliefs and experiences, emphasizing the pressing need to prioritize environmental consciousness and work towards establishing a more sustainable (in the large sense of the word) built environment.

Knut Stockhusen discusses the latest considerations in resource-saving construction. Stockhusen emphasizes the importance of sustainable planning and the careful selection and use of materials in structural design. The modular "kit of parts" system employed in the design of Stadium 974 in Qatar is showcased as an exemplary approach to achieving flexibility and multifunctionality while maintaining resource efficiency.

Elli Mosayebi discusses the responsibility of architects and engineers in minimizing waste and resource depletion in the building sector. She emphasizes the importance of collaboration between architecture and engineering students and the necessity for a culture of exchange within design studios. Mosayebi shares her experiences working with structural engineers, highlighting the value of interdisciplinary collaboration.

Miguel Fernández Ruiz and Duarte M. Viula Faria delve into the significant impact of civil engineering and architecture on the natural environment, emphasizing the need for responsible and sustainable practices in infrastructure planning, design, and construction. The chapter emphasizes the complexity of achieving sustainable solutions, emphasizing the importance of analyzing local resources, and vernacular building traditions, and adapting construction approaches accordingly.

Lee Franck and Jane Wernick explore the evolving role of civil engineers in today's complex and rapidly advancing world. The engineering profession is fragmented, which poses challenges with the new technical advancements. Engineers need to actively participate in public discussions about projects and broader built environment issues. Engineers should be politically engaged and advocate for their representation and understanding in public discourse.

Mario Rinke discusses the critical role of load-bearing structures in sustainable construction and the need for a flexible design philosophy. Optimizing material consumption and reuse are crucial to extending the life span of buildings. The life span of buildings is often overlooked. We need a more adaptable design mind-set.

We bring together a diverse range of perspectives on ethics, with insights and case studies that underscore the importance of ethical considerations in the construction industry. Through systems thinking, interdisciplinary collaboration, and a flexible design philosophy, architects and engineers can contribute to a more environmentally conscious built environment.

Catherine De Wolf

Stadium 974 in Qatar. The steel frame structure with fully pre-equipped containers

CONCEPTUAL DESIGN FOR REUSABLE INFRASTRUCTURES

KNUT STOCKHUSEN IN CONVERSATION WITH PATRICK OLE OHLBROCK AND ROLAND PAWLITSCHKO

OO   Your company, schlaich bergermann partner, is known worldwide for their outstanding lightweight structures that are especially tailored to specific uses and to withstand expected load cases. Do you see a new trend – away from the specific-optimized (lightweight) structure towards a flexible, generic structure that has greater redundancies with respect to different scenarios but also requires more resources to be built in the first place?

KS   No, that would also not be appropriate and in line with the current times. Sustainable planning and an adequate use and selection of materials are elementary components for contemporary resource-saving construction. Flexibility and multifunctionality must therefore be achieved through other concepts or ideas, as the topic is becoming increasingly important and is gaining a foothold in all different building categories.

RP   How did the planning process for Stadium 974 in Qatar differ from conventional planning processes? What did you have to pay particular attention to?

KS   It all started with a competition. Various international teams were invited to propose sustainability improvements for one of the projects already planned in Doha. Our approach was to simply discard the existing design altogether and replace it with a fully modular "building kit" system. However, modular systems had not previously been conceived for permanent large-scale sports venues, and temporary systems were not permitted. So we had to reinvent a system that would consist of components that could be repeated as often as possible and would be easy to transport. In addition, of course, we had to meet all the requirements of a modern first-class venue for an international sporting event – these requirements are high.

The "Container Stadium" is based on the plug-and-play principle with prefabricated components that are repeated in large numbers **[PAGE 176]**. Like a children's assembly kit, it can be used to realize a temporary venue in a short time: manufactured, transported to the site and installed independently of its place of operation. Like a high rack, identical supports are lined up on a uniform grid – connected by tangential and perpendicularly oriented beams **[PAGE 177]**. Depending on their position, these beams carry the modular ceiling panels or the fully equipped containers. After the event period, the building can be easily dismantled and reassembled at another location. It is also possible to disassemble the stadium into many smaller projects and reassemble and use them at different locations for other purposes.

RP   How was the collaboration with Fenwick Iribarren Architects and Hilson Moran? For example, how have objectives been defined and implemented?

KS   The cooperation went great! Our container stadium idea received great interest, motivating all the disciplines to contribute to proving its feasibility. Together, we made an unprecedented concept technically feasible and understandable, allowing the people in charge on-site to get on board with it as well.

OO   Can you describe the main design aspects of the stadium structure? For example, what were the client's requirements? Did any compromises have to be made compared to a "normal" World Cup stadium?

KS   The client's main requirement was to develop sustainable concepts for a FIFA-compatible World Cup stadium as a venue for matches up to the quarter finals. Since FIFA has to approve the planning of a World Cup stadium, all the basic requirements have of course been met. In other words, no compromises were made. The issues of usability and comfort also correspond to those of a conventional sports venue.

OO   What are the stages of development for the load-bearing structure and how does it work?

KS   An overall modular system with a high repetition rate such as Stadium 974 is subject to design parameters that differ from those of a "conventional" building. The task was to develop the optimal grid: to design columns, beams, toothed girders, and floor slabs that function in different places. In addition, there is the design of a roof composed of different modules.

The stadium is built on a footprint of 212 × 200 m and has a maximum height of 46.9 m. The

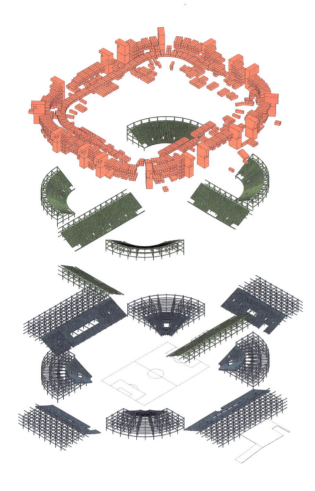

TOP/BOTTOM Exploded view of the main prefabricated components of the Stadium 974 in Qatar. The structure consists of a steel frame construction reminiscent of a high-bay warehouse and carries modified shipping containers that contain all the necessary functions: changing rooms, stands, and sanitary fittings.
Architecture: Fenwick Iribarren Architects with Hilson Moran; Structural design and engineering: schlaich bergermann partner

system is divided into eight sectors: four straight sectors and four curved corner sectors separated by expansion joints. The four straight sectors consist of a series of modular steel frames forming a regular grid of 8.50 × 9.0 m (in tangential and radial directions, respectively) of squared welded columns with modular outer dimensions of 300 × 300 mm, 400 × 400 mm or 500 × 500 mm. They vary from the inner to the outer columns and have different plate thicknesses depending on the stress levels. The corner sectors are arranged in a radial grid, maintaining the radial spacing of 9.0 m between the tangential axes and using the same modular column dimensions. The last bay of the tangential beams and purlins of the straight sectors, on the other hand, is provided with a sliding connection to the first radial frame of the corner sectors so that only vertical forces can be transferred to the adjacent corner frame.

OO   And how is the roof structure conceived?

KS   The roof structure follows the regular grid of the stands and consists of radial main girders supported by V-shaped columns on the outer edge columns and cantilevering from the north and south stands as well as from the east and west stands [PAGE 178]. The cantilever moment is absorbed through a vertical pair of forces and leads, on the one hand, to a compressive force in the columns of the stands. The corresponding tensile force is transferred directly to the foundation level by an external, inclined bracing. Trapezoidal sheets form the roof covering, spanning 4.50 m in the radial direction over tangential purlins. They are rigidly connected to the bottom chords of the radial main trusses and provide stability to these elements. Towards the outer edge, the roof is inclined to drain rainwater via a circumferential gutter.

The modular ceiling system made of thin orthotropic steel plates reduces the means required for assembly and disassembly to a minimum. The stand elements for mounting the seats were also designed as folded steel plates with a thickness of only 7 mm and bolted to the adjacent beams of the stand. The system exhibits sufficient stiffness to meet the high vibration requirements in serviceability limit states. In addition, the legacy, the after-use, had to be conceived. We have showed how the individual parts can be assembled into different new structures. This makes the second and subsequent lives of the whole structural system more likely.

RP   What details were particularly important?

KS   Particularly important were the connecting elements and the assignment of the individual parts – in other words, the logistics. In order to keep the compo-

TOP/BOTTOM The stadium is built on a footprint of 212 × 200 m and has a maximum height of 46.9 m. The main works started on November 1, 2019 and proceeded without major disruptions until the completion of the main structure of the arena in March 2021.

TOP/BOTTOM **The stadium has a seating capacity of 40,000. It can be easily demounted into its components and then rebuilt at another location – as a new stadium or in the form of several smaller stadiums.**

CONCEPTUAL DESIGN FOR REUSABLE INFRASTRUCTURES

nents demountable, the connections must be easily and completely detachable. Plastic deformation must be avoided. In the design and detailed dimensioning, this required a lot of attention and meticulousness in order not to be confronted with unexpected problems later on.

RP How are the components of the stadium transported, assembled, disassembled?

KS All components were principally bolted or pinned – the detailing had to ensure that the connections could also be released again. Optimizing the grid resulted in ideal spans for the individual parts and thus moderate cross sections. And these resulting lengths are easy to stack and transport. In addition, the tribune elements are modularized in lengths and can be transported in standard shipping containers. This is also how the parts arrived on site. All containers with functions were delivered fully equipped and will be used in this way.

OO What sustainability-relevant changes occurred during the design phase?

KS The energy used to manufacture the individual parts is comparable to that of conventional projects. The reusability and clear allocation of capacities and use cases for each element creates an overarching sustainability aspect. However, this only unfolds if the systems can be reasonably reused elsewhere, thus avoiding new construction and renewed consumption of primary resources.

RP What design aspects are mandatory to consider when reuse is planned?

KS If composition, material, resistance and geometry for building components in general could be quickly captured or even digitally read (as is the case with the container stadium), a second life would become easier for many buildings or parts of buildings. This would simplify time-consuming structural assessments and recalculations. Just as important as the knowledge of the materiality, structural capacity, etc. of the components is the knowledge of their deconstructability. This is where the detailing of the connections comes into play.

OO What will happen to the building when it is dismantled in Qatar? Are there concrete plans for subsequent use? Who "owns" the components?

KS Yes, there are precise plans. But these are confidential and are the responsibility of the Supreme Committee. In other countries, too, operators are responsible for developing reasonable concepts for their major sports facilities. Unfortunately, this sometimes goes wrong. In the case of the modular Stadium 974, however, the chances are good that a suitable reuse will follow, no matter where the stadium or parts of it will be rebuilt. In any case, a redesign or verification according to the then new local standards will be necessary. The soil conditions will be different, wind loads will change and earthquakes will also have a different impact. Likewise, the building services will have to be verified for the new location.

RP Can the steel-frame structure be reused for entirely different purposes – not as a stadium, but as a high-rack warehouse, for example?

KS Yes, sure. These are steel components that do not know what they are used for. They only "know" their structural capacity. So any conceivable use that results in similar utilization is possible.

RP In general, where do you see the greatest opportunities and where do you see the greatest obstacles in the context of reuse?

KS A major challenge is the availability of catalogued parts and the risk of misjudging the load-bearing capacity. In the case of Stadium 974, reuse was an issue from the beginning. In principle, however, structures do not have a reuse plan, so the first step is to record the condition and capacity of each component. This is even easier for secondary components than for primary ones.

RP What lessons can be transferred from this project to other projects?

KS From my point of view, mainly the fact that the after-use influenced the planning of the initial use and was already part of it. An approach like this would be useful for many projects. It also affects the process of building and documentation. However, one must not forget the innovation, courage, and determination of project teams and clients as key factors. Because without them, projects like this cannot be realized.

NEXT PAGE Stadium 974 at the bay of Doha. The venue has already been completely dismantled and is now ready for its next use.

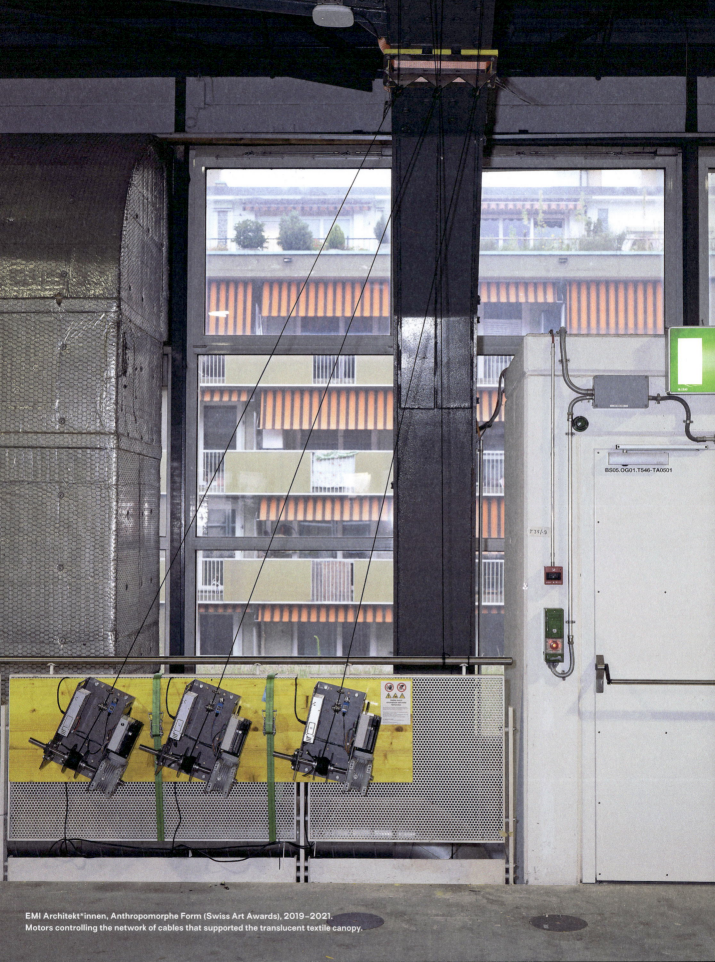

EMI Architekt*innen, Anthropomorphe Form (Swiss Art Awards), 2019–2021.
Motors controlling the network of cables that supported the translucent textile canopy.

THE INTERDISCIPLINARY NATURE OF ARCHITECTURE: CHALLENGES AND OPPORTUNITIES BETWEEN ACADEMIA AND PRACTICE

ELLI MOSAYEBI IN CONVERSATION WITH FEDERICO BERTAGNA AND PATRICK OLE OHLBROCK

OO Let's start with a question on the interaction between architects and structural engineers: what role do structures play in your daily work as an architect? Is there a difference in the way you interact with structural engineering as a discipline in academia compared to practice?

EM In 2019 we collaborated with Joseph [Schwartz] in our design studio at ETH, and that was very productive. I really experienced Joseph as an "architect" with a specific focus on structure, so to speak. This was an interesting and somewhat new experience for me. On a day-to-day basis, we build a lot of residential buildings in the Zurich area. With the limited spans of houses, the structural aspects of the projects are often not that challenging. The collaboration revealed how much more is actually possible in terms of collaboration.

Incorporating engineering aspects into a design process is a unique way of developing and explaining form, which is determined by factors that we as architects give too little attention. And yet a large part of the CO_2 is emitted with the structure and thus in the poorly dimensioned statics. Refinement in the structure thus is not only an aesthetic criterion, but also an ecological one.

OO What do you see as the main features of a fruitful interdisciplinary design session?

EM The best projects are often the result of a dynamic process of negotiation between science, art, and architecture. From the natural sciences (such as structural engineering or building physics) come the fixed components, usually in the form of immutable theorems. This does not mean that they cannot be experimented with, but their rules preexist in a certain way. The artists bring in other points of view, which are characterized by positions and interpretations. They are definitely negotiable and more open. Combining both aspects and creating a meaningful whole is the attraction of architecture.

Trusting the other disciplines and wanting to experiment is thus essential.

FB One crucial element is finding a common language between professionals from different disciplines. This very much lays the ground for a good collaboration. It seems that you have found effective ways to do that both in practice and in academia, where you always invite professors from different disciplines to contribute in the design studios.

EM The "trick" is not to have a predefined common language, but to be open to new languages. Each design studio serves both to teach the students and to broaden our own horizons as a teaching team. Looking back, I can say that each collaboration was also a memorable experience for us. As amateurs, we found ourselves learning new principles and applying them to projects. The intensity of these experiences has left us with fond memories and a desire for new ones.

FB Academia is the perfect testing ground for this kind of experiment. This might be different in practice, but how different would it be, precisely?

EM I feel that these collaborations take us to a different point. Perhaps we are even further ahead in science than we are in practice, because practice is generally very slow and ambivalent about new findings for a variety of reasons. In practice, when you try to convince clients of certain issues, they often refuse because they are afraid of the risks they have to take. In academia you can be much more radical. For me, the relationship between practice and academia has changed over the last ten years. I used to feel that I was bringing my knowledge from practice to academia, but that feeling has become reversed.

OO At the Chair you developed a Thesaurus,[1] which together with "12 theses,"[2] outlines the philosophy of the Second Modernity. One of the keywords is *experimentalism*. For engineers, this word might have conflicting connotations: on the one hand, experiments

---

[1] https://mosayebi.arch.ethz.ch/en/thesaurus.

[2] https://mosayebi.arch.ethz.ch/en/twelve-theses.

are very important to prove a theory; on the other hand, it might have a negative connotation in certain scientific fields where rationality appears to be all you need to derive your conclusions. What you just described seems to suggest that you are building these experiments in a very strategic way to learn the maximum from them…

EM It is an empirical way of learning. It's about arranging, trying and testing, using models, films, and drawings. Every studio is a laboratory in a way…the project itself is an experiment that allows you to think radically about a particular question. You can fail; that's fine, as long as it's clear how you got there and what caused the failure. Experimentation is not only about the outcome, but equally about the process. In this sense, I think that design has perhaps been taught too intuitively in the past and that a certain rationality and method – which does exist – should be made clearer in the design process.

FB What you said about this relationship with engineers is that they introduce more rationality to a process that often seems to be exclusively intuitive. That's interesting, because on the other hand one could also say that engineers need to develop more design intuition. What's your experience there? Are the engineers you work with notably more rational than intuitive?

EM I wouldn't say that. It really depends. I worked with both: intuitive and rational engineers. We also have to be careful not to fall into clichés. When I was writing my dissertation, I realized that there is a big difference in the thinking process between designing a project and writing scientifically. In a PhD, or in any kind of systematic work on a certain topic, you have to go through all the layers of every facet. You have to open it up, show the different categories of each field … On the contrary, design is always a kind of movement – it's a convergence, it synthesizes everything into a specific object. Design intuition means being very attentive and observant. It doesn't mean deducing from a theory. You have to be extremely attentive and you have to know that every detail is specific and can become a generative part of the project. That's something you could call intuition: being very attentive and having an open mind.

OO When looking at the results of your studios, I think it would be worth trying to extend similar approaches to the whole ETH or even to other architecture schools. Have you seen any development in this direction? Do you see a closer collaboration between engineering and architectural students as already being possible at the studio level?

EM Architecture has always been an interdisciplinary field. I think we should really acknowledge that and just work that way. Architecture students need to know a lot to be able to deal with the complexity of design tasks. I really believe that this culture of collaboration should be implemented in the design studios. Because you have to develop this mind-set of exchange. It's something I didn't learn at school but only later in my own practice. In fact, if you can put your ego aside and say that it's all about making things better together, and you allow those inputs to happen, it can be extremely productive most of the time. It's really about the mind-set, and that's something we should train for.

OO In addition to the Department of Architecture, we also teach structural design courses at the Department of Civil Engineering. There, it seems to be even more the case that people exclusively focused on their own discipline. Interdisciplinary exchanges in education would probably bring more benefit to the engineering students compared to architecture students because architects already have a much broader curriculum than most of the engineers. At ETH, we have always tried to bridge the two departments. Among the architecture professors I know, you're one of the few who really tries to include some of the engineers. It would be great if other architects or even some engineers would acknowledge the importance of these collaborations as part of the curricula and push that a bit more.

EM That would be very interesting. Actually, I invite them to the studios. They have never invited me back [*laughs*]…I recently saw a small exhibition by civil engineering students at ETH. The intention was indeed quite good, because it was really about designing something. So it attracted me. Then I also thought that I would be very open to supporting them, and that this might be a very interesting experiment too.

FB If design-related activities like these took place more frequently in the engineering department, there would be more opportunities for collaborations with professors from architecture. I'm quite sure that the reason why you were not invited back is that what engineering students do in the classroom is very different in terms of content and atmosphere compared to an architecture design studio. Nevertheless, there are some attempts being made at ETH, with some more design-related classes for civil engineers. In these contexts, even a single input lecture from an architect would give an early hint to the students that yes, you have to make sure that the structure is sound and safe, but there is more to that…

OO Another topic that we would like to discuss is connected to the *redundancy* and *adaptability* of buildings. We know that the movable interior partitions idea

EMI Architekt*innen, House Stampfenbachstrasse, 2018–2022. A residential building designed to adapt to the users' need. The building combines several types of units including top-floor apartments with roof sheds and 23 apartments with flexible rotating elements.

Professorship Mosayebi (ETH Zurich), vacancy–no vacancy, 2019–2021. The "performative room" embodies the idea of a space that adapts to users' need by means of a set of movable elements that users can adjust to configure the space they live in.

that you initially designed as a demonstrator on the roof terrace at ETH [PICTURES ON THIS DOUBLE PAGE] has now been applied to a real apartment building [PAGE 185] in Zurich. Was this just an experiment in the beginning?

EM   The idea developed from the observation that single households were extremely diverse, and not knowing how these people might actually live. With this project, we wanted to find out how these apartments could become adaptable – to a certain extent – to be used by people according to their actual needs. That was one aspect. The other aspect was investigating a much more playful understanding of what housing might be. It's a typology that tends to be very conservative and rigid, but could it be something playful and changeable instead?

OO   How did the client react to the idea of installing movable walls?

EM   The client was open to this because we have worked together a lot and a certain level of trust existed. But movable elements are quite rare in this context, and the risk is even higher when you consider that they are designed for rental apartments. There are a lot of changes, and these movable elements have to be very robust. We were also a bit nervous about these aspects ourselves, so we thought about building a prototype first. That was actually the first reason why we did the one on the ETH roof. The second reason was that it's a timber construction. The slabs are also made of wood, and the main question regarding them was acoustics: how do we avoid noise transmission from one apartment to another? Normally you have these heavy concrete slabs in the ceiling, but we didn't want to do that. So we tried to separate the wooden walls from the slabs: the walls are not directly connected to the slab, they are connected with dowels. We built the prototype with a temporary second floor to measure the sound transmission. The system worked and met the standards.

OO   In terms of use of space, I think we all agree that it would make sense to have a certain level of adaptability in our buildings. In this case, you had movable partitioning walls, but static walls can also result in the creation of a flexible space. I consider that the Kalkbreite is also an adaptable building because you can use the space in many different ways…

EM   You also mentioned the concept of redundancy. If you have enough space in your home that you can just rent space out when you don't need it, that's also a way of being flexible. I think a question we are very interested in is more how to build apartments that can breathe, that can become bigger or smaller depend-

Professorship Mosayebi (ETH Zurich), vacancy–no vacancy, 2019–2021. The 1:1 scale mock-up was used to test the construction system as well as the user's response to the possibility of adapting the living space. Volunteers lived in the "performative room" for a week while sensors were recording the different spatial configurations they created.

TOP/BOTTOM, RIGHT PAGE EMI Architekt*innen, Residential building in Hottingen, 2011–2015. The floor plan is the result of a complex blend of shaping forces, including the presence of preexisting trees on the site. As such, each interior space gains a specific character due to the need to respond to diverse boundary conditions in an individual yet coordinated manner.

ing on needs. In this project, adaptability is materialized through these movable elements or performative spaces, but it's just one possible way. I really liked it for the smaller apartments, but I don't know if it would be suitable for larger apartments, because you have a lot of people living together and maybe it would be more difficult. Who decides when to move what?

Another way of realizing this concept of flexibility and redundancy was undertaken by us in the Freihofstrasse project. It is a low-cost residential building with a layout based on many rooms. We decided not to differentiate even between living and sleeping rooms – they're all the same. So the tenant can decide whether he or she wants to use this room as an extra workroom, a living room or a private room.

OO   But is it still interesting for you as an architect? Or does it become at some point just a generic floor plan where everything is the same?

EM   Yes, that risk exists. The question is: how can we be specific and still take everything into account? During the development of the Freihofstrasse project, we talked about the qualities of old houses. One of the specific qualities is their "grown" character, which distinguishes them from the smoothness and seriality of new buildings. Old houses are often rebuilt and adapted over time. In Freihofstrasse, for example, all the rooms are the same, but they have different doors to give them a special character... Some have lintels, others do not, creating almost surreal moments.

OO   Even though I'm not an architect, I can imagine that in order to enhance spatial flexibility a skeleton structure would work just fine, but it might be very boring...

EM   Not necessarily. In another project we're carrying out for the city of Zurich, the Stiftung "Einfach Wohnen," we're actually using a skeleton structure, because the building has to be both economical and ecological at the same time. But the site, with its beautiful mature trees, articulates the external form of the building. Thankfully, it's not just the interior: the site has its own difficulties that will have an impact on the building and create specific solutions.

OO   Going back to keywords, a pair of keywords that we would like to discuss are *high-tech* and *low-tech*. What is your opinion on that? Do you have a clear strategy in that regard?

EM   I think low-tech always beats high-tech. If you're going to rely on high-tech solutions as the main strategy for solving design problems, you need to be aware that those solutions have to be produced somewhere, and that they have a cost in grey energy. Also their maintenance is often underestimated. I have to say that I'm really fascinated by high-tech in terms of the imagination, but are there good examples for ecological solutions? In the end, a very simple rule could be just to build as light as possible and as low-tech as possible. I think that making things as simple as possible may be the best way.

FB   What about the use of concrete? On the one hand it is somehow becoming a taboo, but it is also a very simple and effective solution in many cases.

EM   In the house that I showed you with the skeleton structure, of course we have a concrete structure, but we have managed to reduce the thickness of the slabs to 20 centimeters and use wooden elements for the façade. In most cases today the slabs are 25–26 centimeters,

EMI Architekt*innen, Anthropomorphe Form (Swiss Art Awards), 2019–2021.
The installation consisted of a translucent textile canopy supported by a network of cables floating above the exhibition hall. The length of the cables was controlled by a series of motors triggered by sensors monitoring environmental parameters such as noise level, number and distribution of visitors, and so on.

and that is really very thick. If you go back to the 50s or 60s, you'll see that it was only 16 centimeters. It has grown a lot, but why? It would still make sense to use concrete, absolutely, but it doesn't make sense to put so much material into a slab, for example. These are really structural issues and there is so much to discuss and understand, such as the reasons why we currently have certain norms. This is something that architects and engineers may also need to do collaboratively.

FB You mentioned that you used timber elements for the façade. What were the challenges in that case? The building envelope, together with the structural system, is also a crucial element in building design. This is another area where the struggle between low-tech and high-tech solutions is very prominent.

EM For the timber elements of the façade, the aim was to have prefabricated, interchangeable and repairable elements that could even be replaced one day. We know that the concrete skeleton structure is more durable than the façade. We also wanted to avoid the use of oil-based products such as foils and glues for the timber elements. After all, we don't even know what will happen to these products after 20 years. There is this obsession in the building sector for structures being as airtight as possible. You have to seal everything. In this project, we decided to challenge that and give it the climate of an old building, so that you feel a bit of the weather outside.

Another issue is the actual need for triple glazing. We don't want to use triple glazing if it's not necessary. It's just the new norm that everybody uses triple glazing, but what is the need for that? If you've got an acoustic problem, I understand, but when it comes to thermal insulation, we all know that after 20 years the gas is out. You put in so much embodied energy, you triple the amount of glass, you put the gas in, and then it's out …

FB There are also so many qualitative aspects that are crucial parts of the design process. However, they are very difficult to evaluate exactly because of their inherent qualitative nature. If we look at energy standards and energy rating systems, such as the Swiss Minergie, all these standards are necessarily built on a quantitative basis. But in a way that's a little bit at odds with design itself, isn't it?

EM Exactly. You cannot measure a good layout or a good urban design. I tell my students that the life cycle of a building is not measured by quantitative data, but mainly by quality, by architectural beauty. If the design is not good enough, the building will be demolished after 20 years, and then the life cycle has not been achieved. I have serious doubts about labels. The Minergie-P-Eco label somehow reassures the client because he or she thinks everything is in order. Unfortunately, this is a deception.

FB So that's something that you don't use at all in the design process.

EM Not at all.

OO What about the role of computational tools instead? For instance, there are now machine learning algorithms that can automatically generate floor plans. Have you ever experimented with that? Do you think this will change the way you work in the future?

EM I'm very critical of these tools. The problem is this kind of idea that everything happens automatically. Design is an intellectual activity and why should you trust the algorithm to do it for you?

OO Nevertheless, I think we will all be confronted with that sooner or later. At some point people will claim that they have a machine that can do our job just fine, and clients will not be willing to pay anymore for that floor plan development or wall calculation, even though the intellectual part of the process is completely absent.

EM Yes, maybe. It's going to be ChatGPT drawing floor plans for us. I find it very dystopian. It completely undermines culture, authorship, and the individual.

FB In your thesaurus, and we found that "comfort" is not included as a keyword. If we look at indoor thermal comfort in the early development of modern architecture, that was often not an issue as technology could compensate for almost any architectural choice. All the problems related to an extensive use of glass in building envelopes were solved through mechanical climate control systems. Now it's clear that we cannot persist with this kind of approach. What is the strategy of the "Second Modernity"? Do we have to rethink our idea of comfort?

EM The words in the thesaurus are put together in such a way that they relate precisely to the present and to what interests us in the present. "Comfort" would be a word that could be included, that's absolutely right – perhaps in conjunction with the concept of sufficiency. This is about comfort in terms of what we actually need as a minimum. Less comfort always feels like we are going backward, when in fact we are going forward. But the question of comfort in our present day might need to be discussed with a sociologist and a psychologist!

MIGUEL FERNÁNDEZ RUIZ
DUARTE M. VIULA FARIA

THE ROLE OF ENGINEERING AND CONCEPTUAL DESIGN ON SUSTAINABILITY

Our common trail, looking back

The professions of civil engineering and architecture are amongst the most influential regarding the manner in which human society interacts with and transforms our natural environment. Its associated works (be they bridges, dams, buildings or any other civil construction) require large amounts of resources, which are normally provided and financed in a collective manner by communities. They are also intended to be durable and safe, lasting longer than the generation that contributed to building them and thus being part of our heritage.

When looking at the history of civil engineering, one realizes that architecture and civil engineering projects have continuously evolved, in terms of needs, aesthetics, and also technique. Traditionally, these projects were governed by an ethics of conserving materials and resources and their design was determined by the available accumulated (empirical) knowledge. Major changes are associated with the discovery or invention of new construction materials such as iron, steel or concrete (occurring in the 18th and 19th centuries). Also, the introduction of the scientific method in the 18th century inspired engineering initiatives and created a major breakthrough in terms of opportunities and creative freedom. All the enhanced potential in technical terms (in terms of material and design approach alike) was also influenced in the second half of the 20th century by a change in the economic significance of material costs and labor wages. This allowed for new perspectives, particularly in architecture, where the quantity of consumed materials was less significant. Concerning large civil infrastructures, however, the fulfillment of static requirements still imposed a logics of saving, consistently with the historical approach for these structures.

As we approach the conclusion of the first quarter of the 21st century, we may take a look at our history and critically consider whether the manner in which construction has evolved over the last fifty years is reasonable and whether it can continue as it is. In other terms, we might consider whether our current building culture is sustainable in the context of the present and the future, and whether, by implication, future generations will be able to continue building in a comparable manner.

The concern on sustainability

Although every generation of engineers has dealt, implicitly or explicitly, with concerns relating to sustainability, the modern conception of this term was formalized in a clear manner at a relatively late stage. In 1987, the Brundtland report[1] first described sustainability as "development that meets the needs of the present without compromising the ability of future generations to meet their own needs."

1 World Commission on Environment and Development: (1987) Our Common Future, Oxford University Press, p. 383.

LEFT PAGE Use of prestressed girders for roof systems. Nouveau groupe scolaire à Bussigny Ouest, Bussigny, Switzerland, Architecture: GNWA Gonzalo, Neck, Weri Architectes; Structural design and engineering: Muttoni et Fernández, ingénieurs conseils SA

The concept of sustainability has since been agreed to rest on three pillars: social, economic, and environmental (as well as the governance frame). Considering every solution in alignment with sustainability considerations requires that it must optimally satisfy the different aspects (which might in some cases be in conflict). Typically, the performance of a solution with respect to the different criteria are evaluated through the entire life span of a structure and their result weighted in order to obtain a global picture – what is usually called a life cycle analysis.

The concept of the pillars (despite its implicit and explicit limitations) is instrumental in the understanding of the holistic approach required by a sustainable solution during the conceptual design phase. Also, in clarifying that social and economic aspects are relevant too, and that sustainability is not only linked to our environmental footprint. This latter concept, traditionally considered in a secondary manner, has nonetheless gained significant relevance following increased awareness of the human footprint and its impact on the environment. For instance, the construction industry is responsible for a large fraction of total greenhouse gases (estimated to be close to 10% of total human footprint) and consumption of resources (estimated to be close to 50% of produced materials).[2,3] Satisfying multiple different sustainability criteria is intellectually a difficult task, and there is no simple solution that applies to all the relevant aspects. Every project and every context is different. What is probably required is a change in the building paradigm as well as in the architectural and engineering culture. This requires careful analysis of the availability of local resources and of the vernacular building tradition of communities, as well as to adapt our construction approach to take as much advantage of them as possible. Perhaps, then, one of the most relevant changes that must take place is a new mentality of using and combining the available resources in the most efficient possible manner and cutting unnecessary use of material, which may even imply redefinition of programs and requirements for reliability.[4]

It is also interesting to refer to the relationship between sustainability and durability of structures. The durability of a structure refers to its capacity to resist environmental conditions and normal use. It requires careful consideration during all stages of the project, starting with the conceptual design, the selection of materials, and detailing. Special attention must also be paid during the execution phase. Durability aspects have attracted more interest since the 1980s, with the evolution of knowledge relating to materials and based upon previous experiences. In general, a more durable structure is aligned with the concepts of sustainability, since the structure will require less maintenance. However, in some situations, the requirements linked to durability aspects (effect of environment on the structure) contradict those of sustainability (effect of the structure on the environment). A typical example of this refers to cases where higher durability is achieved by using construction materials with higher CO_2-eq emissions. Thus, a balance must be found between the needs for durability and sustainability, with the correct selection of materials being made according to the structural design.

Concerning the responsibilities of the architects and civil engineers regarding sustainability, they are engaged at different stages of a project: planning, designing, and building. Such responsibilities start with the planning duties, during which some fundamental overarching questions may be raised: is an infrastructure really needed? To what extent can existing infrastructure be upgraded to satisfy the expected needs? The role of the planner, and particularly of those with a public role, is instrumental in the

[2] Fivet, C.: (2022) "Bauen, ohne zu konsumieren: eine ethische Verantwortung," Schweizer Ingenieurbaukunst 4, pp. 99–103.

[3] Regúlez, B., Faria, D. V., Todisco, L., Fernández Ruiz, M., Corres Peiretti, H.: (2022) Sustainability in construction: the urgent need for a new ethics," Structural Concrete 24(2), pp. 1–21.

[4] Fernández Ruiz, M., Regúlez, B., Todisco, L., Faria, D. V., Corres Peiretti, H.: (2023) Reliability- and sustainability-driven strategies for the maintenance of existing structures," Structural Concrete 24(4), pp. 1–19.

responsible and sustainable construction of infrastructure. Once a piece of infrastructure has been planned out, the responsibility is passed on to the designer, whose role is to use and to combine the available resources in an efficient manner [PAGE 195, TOP AND BOTTOM]. This is probably the phase that is most influenced by the education, culture, and sensitivity of the authors, and where the role of conceptual design is most instrumental. Finally, last but not least, the engagement of contractors during the construction phase is also a necessary step to ensure due diligence for the whole chain of production.

All of these stages require individuals with a sense of ethics (individual responsibility) and also require that such ethics is consistent through the whole process (social responsibility). Ethics can be defined as the set of moral principles that drives us to action. Although the principles of ethics can be studied, finding or defining them is a personal process, influenced by education, societal values, and self-reasoning, and may evolve during our lifetime. Although most of us were not taught the values behind the word "sustainability" (which was not even defined in its modern conception at the time the authors were born), we are now fully aware of its real meaning, and it is our responsibility to implement it and to transfer it to future generations through action, education and research.

Approaches for during the conceptual design for new structures and interventions on existing structures

During the design process, several aspects play a key role in driving our actions towards a sustainability perspective. They largely depend, however, on the type of project and particularly on whether it deals with an existing structure or a new one.

For existing structures, the main question is to what extent one can reuse or upgrade the existing structure. In many cases, existing structures are fully functional, and limiting or adapting the actions ensures a convenient level of safety. When the actions cannot be limited to comply with the resistance of the structure, instead of demolishing them, one should investigate possible means to strengthen, increasing the capacity of the governing load-carrying mechanisms. This saves significant amounts of materials as well as their associated economic resources and energy for production and building. It is truly a change of paradigm, with engineering works addressed at a high level of added value expertise and assessment. This approach is not simple or exempt from risks, as the knowledge of the properties of an existing structure is never perfect and more sophisticated analysis methods are required, implying a higher level of education. However, it is the only way of protecting our heritage and reusing it in a sound and safe manner, and is the track implemented currently by most codes of practice. Today, different analysis tools are available, allowing us to take into account all potential resistances of structural elements. Experience gained from the use of different advanced analysis methods showed that these methods are reliable, and consequently several codes already allow for their use (these methods allow us to estimate the resistance in a more accurate and less conservative manner than those commonly used for design of new structures). In general, this allows for less intrusive intervention or even no intervention at all.

For new structures, inconsistent or incomplete information has been circulating for the past decade at least concerning the sustainability of our new constructions (related to many "green-washing issues").

Examples of ribbed slabs:

TOP Lanificio Gatti (Rome, Italy, Pier Luigi Nervi)

BOTTOM Logytel headquarters office building (Alcalá de Henares, Spain, using Holedeck(R) system for voided ribbed slabs)

This has misled many designers and owners concerning how sustainable projects should be developed. The most critical aspect is the unfair notion that sustainability is directly related to the choice of the construction material.[5] This has, however, been argued to be a false principle. Scientific studies have clearly shown that a structure, be it in timber, concrete, or steel, can have a comparable environmental footprint provided that it is designed with an efficient typology minimizing the materials used for its construction.[3] In fact, seeking for direct load transfers and following the natural path of forces are the key aspects for designing efficiently. Our CO_2 footprint is thus related to the selection of an efficient structural typology and to the sensitivity to saving resources, rather than adopting a specific material before the project is even defined. In this respect, the rational use of concrete is still the most reasonable approach to address the massive demands of housing and infrastructure.[6,7] This material is available worldwide and can have a relatively low specific environmental footprint. It only has to be used in a rational manner (structural typology, choice of cement type, using local aggregates, additives, types of reinforcement bars...) to avoid unnecessary waste. Even more important, designers (architects and engineers) should assume a humble strategy while performing the conceptual design with owners. Lower spans, for instance, are associated with lower consumption of materials in buildings. For example, as shown in **PAGE 197, BOTTOM**, a reinforced concrete waffle slab of 7–8 m of span is much more efficient than a reinforced concrete flat slab of 11–12 m span (with approximately half the CO_2-eq emissions), and also clearly has a lower footprint than a full-timber ribbed slab of 11–12 m span. Also, the design shall take account of the energy consumption during the lifetime of a structure, related to issues such as, for instance, thermal inertia and insulation. Finally, another important aspect to consider is accounting for the peculiarities of the construction site during the conceptual design process: in particular, the building tradition and the local industries and communities. Activating local resources by means of projects that are consistent with them is a way of reducing transport-related emissions and also of satisfying the objectives of the social pillar of sustainability, providing local employment, and involving communities in the projects that they are going to be using.

Our common trail, looking ahead

Our decisions will influence our current and future welfare. We have to be aware of this. Our moment is decisive, just as much as many others in the past, and our community of engineers and architects should surpass expectations to provide reasonable and sensitive answers. The current demands in terms of infrastructure needs are so high that resources are precious and should be saved by all means. This sensitivity has yet to be infused into education and into society.

It is very likely that the way in which we have undertaken construction over past decades will evolve again, as it is far from being sustainable. Building with less will require rethinking of the technique and the developing of new solutions, ranging from materials to structural typology. These should, however, not remain as expensive laboratory toys, but should be turned into real solutions that can be adapted both to high-tech and to low-tech contexts (like those currently used nowadays). There is a bright future ahead, waiting for us to walk it with wisdom and responsibility.

---

5 The Guardian: (2019) "Concrete: the most destructive material on Earth," The Guardian, https://www.theguardian.com/cities/2019/feb/25/con-crete-the-mostdestructive-material-on-earth.

6 United Nations Environment Programme: (2017) Eco-efficient cements: Potential economically viable solutions for a low-CO_2 cement-based materials industry.

7 Favier, A., De Wolf, C., Scrivener, K., Habert, G.: (2018) A sustainable future for the European Cement and Concrete Industry – Technology assessment for full decarbonisation of the industry by 2050, ETHZ – EPFL report, p. 93.

RIGHT PAGE, TOP Combining materials in construction, beams in timber for long spans, and prestressed walls as diaphragms (Cycle d'Orientation de la Glâne, Romont, Switzerland, Architecture: GNWA Gonzalo, Neck, Weri Architectes; Structural design and engineering: Muttoni et Fernández, ingénieurs conseils SA)

RIGHT PAGE, BOTTOM Impact on carbon footprint of structural typologies and materials: (a) section of investigated building; (b) span dimensions; and (c) carbon footprint as a function of the span length for different structural solutions

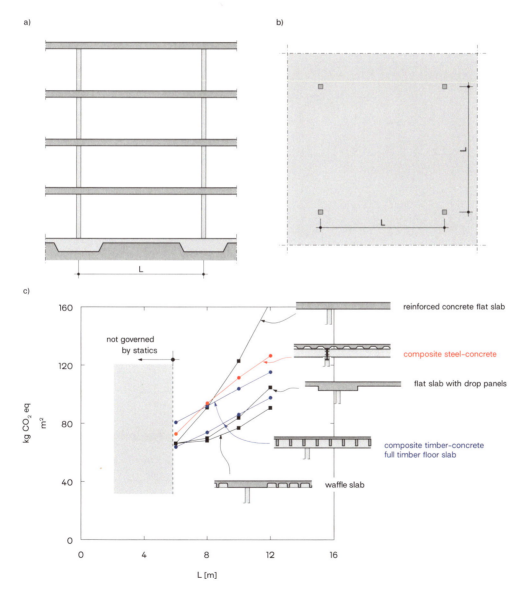

a)

b)

c)

kg CO_2 eq / m^2

not governed by statics

reinforced concrete flat slab
composite steel-concrete
flat slab with drop panels
composite timber-concrete
full timber floor slab
waffle slab

L [m]

COMMON RESPONSIBILITIES

Re-use of a peat barn in Schechen, Germany, 2015
Structural design and engineering / Architecture: ZRS Architekten Ingenieure

RESPONSIBILITIES OF CIVIL ENGINEERS IN SOCIETY

LEE FRANCK AND JANE WERNICK IN CONVERSATION WITH ROLAND PAWLITSCHKO

RP In the 18th and 19th centuries, civil engineers were the ones who changed the world (after the invention of the steam engine and the railway). How could it happen that this profession is so little in focus today by comparison?

LF When you decide to become an engineer today, you might have the image of renowned engineers in mind who had a very big impact. Unfortunately, the reality today is usually different. The fact that engineers like John Augustus Roebling or Isambard Kingdom Brunel had so much influence is also due to the fact that they were responsible for virtually everything. They were responsible for the technical matters and the design, they were the main interface with customers and were perhaps even involved in projects on a business level themselves. Over the years, with the arrival of greater complexity, but also due to new technical and research advances, this has become more and more fragmented. Today, there are an insane number of specialists: structural engineers, civil engineers, technicians, façade engineers, etc., plus all the other design disciplines. There might be project managers who still have a kind of generalists' view, but they are too far away from the design and technical aspects. We no longer have people who are able to play an overarching role. And I often have the feeling that you can see this in the results.

JW It is so rare that engineers are mentioned when projects are discussed publicly. We have to make sure that we are represented and that everybody understands who is involved in the process. We want the public to realize that there are engineers behind the solutions. One thing we can do is keep on speaking up at every opportunity. Engineers should be prepared to be political, and to speak up about the broader built environment issues. We are members of society as well as being engineers.

At the same time, we are frustrated about how undergraduate students are educated. There is virtually no collaboration between the disciplines. Instead, we have a kind of silo definition of the degree a student graduates with – this is an idea that is completely outdated. The requirements to become an engineer in the UK – and I think this is pretty universal – are defined very narrowly. You are tested solely on your technical ability. That is to some extent essential because you don't want to have an engineer who doesn't understand stability. On the other hand, however, undergraduate level students should learn to collaborate across many disciplines – economics, psychology, sociology, geology, etc. What we need in education are broad-based projects for student groups of perhaps ten people that address ethical issues as well as the economy and sociology etc. I'm sure students will be enthusiastic about this, even if they spent only one month a year in this way, because they will learn how to contribute their own specialist knowledge. And they will also be able to start friendships and collaborations with people in many different fields that will continue through their working lives.

LF I agree with Jane. The topics we are taught in structural engineering and civil engineering are not broad enough. I remember when I came from Luxembourg to Switzerland – my future university looked only at my results in mathematics and physics. That way, you attract young people who are very passionate about these two subjects, but often nothing more. And then, over the following years, you want to teach them about philosophy, about art and all these much more humanity-based things, and that's really hard. I remember Prof. Tim Ibell once saying something at a conference that really stuck with me: "If you want to teach someone who is already good at math to get better at it, that's easy. But if you want to teach someone who has absolutely no interest in all these other topics to develop a feeling for them, that's super hard."

RP Do you see better conditions in the early years of young engineers' office careers?

LF There are many graduates who, after a course of study in which they showed great interdisciplinary interest at a broad level and perhaps in climate change, end up in larger offices where they spend the first five years doing mainly detailed and sometimes repetitive calculation work. Also, when I started working, I was surrounded by quite a few people who actually found

this quite discouraging – including myself. A lot of them left the office, also for financial reasons, and went to work in consulting, where they felt like they could engage in these wider topics. One way of retaining these people is to have a good mentor who can introduce them to all of this thinking and push them to think beyond the calculations on their desks. For me, this was very much the key. I think we have to give new meaning to the job of engineers. So that people who choose this profession do it not because it gives them a safe job or a certain status but more because they really feel that it is a way for them to contribute to our society.

RP Which principles have to be taken into account to make a construction design better and more interdisciplinary in every respect?

LF The key point is to realize where you will have the biggest impact. And if you ask me when a structural engineer should be involved in a project, there can be only one answer: As soon as possible – not at a time when the opportunities have gone. Afterward, you can do much less and it's going to be more painful and costs you more and takes more time. The first thing, really, is the brief: What do you need? Do you even need to build? Mostly we help a client to build. But in the end we are problem solvers, and perhaps we should help by defining the problems better and setting the scene. Sometimes the solution may be not to build at all. With this thinking in mind, you can go forward step by step **[PAGE 201]**. If we are convinced that we have to build, then how much do we build? Do we really need to build a basement, or can we create a different solution? Can we perhaps reuse something that's already there **[PAGE 202]**? Or can we take materials from other projects **[PAGES 198, 200]**? I think that in the future this will completely change the way we design. Right now, at the beginning of a project, we have a blank sheet of paper, but I think that in future we can go and look in a catalogue database to see if there is a project not so far away that is getting dismantled. This is how we are going to design. It's a kind of reverse design process: You look at what's available and you incorporate it – instead of defining what you need and then going to the market to search for someone who provides this. The next step is building cleverer, and this has absolutely nothing to do with optimizing this one millimeter on a steel plate.

JW We as engineers need to have the confidence to be able to contribute value to the conceptual decisions. Therefore, we have to speak up at the very first meetings. The most important thing is to avoid demolition. And, of course, we should make every structural element as small as possible. But we also have to make sure that buildings

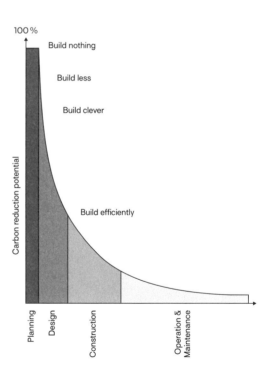

LEFT PAGE Peat barn in Schechen, Germany, 2015. A historical peat barn in Kolbermoor was threatened with demolition and disposal. It was dismantled, extensively repaired, and then rebuilt 15 km away in Schechen – as part of a new home with workshop. Structural design and engineering / Architecture: ZRS Architekten Ingenieure

TOP Lean Design Principles – build nothing, build less, build clever, build efficiently

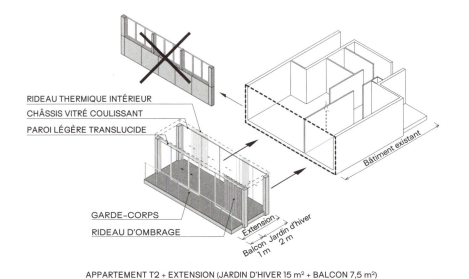

APPARTEMENT T2 + EXTENSION (JARDIN D'HIVER 15 m² + BALCON 7,5 m²)

Tour Bois le Prêtre – Transformation of a housing block in Paris, France, 2011. Architecture: Druot, Lacaton & Vassal; Structural design and engineering: VP & Green
Built in the early 1960s in the north of Paris, this high-rise has 16 floors with a total of 96 apartments. The initially planned demolition could be avoided and instead a project for remodeling was decided. Among other things, the project provides for a generous extension of the apartments.

can be reused in a completely different way to the ways we thought they would be used in the beginning. When we build housing projects, the buildings should also be capable of being used as offices. The floor-to-floor height has to be generous enough to accommodate this. We have to take the long-term view.

RP The construction industry is responsible for a good 40% of carbon emissions. When two-thirds of embodied carbon is contained in superstructure and substructure, the engineer's work is extremely important in terms of reducing carbon emissions. Which (new) materials are particularly suitable for sustainable constructions? Timber?

JW Timber is one option. I think we always have to think through all of the options and see which is the most appropriate. Concrete is still probably the most problematic structure material on the planet, while clay is really interesting, because clay is the most abundant material on the planet. We will be using concrete in some way for a very long time, so we need to keep working to make sure that it is really put to good use, and to reduce the amount of carbon used in the process as much as possible. At the same time, we need to find ways to introduce new materials and facilitate their approval.

LF While we are on the subject, it is important to understand the time value of carbon. A ton of CO_2 today has more impact than the same amount in 20–30 years. As much as I agree that we have to keep on doing the research and the industrial development on the new materials side, it's not going to change the way we design and build today. And it's today that we really have to do things in a drastically different way. It's absolutely possible to cut from every project 10–20% of CO_2 emission today. Also, it's very important to demonstrate to our clients that this is actually going to save money. I'm saying this because they still have this notion in their head that green must necessarily mean more expensive.

RP How do you deal with this notion that steps to improve the sustainability of a building usually cost more money?

LF In the case of energy-efficiency, it is indeed the case that more needs to be invested first. But it should not be the same with material efficiency and reduction of embodied carbon – at least not for the first 10–20%, where you can work with the conventional methods. If we as structural engineers are able to demonstrate to our clients that we will save them money – this could change everything. And this is directly connected to another financial topic: how we are paid for our job. It's crazy that I'm getting paid more as an engineer when I make a greater quantity in my project. Which other industry works like that? That's like paying a lawyer more money to go to jail longer. The question is: how are we going to change it? Perhaps there should be a benchmark that is the starting point, and the fees should be somehow calibrated against that. Additionally, there could be a kind of performance fee that depends on how much CO_2 you save. You would have to share this with the architects and others as well as with the construction firms, so everyone in the design team benefits financially by doing better.

RP Can there be construction materials that are truly net zero carbon?

LF There will always be some CO_2 left. Beside this, there is the option of offsetting. But we know that it's not the right solution because there are not enough opportunities to solve the problem with that approach. Furthermore, it takes us away from the real things we should do: cutting down the emissions as much as we can. So personally, I'm not interested in this discussion, because even if we do reach certain future goals with that, I think it's more important to be focused on what we can do today.

RP High-rise buildings are often mentioned as a solution in the context of sustainability. They seal only a small amount of ground area. At the same time, they will always be more carbon-intensive to construct, operate and maintain than lower-rise buildings of the same specification. How do you deal with this conflict?

JW First of all, taller buildings always need more construction material because the load-bearing structure has to be bigger to carry all the weight. And then there are much larger wind forces to resist. For the whole life of the building, you have to lift people and water up the building, which needs quite a lot of energy. In the end, embodied carbon and carbon in use is much higher the higher you build.

LF In a way, it's tragic that high-rise buildings in particular fascinate engineers so much. Special courses are taught on them at university, and, later, highly regarded architecture prizes are awarded for them. In terms of sustainability, there are fields in an engineer's practice that require far more attention – especially with regard to sustainability, CO_2 reduction and a more interdisciplinary design process.

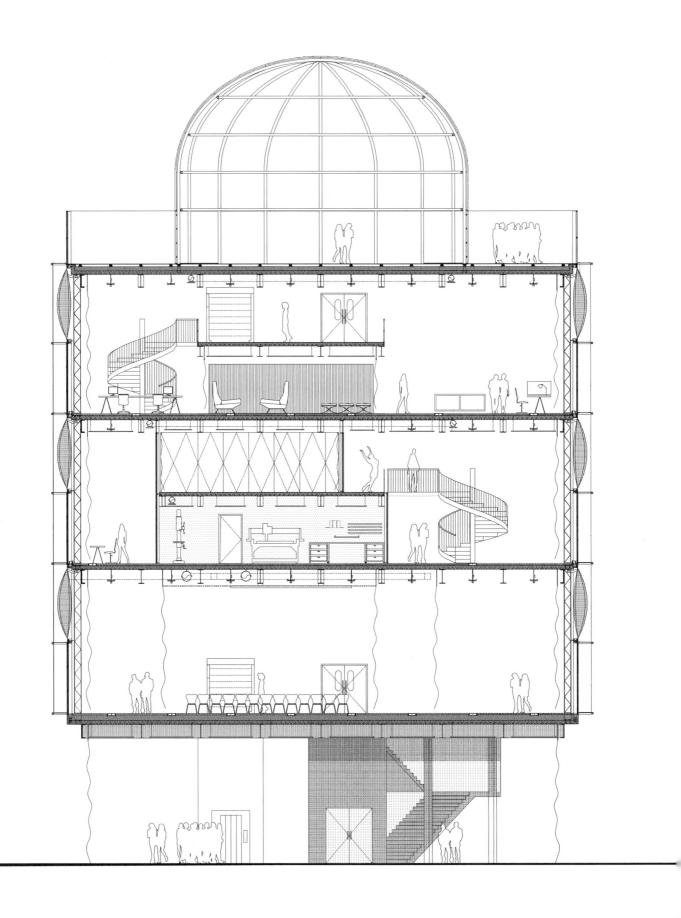

MARIO RINKE

CONCEPTUALIZING STRUCTURAL PERMANENCIES

[1] De Wolf, C., Brütting, J., and Fivet, C.: (2018) Embodied Carbon Benefits of Reusing Structural Components in the Built Environment: A Medium-Rise Office Building Case Study, PLEA Conference (Hong-Kong).

[2] Issue "Knochenarchitektur" of werk, bauen + wohnen, 3, 2018, or Otto, F. (1987) "Der Knochen, eine komplexe Konstruktion. Gedanken eines Architekten," Anthropologischer Anzeiger 45(3), pp. 289–301.

[3] Rinke, M.: (2019) "Structure as an Organizing Tool for Possibilities," in The Bones of Architecture, ed. Mario Rinke, Triest, Zurich, pp. 195–199.

[4] Vividly discussed, for example, in a conference of the Getty Conservation Institute Los Angeles: Kyle Normandin & Susan Macdonald, A Colloquium to Advance the Practice of Conserving Modern Heritage, March 6–7, 2013, www.getty.edu/conservation.

LEFT PAGE Mixed-use laboratory building, designed to constantly adapt, New Generation Research Center, Caen, France, 2015 Architecture: Bruther Architects

In the current debate on sustainable construction, the load-bearing structure occupies a special position. Mainly because of its embodied carbon, relatively large volume, high mass and energy-intensive manufacturing process, it has a large share in the ecological footprint of buildings.[1] To address this, it has been proposed that we should optimize the material consumption of the structure or use more sustainable materials. Other concepts seek to reuse the components, which requires a correspondingly different design philosophy. Apart from the use of materials, however, the life span of a building is often left out of the sustainability discussion, as is the far-too-strong link between the building design and its use. As a result, in times of increasing scarcity of resources, there is simultaneously a need for buildings and a vacancy rate, often close to each other. The globally absurd problem of the astonishingly short life span of many buildings can be traced back to the very limited sustainability of the architecture itself, not that of its building materials. For robust architecture to establish itself in a sustainable building, its relationship to use must change. It must be able to demand a more intelligent contribution from the structure that participates not only in enabling architectural spaces, but also in enabling possibilities for other architectures later. The interaction between architects and engineers will expand, oriented towards a more complex determination of the building's trajectories of possibilities, planned by them jointly.

Functional layers and time layers

With modernism's programmatic detachment of the building envelope from the supporting structure, the skeleton has moved to the center of architectural production as a space-forming factor. The central role of the skeleton becomes visible when we are dealing with the conversion of existing buildings or *ruins*. Conversion, retrofitting, and stripping away to the core exposes the skeleton, and this unchangeable element of the building is then used to operate, to continue building. The stripping can be compared to the work of archaeologists, the intervention to that of surgeons. The supporting structure has often been compared to bones – the fact that it is frequently referred to as a skeleton clearly indicates this.[2] Inside the body, the bones provide support and stability. However, important as they are, their purpose is limited. Bones alone have no meaning in relation to the whole of which they are a part; they are always part of a complex system.[3] Just like bones, load-bearing structures only make sense in their context and for a function. Only when they are embedded in a functional setting do they make sense in terms of what they were set up for. This can be seen in recurring discussions in heritage conservation circles concerning the survival of unused cultural monuments[4] or the acute vacancy of office buildings in many city centers.

But buildings and their structures don't just need a function, they also need a flexibility in terms of functional change. Stewart Brand concluded in his influential study of how buildings change over time: "All buildings are predictions. All predictions are wrong."[5] The narrow functional-spatial planning does not stand up to the actual use that follows. In their close constructional entanglement, façade, building services, load-bearing structure or fittings are very often responsible for problems in the event of a later necessary adaptation. Depending on the frequency of adaptations due to changes in use or maintenance, these functional layers can also be regarded as intertwined time layers, each of which is subject to its own rhythm of existence [PAGE 207, TOP]. Brand called them "shearing layers of change." The more connected they are, and the more firmly they are connected, the greater the problem: "Because of the different rates of change of its parts," says Brand, "a building always tears itself apart." Ideally, therefore, components of different functions within the building should remain workable, which means, for example, that the supporting structure should remain separate from the building services.

Of course, for Brand, the supporting structure is only one of the many functional layers. In its permanence, it must allow for swift change around it – through spatial generosity, for example. Accordingly, the structural designer should strive to think of the structure as a framework of possibilities for various specific architectures, to each of which it contributes particular qualities – it will, however, always outlast these architectural constellations. In this way, the supporting structure and architecture do not become spatially and sensually separated, but only separated in terms of time.

Now, what do the possibilities for change mean, in practical terms, for the supporting structure? Since it is so much firmer than the soft layers, it must also be thought of in terms of what can be expected of it in a later context. How can that change around the supporting structure and how does the skeleton determine this process? It is precisely in the structural setting that we are aware of in dealing with existing buildings that we can see, very well, the great importance of the inner structure not only in its (first) lifetime, during its firm and stable support of the spaces and uses laid out, but its appropriation in connection with the need or desire to change the building. In this reading, the structure depicts what is currently happening (what it is used for), but also what may have had to be dealt with earlier or what is yet to come in terms of future demands. As a circular strategy, this kind of structural design means that the skeleton remains in place, so that it is available once again as a framework for each subsequent use. Only the lighter components for the skin and interior partitioning would be dismantled or added. The radius of movement of the most energy-intensive functional layer is thus kept as minimal as possible.

Change as a load case

This simultaneity of the nonsimultaneous is, essentially, also the practice of scientific, and indeed modern, structural design today.[6] Unfortunately, it is usually limited to modeling loads. We define requirements that arise from uses, from wind or earthquake effects, and equip the building with a structure that then has appropriate capacities for precisely these requirements. This affects the shape of the parts and the entire structure, as well as the construction materials. However, it is precisely in this purely technical consideration that the banality of a supporting structure often lies. Thus, while we project the external effects onto our present building as a future possibility, we accept its internal use-related layout as a series of narrow corridors of possibility that hardly allow any alternatives. Structural design

[5] Brand, S.: (1995) How Buildings Learn. What Happens After They're Built, Penguin Books, London, 1995.

[6] Rinke, M.: (2016) "Konstruktion im Zwiespalt," Trans 28, pp. 25–26.

RIGHT PAGE, TOP Brand's shear layer diagram. See footnote 5.

RIGHT PAGE, BOTTOM Nolli-Plan, Giambattista Nolli, Nuova Topografia di Roma, 1748

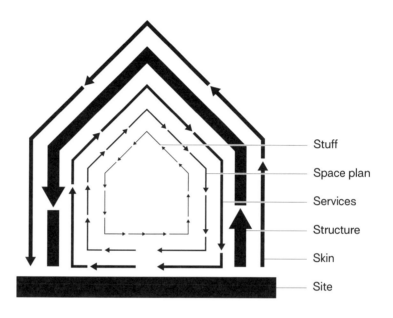

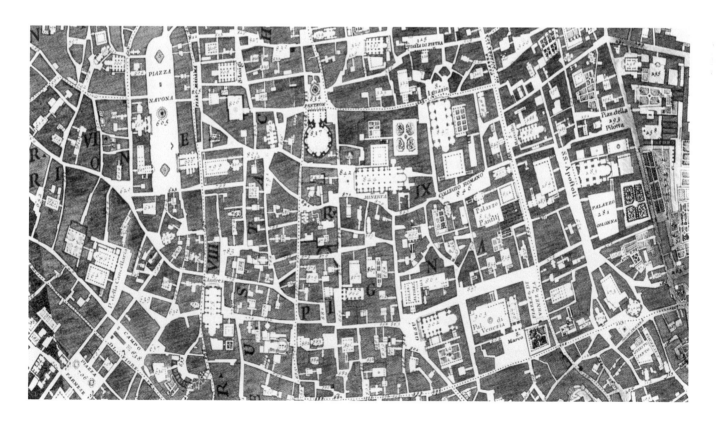

COMMON RESPONSIBILITIES 207

is still mostly concerned with the robustness of generously dimensioned building components or resilient building materials, instead of engaging with the spatial and, above all, temporal variation strategies of the building. This is because technical structural design relates, above all, to point zero of the building's existence. The supporting structure developed from a superordinate architectural concept is a direct translation, often even a diagram of its requirements for the specified (first) building use.

This is precisely where the overarching – and in fact creative – approach of the engineer in drawing up the structural design for an adaptable building becomes apparent: instead of translating uses into loads and structural dimensions, spatial spectra of use should determine the component arrangements and dimensions and allow possible subsequent breakthroughs to be strategically contained in the components in readiness. For the given floor plans, what other subsequent uses are possible and likely? What is the impact on circulation if different user groups want to move around within one floor? Which of the possible subsequent vertical connections of services or circulation are plausible, probable, and can already be implemented easily? It is then also a question of determining what these capacities represent in terms of costs and effort, and where these contingencies make sense in the specifications. What might a sustainable supporting structure that emerges from a stable architecture and use look like? How could a functionally stable structure be set up that would function for as many conceivable demands upon the building and probable conversions as possible without costly adaptations? And how can it be sustainable beyond its material properties? Strong structures are so architecturally valuable that they significantly shape the identity of spaces and buildings. This means that we must understand a supporting structure not only as a technical apparatus that silently solves problems, but also as a carrier of meaning in the long term within the building over generations of use.

The building skeleton as a porous mass

The supporting structure, which is a self-evident part of the architecture, embraces all areas of the building, permeating it. It is thus the great connective element in the layers of meaning of the building, in that it not only proverbially holds the building together, but also acts with the necessary permanence throughout the episodes of a building's history. In its pervasiveness and homogeneous presence, but above all in its nonnegotiable physical existence (alongside the many changing ideational values), the structure itself becomes the rigid body within which any given architecture takes place. The arrangement of components and cavities resembles the modeling of a porous mass.[7] In this sense, the skeleton is the maximally dissolved mass.

To describe how a building can be reconfigured, appropriated, and adapted – ideally in line with a variety of different users – it must also be understood as a permeable structure. This approach conforms to Richard Sennett's thoughts on the porosity of the city, describing the permeability of buildings and their role in separating private and public spaces within the city.[8] Sennett uses the Nolli Plan to describe building blocks as closed or permeable bodies that make the boundaries of the built environment visible **[PAGE 207, BOTTOM]**. In this sense, the building can also be thought of as a mass broken up by perforations which, depending on its configuration, allows varying levels of access, different interior spatial qualities and connections. For Herman Hertzberger, it is the public space that holds

[7] Castellón, J.J., D'Acunto, P.: (2017) "The Architectural and Performative Potential of Porous Structures," in Thermodynamic Interactions. An Architectural Exploration into Physiological, Material, Territorial Atmospheres, ed. Javier Garcia-German, pp. 133–137.

[8] Sennett, R.: (2019) Building and Dwelling. Ethics for the City, London, pp. 218–221.

the city together and is subject to a minor dynamic. The streets even form the most enduring part of the urban fabric.[9] Thus, if we understand corridors on the one hand as the dividing lines between private and less private spaces in buildings and on the other hand as being themselves the most enduring functional zones dedicated to facilitating circulation, then the interplay between circulation and structure in conjunction with associated spectra of use becomes the actual configuration of building possibilities [PAGES 204, 210 TOP].

Like building blocks, street façades or the volume of a building, the walls and slabs of a structure are not completely sealed, but have numerous openings for various reasons – e.g., for service shafts or doors. More than that, however, these structural surfaces (especially those built from the first half of the 20th century onward) often have an internal substructure, as they consist of a skeleton filled in with additional elements. As a porous structure, the skeleton, which was preferred at the time of its construction primarily for reasons of material savings, allows for much greater flexibility in later conversions, as openings can be made more quickly and easily. The structurally hierarchical ribbed ceilings would thus become architectural membranes that allowed for specific forms of permeability as needed. This generic, nonspecific dissolution is the real intelligence of the building component, which does not respond to rigid load ideas, but instead creates windows of possibility that are interwoven with the structural idea and the building process. These internal possibilities for change by means of potential penetrations – without compromising the overall integrity of the structure, of course – must be included in the discussion of the porous structure during the structural design process.[10] Consequently, the permeability of the building can be read in three ways: (1) relative to the surroundings through possible entrances and exits but also through open or closed façades in general; (2) in terms of the traversing of the building by corridors to connect functions; and (3) as the possible permeability of space-enclosing components such as slabs or walls to connect units of use horizontally and vertically. The concept of porosity can help in identifying permanent structural features and translating them into an appropriate material concept. This means, for example, that within a floor slab the corridor around the core and the staircase could be solid, while the floor areas next to it would consist of lighter elements inserted between solid beams of the skeleton. The identified permanent features of the structure are thus matched with a corresponding material mobility. This means that the load-bearing skeleton itself does not necessarily have to consist of demountable, circular components, because it necessarily remains in place. All the other softer layers, on the other hand, should be contained for purposes of circulation.

An interesting open-structure building typology has been discussed in the context of public and private spaces.[11] The concrete skeletons from the so-called Polykatoikia, literally "multiresidence" – a structure intended to shape modern Athens – created a structural framework often set back at street level, creating open colonnades and gradually receding on top to create terraces. The structure is filled with bricks or windows to form apartments or shops – in this respect, it links with Le Corbusier's Dom-ino construction system.[12]

The intelligent ruin

However, the structure can also be transposed into a larger scale of thought in a reverse manner. In its enduring presence, it then quite naturally detach-

---

[9] Hertzberger, H.: (2013) Social Space and Structuralism, OASE 90, p. 20.

[10] Rinke, M., Pacquée R.: (2022) Structures and change. Tracing adaptability based on structural porosity in converted buildings, Architecture Structure and Construction.

[11] Richard Woditsch (ed.): (2018) The Public Private House: Modern Athens and Its Polykatoikia, Park Books, Zurich.

[12] Vittorio Aureli, P., Giudici, M.S, Issaias, P.: (2012) From Domino to Polykatoikia, Domus 962.

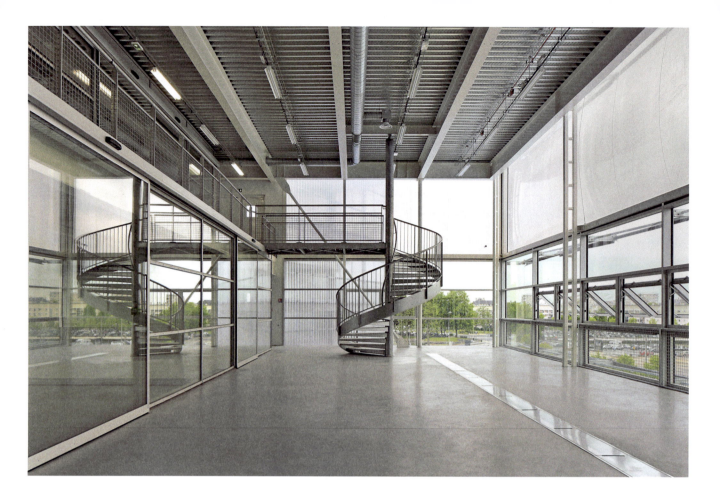

CONCEPTUALIZING STRUCTURAL PERMANENCIES

[13] Van Reeth, B.: (2013) "Good architecture?" OASE 90, p. 42.

[14] Ingold, T.: (1993) "The Temporality of the Landscape," World Archaeology 25(2), pp. 152–174.

es itself from the current building in terms of its overarching significance. As the most rigid part of the building, it belongs more to the outside, to the urban environment, than to the inside, to its current use. From a macro perspective, the supporting structure becomes an element of the neighborhood and urban development, containing a spectrum of uses and enabling appropriations. These respond to those of the neighbors, allowing continuity between buildings and controlling them through their own internal order. The orientation of the building and thus the order of accesses can change, while users and user combinations can fluctuate and floor plans can shift owing to fit-outs or new cross-connections. The structures of buildings can thus be read as a meta-landscape that determines usability and relationships, but can also be adapted at any time, and that has an effect both internally on its own spaces and externally upon its neighborhood. Following Brand's model of shearing layers – the almost permanent structure thus merges with the permanent site – it becomes an extended building site with all the preconditions for (further) building **[PAGE 210, BOTTOM]**.

The Belgian architect Bob Van Reeth has described changeable structures of this type as intelligent ruins. "A building is a possibility, is conducive, preferably taciturn, silent, is willing, liberates space, mediates. Building as intelligent ruins. [...] Good buildings conceal daily use – they are stable and stubborn, obstinately distributive and (to echo Kant) 'purposive without a purpose'. Therein lies the quality of their durability, or their cultural durability, which yields dignity. Expediency calls for the right scale, an extreme precision that leaves everything open that cannot be predicted."[13] In this sense, the design of the building structure is not only the conceptual connective element of space, time and scale, but also the essential tactile ordering element that transcends the episodes of a place's existence: uses, materials, the flow of people through it – all of these condense, grow, and reinvent themselves anew.

Today, given the ongoing efforts to achieve sustainable architectures (and structures), we have some new requirements: namely, to meaningfully extend the use cycles of buildings and components. The structure can make a particular contribution to this by providing the framework for a constantly transforming urban landscape, which is always only temporary and thus bears traces of previous uses.[14] In addition to the urgent discussions concerning sustainable materials and the expected focus on reusable building components, we also urgently need to rethink the currently far-too-narrow concept of durability for structures and function. The structural engineer can contribute in ways that are far more profound than merely making structures more slender as well as connections more flexible. After all this can lead to differentiated structures – i.e., link them to spectra of use and changing contexts, and thus gain an understanding of them as easily appropriated, intelligent ruins. In this, support is required of those who conceptualize the building and those who determine trajectories of the city and the neighborhood. Structures are a natural part of architecture: neither one of the two can make sense without the other, nor can it be long-lasting.

LEFT PAGE, TOP **Mixed-use laboratory building, designed to constantly adapt, New Generation Research Center, Caen, France, 2015. Architecture: Bruther Architects**

LEFT PAGE, BOTTOM **Ruin as shell of the new, Naxos, Greece, 2023**

APPENDIX

AUTHORS

WILLIAM BAKER is a Consulting Structural Engineering Partner at SOM. Throughout his career, Baker has dedicated himself to innovative structural engineering design and research, with expertise across a variety of structures around the world. He developed the "buttressed core" structural system for the Burj Khalifa, the world's tallest human-made structure, as well as the Broadgate Exchange House, a 10-story office building with an iconic structure that spans a 78-meter-long rail yard in London. Baker has also advanced a range of engineering collaborations with architects and artists from around the world, including projects such as the Fishers Island Residence single-family home in New York, with architect Thomas Phifer and Partners; and Skyspace, a permanent art installation with artist James Turrell at Rice University.

ALESSANDRO BEGHINI is a Structural Engineering Senior Associate Principal with SOM. Alessandro works to develop innovative structural design for projects in coordination with the architectural and building services teams. Recent projects include the 530m tall Tianjin CTF project and collaborations with Atelier Peter Zumthor for the LACMA Museum and with Janet Echelman for Current. Throughout his career, Alessandro has been conducting research in the field of optimal structural topologies and development of innovative methodologies for structural analysis. To this end, he maintains ongoing collaborations with academic institutions and has served as Adjunct Professor at Northwestern University.

ALEJANDRO BERNABEU, Ph. Civil Engineer and Professor at the School of Architecture (UPM), is an expert in structures of singular buildings with more than 20 years of experience. CEO of Bernabeu Ingenieros, he has developed projects worldwide working in collaboration with well-known architects such as Herzog & de Meuron, David Chipperfield, Dominique Perrault, Nieto Sobejano, Rafael de La Hoz or Burgos & Garrido. His work focusses on structural design and the relationship between structure and architecture. He has been awarded with the IABSE prize.

FEDERICO BERTAGNA is a post-doctoral researcher and lecturer at the Chair of Structural Design led by Prof. Dr. Jacqueline Pauli at ETH Zurich. Originally trained as a structural engineer, he later obtained a doctorate from the Department of Architecture at ETH Zurich under the supervision of Prof. Dr. Joseph Schwartz. His research focuses on geometry-based graphical methods as a way to establish holistic design approaches that reconcile spatial, structural, and environmental aspects.

KAI-UWE BLETZINGER works in the field of computational mechanics for static-dynamic analysis, simulation and optimization and their integration into the digital design chain. He studied civil engineering in Stuttgart and Calgary (Canada) and received his PhD in 1990 in Stuttgart. In 1996, he was appointed to a professorship at the University of Karlsruhe before joining the faculty of TUM in 1999. He is a member of numerous committees for basic and applied research, European standardization, the German Research Foundation, and the Bavarian Construction Administration's examination board for the recognition of test engineers

GIULIA BOLLER is a scientific assistant and postdoctoral researcher at the Chair of the Theory of Architecture at ETH Zurich. She is both an engineer and an architect. Her research interests lie at the interface between history, architecture and structural engineering disciplines. In 2022 she completed a doctoral thesis at the Chair of Structural Design at ETH Zurich. She gained professional experience at Renzo Piano Building Workshop. Giulia graduated with honors in Building Engineering-Architecture at the University of Trento (Italy) in 2015.

JÜRG CONZETT studied civil engineering at EPF Lausanne and ETH Zurich. After receiving his diploma in 1980 he worked for several years in the office of architect Peter Zumthor. In 1988 he started his own office as a structural engineer. Today, the firm Conzett Bronzini Partner in Chur (Grisons) investigates existing constructions and designs new bridges and buildings, often in collaboration with architects.

PIERLUIGI D'ACUNTO is an Assistant Professor of Structural Design at the School of Engineering and Design of the Technical University of Munich (TUM). His research explores the convergence of architecture and structural engineering through computer-aided design and emerging construction technologies. Pierluigi graduated with honors in Building Engineering-Architecture from the University of Pisa in 2007 and received a Master of Architecture from the Architectural Association in London in 2012. In 2018 he completed his doctorate with distinction at ETH Zurich.

CATHERINE DE WOLF is the director of ETH Zurich's Chair of Circular Engineering for Architecture (CEA), where she leverages digital innovations to promote a circular economy in the built environment. With a dual background in civil engineering and architecture and a PhD in building technology from MIT, Catherine has contributed to real-world projects globally and collaborated with organizations like the European Commission and Arup. She is a faculty at EMPA, ETH AI Center, the NCCR on digital fabrication, and Design++.

JANET ECHELMAN sculpts at the scale of buildings and city blocks. Echelman's work defies categorization, as it intersects sculpture, architecture, urban design, material science, structural and aeronautical engineering, and computer science. Her art transforms with wind and light, and shifts from being "an object you look at, into an experience you can get lost in." Recipient of the Guggenheim Fellowship, Smithsonian American Ingenuity Award, and #1 on Oprah's "List of 50 Things That Make You Say Wow!", Echelman has taught at Harvard Graduate School of Design, Princeton University, and Massachusetts Institute of Technology (MIT), where she is currently the Mellon Distinguished Visiting Artist.

MIGUEL FERNÁNDEZ RUIZ obtained his diploma in civil engineering from Universidad Politécnica de Madrid (UPM, Spain) in 2001 and later his PhD in 2004. In 2004 he joined École Polytechnique Fédérale de Lausanne (Switzerland), where he was later promoted to Senior Scientist and worked part-time until 2022, developing also a professional career as partner of a consulting firm specialized in structural design. Since 2021 he is full professor at UPM.

LEE FRANCK is a structural engineer who graduated from EPFL in 2009. She worked at Arup in London from 2009 to 2015 and at Guy Nordenson and Associates in New York City from 2015 to 2018. Since 2019 she has been working independently and founded LEEN, a consultancy that collaborates with both public and private clients to reduce embodied carbon and advocate for the circular economy through strategy development and lean design thinking. Additionally, she lectures to industry professionals and university students.

ROBERTO GARGIANI was educated at the Faculty of Architecture of the University of Florence where he graduated in architecture in 1983 and received his PhD in 1992. Between 1994 and 2004 he was professor in various universities in France and Italy. Since 2005 he was professor at the École Polytechnique Fédérale de Lausanne (EPFL), where he was the head of the Laboratory of Theory and History of Architecture 3 (LTH3) and where he served as Director of the Architecture Department (2011–2015) and of the Archives de la construction moderne (2015–2017). Today he is guest professor at Polytecnico di Bari.

PAUL GAUVREAU was educated at the University of Victoria (B. Sc.), Princeton University (M. S. E.), and the ETH Zurich (Dr. sc. techn.). He entered bridge design practice in 1983 and worked with firms in Canada and the US, rising to Principal at J. Muller International. He was appointed Professor at the University of Toronto in 2002, where he teaches concrete structures, drawing, and bridge design, and conducts research into the bridge design process. He maintains an active consulting practice, providing clients with bridge design concepts, peer review, and expert testimony.

ANN-KATHRIN GOLDBACH focuses on various advanced computational design, analysis, and optimization aspects towards an integrated digital simulation environment for engineering structures. She studied civil engineering at the Technical University of Munich and KTH Stockholm (Sweden). In 2021 she received her PhD at TUM and since then works as a postdoc and deputy head of the chair of Structural Analysis. Her current role includes the participation in several research and standardization committees. In addition, she has multiple teaching activities at TUM as well as international partner institutions, ranging from lectures to seminars and workshops.

CLEMENTINE HEGNER-VAN ROODEN graduated in civil engineering at ETH Zurich and first worked as an assistant at the Chair of Structural Design of the Department of Architecture. At the same time, she completed the Higher Teaching Qualification at ETH. This was followed by years of practical experience as a project manager in structural engineering at Stocker & Partner in Bern and Zurich and as a specialist didactician at Höhere Fachschule Hochbau in Winterthur, before she became editor at Schweizerische Bauzeitung TEC21 in 2006. Since 2013 she has been a freelance publicist in the field of structural engineering and civil engineering, correspondent for TEC21, and managing director of the Swiss Society for the Art of Engineering.

THORSTEN HELBIG is a founder and Managing Partner at knippershelbig. Under his supervision, knippershelbig has become one of the leading engineering consultants for innovative specialty structures and façades. Since 2018 Helbig is an Associate Professor at the Irwin S. Chanin School of Architecture at The Cooper Union, New York, and since 2022 Professor for structural design at the University of Applied Sciences in Darmstadt.

TULLIA IORI is professor at the University of Rome Tor Vergata, where she is pro-rector for teaching and coordinator of the PhD in Civil Engineering. She has coordinated, with Sergio Poretti, the research SIXXI – History of Structural Engineering in Italy, funded by an ERC Advanced Grant in 2012. She has conducted research on the history of reinforced concrete in Italy, on Pier Luigi Nervi and Sergio Musmeci (also curating exhibitions at the MAXXI Museum in Rome) and, more generally, on the history of engineering in Italy with the SIXXI series of 5 volumes.

CHRISTIAN KEREZ was born in 1962 in Maracaibo, Venezuela and educated at the Swiss Federal Institute of Technology Zurich. After extensive published work in the field of architectural photography, he opened his own architectural office in Zurich, Switzerland, in 1993 and in 2017 in Berlin, Germany. In 2021 he moved to Milan, Italy. His work includes several projects in various scales in France, Bahrain, the Czech Republic, Switzerland, Austria, Dubai, and China.

JEANNETTE KUO is founding partner of KARAMUK KUO in Zurich, and Professor of Architecture and Construction at TU Munich. Prior to teaching at TUM, Kuo taught for many years at Harvard Graduate School of Design, at EPF Lausanne and at MIT. Her work and research focus on the intersection of architecture, culture, and construction, foregrounding sustainable principles. Publications include the critically acclaimed *A-Typical Plan* (Park Books, 2013) and *Space of Production* (Park Books, 2015).

MASSIMO LAFFRANCHI has been educated at the Swiss Federal Institute of Technology (ETH) in Zurich. There, he graduated in 1993 and published his PhD thesis about conceptual design of curved bridges in 1999. In 2000 he founded with Dr. Armand Fürst the company Fürst Laffranchi Bauingenieure GmbH. The office realized numerous bridges and structures for buildings resulting from successful competitions. From 2000 to 2013, he was a professor at the USI, Accademia di architettura in Mendrisio, CH. He has been a member of the board since 2001 and he has been president of the Swiss Society for the Art of Engineering since 2019.

CHRISTIAN MENN was a renowned Swiss civil engineer and bridge designer. He graduated in civil engineering from ETH Zurich in 1950. He was involved in the construction of around 100 bridges worldwide. Menn led his own engineering company in Chur from 1957 to 1971. From 1971 until his retirement in 1992, he was a professor of structural engineering at ETH Zurich, specializing in bridge design. After his retirement as professor, he continued to be a consulting engineer in private practice.

FLORIAN MEIER, P. E., is a Director with knippershelbig and is leading the New York office. He was trained at the Technical University of Munich, with a focus on structural optimization, and has experience in a variety of materials and structural typologies. He is co-teaching a structures class at the Irwin S. Chanin School of Architecture of Cooper Union, New York, focusing on the collaboration between architects and engineers, innovative structural systems, building technologies, and materials.

ELLI MOSAYEBI'S career is characterized by the close connection between practice, research, and teaching. Since 2004 she has led the Zurich-based architecture office Edelaar Mosayebi Inderbitzin together with Ron Edelaar and Christian Inderbitzin. From 2004 to 2008 she was research assistant at the Chair for Architecture Theory under Prof. Dr. Ákos Moravánszky, in which she completed her doctoral dissertation on the work of the Milanese architect Luigi Caccia Dominioni. From 2012 to 2018 she was Professor for Design and Housing at TU Darmstadt, and since 2018 she has held the position of Professor for Architecture and Design at ETH Zurich.

AURELIO MUTTONI received his diploma and PhD in civil engineering from ETHZ, Switzerland, in 1982 and 1989, respectively. Since then, he practices as a structural designer in engineering offices based in Switzerland. At the same time, he was professor of structural design at the Academy of Architecture in Mendrisio from its foundation until 2001 and is part-time professor of structural engineering (concrete structures and bridge design) at EPFL, Switzerland, since 2000. He is also often called upon as an expert in the verification of complex structures and the analysis of structural collapses.

REZA NAJIAN ASL recently completed his postdoctoral research at the Technical University of Munich (TUM), focusing on computational mechanics and optimization. With academic roots at the University of Tehran and TUM, he has developed skills in FEM/FVM-based simulation and optimization for structures and fluids. During his time as a Research Assistant, he worked on optimization frameworks for companies like BMW and Volkswagen. In his postdoctoral role, he explored the simulation and optimization of large-scale additively manufactured structures. Dr. Najian Asl's work aims to bridge theoretical advancements with practical applications in computational optimization, contributing to both academia and the industry.

PATRICK OLE OHLBROCK is a structural engineer at Dr. Schwartz Consulting AG and in parallel post-doctoral researcher at the Chair of Structural Design at the School of Engineering and Design of the Technical University of Munich (TUM). His research interests are geometry-based methods for structural design, design-oriented computational modeling of structures, natural building materials, and form finding coupled with machine learning. Ole graduated from the Technical University of Munich in 2013 and completed his doctorate in 2020 with distinction at ETH Zurich.

ROLAND PAWLITSCHKO is an architect, freelance author, editor, translator, and architectural critic. After studying architecture in Karlsruhe and Vienna he worked with various German and Austrian architectural firms. Today he curates exhibitions, organizes architecture excursions, and publishes articles and essays on architecture and structural engineering in books, magazines, and daily newspapers.

STEFAN POLÓNYI studied civil engineering at the Budapest University of Technology and Economics. He left Budapest for Cologne in 1956 and opened his own office the following year. In 1965 he became a professor of engineering at the Technical University of Berlin before he held the similar position at the Technical University of Dortmund starting in 1971. In Dortmund, he invented the "Dortmunder Modell" in which engineering and architectural students were trained together. Stefan Polónyi died in Cologne on April 9, 2021, at the age of ninety.

CECILIA PUGA is the Director and founding partner of CECILIA PUGA – PAULA VELASCO ARQUITECTURA. Since 1995 she has developed her professional practice independently in Santiago, where she has carried out design projects at different scales and programs, from single-family homes (most notably the House in Bahia Azul), to collective housing, educational and industrial equipment, and urban design such as the renovation of public spaces in Cerro Toro. She has developed her academic activity at Universidad Católica de Santiago, at ETH Zurich's School of Architecture, Austin's University of Texas, GSD Harvard, and at BI-Aarch in Barcelona.

MARIO RINKE is a professor at the University of Antwerp and researches and teaches structures and construction in architecture, focusing on adaptable buildings and the interplay of materials and institutions. He worked for engineering offices in London and Zurich and edited and co-authored several books, among others *The Bones of Architecture,* 2019, as part of the international exhibition in Lisbon, which he curated. He will host and co-chair the next International Conference on Structures and Architecture 2025 in Antwerp.

BJØRN NORMANN SANDAKER has a background in structural engineering (M.Sc.) from the Norwegian University of Science and Technology (NTNU), as well as from studies of architectural history and theory at The Oslo School of Architecture and Design (AHO), where he also received his PhD. He is now an emeritus professor at both institutions. Sandaker has numerous publications (books, papers) within his particular field of interest that focuses on the borderline between architecture and engineering.

JOSEPH SCHWARTZ studied civil engineering at ETH Zurich. After his studies, Schwartz researched and taught at ETH Zurich under Bruno Thürlimann. In 1989 he finished his doctorate with a thesis on the nonlinear design of masonry walls and reinforced concrete columns under normal force. Between 2000 and 2008 he was a professor at the University of Applied Sciences of Central Switzerland. Between 2008 and 2023 he was full professor for Structural Design at ETH Zurich. From 1991 to 2001 he was co-owner of an engineering office in Zug, and since 2002 he has been running his own engineering firm Dr. Schwartz Consulting AG.

KNUT STOCKHUSEN studied civil engineering at the University of Stuttgart and started working as an engineer at sbp in 2000. There he is Partner and Managing Director since 2015. Together with his team, he is among the leading experts in the field of special and lightweight structures focusing on stadium roofs and façades, sports and multipurpose venues, movable structures, and long-span structures. For his work he has received numerous awards on national and international level.

LEONARDO TODISCO is an Associate Professor in Structural Engineering at the Universidad Politécnica de Madrid (UPM), where he carries out his activity as lecturer, researcher, and provides consultancy services on structural design. The main contribution provided by his research has allowed him to be awarded the 13th IASS Hangai Prize and the UPM PhD Excellence Award. From 2018 to 2022 he was president of the Young Member Group of ACHE (Spanish Association of Structural Engineering).

DUARTE M. VIULA FARIA received his civil engineering degree from Universidade Nova de Lisboa (UNL, Portugal) in 2000. After working in practice for several years, he performed his PhD at UNL (2007–2011) and was later assistant professor at UNL (2012–2013) and postdoctoral fellow at École Polytechnique Fédérale de Lausanne (Switzerland, 2013–2014). After, he started working in the design office Muttoni et Fernández IC in Ecublens (Switzerland) where he is currently a partner.

JANE WERNICK CBE FREng HonFRIBA is a structural engineer. She worked for Arup, setting up their Los Angeles Office 1986 (notable Arup project: The Millennium Wheel). In 1998 she founded Jane Wernick Associates (notable projects: Young Vic Theatre; treetop walkway Kew Gardens; Living Architecture Houses). Today she is consultant to engineersHRW. She taught architects and engineers, won the 2013 CBI First Woman of the Built Environment Award and serves on Design Review Panels and multidisciplinary think tank, the Edge (www.edgedebate.com).

IMAGE CREDITS

PAGE 8 Courtesy of Mauricio Pezo and Sofia von Ellrichshausen
PAGE 12, TOP Südwestdeutsches Archiv für Architektur und Ingenieurbau (SAAI): Werkarchiv Behnisch. Photographer: Herbert Seiler
PAGE 12, BOTTOM ETH-Bibliothek Zurich, Photo archive / photo: Unknown / Hs_1085-1929-30-1-45-C / Public Domain Mark: https://ba.e-pics.ethz.ch/catalog/ETHBIB.Bildarchiv/r/103715/viewmode=infoview
PAGE 13 Source: Isler, H.: (1993) "The way to shape," in Proceedings of the International Symposium on Innovative World of Concrete, p. 153.
PAGE 15 TOP Iwan Baan
PAGE 15 BOTTOM Anna Heringer / Kurt Hoerbst

PAGE 16 Aurelio Muttoni
PAGE 22 TOP Muttoni et Fernández
PAGE 23 FIRST ROW Grignoli Muttoni Partner, Aurelio Muttoni
PAGE 23 SECOND ROW Lurati Muttoni Partner, Aurelio Muttoni
PAGE 23 THIRD ROW Lurati Muttoni Partner, TEC21
PAGE 23 FOURTH ROW Graber & Steiger Architekten
PAGE 24 TOP ROW Gauch & Schwartz GmbH
PAGE 24 CENTER ROW LEFT Giuliani Hönger Architekten
PAGE 24 CENTER ROW RIGHT Walter Mair
PAGE 24 BOTTOM ROW LEFT Kuster Frey
PAGE 24 BOTTOM ROW RIGHT Deon AG
PAGE 26 Muttoni, Aurelio: The Art of Structures, EPFL Press, 2011

PAGE 32 Studio Janet Echelman
PAGE 34 Kevin MacCormack
PAGE 36 TOP SOM
PAGE 36 BOTTOM formTL
PAGE 38 SOM
PAGE 39 Studio Janet Echelman
PAGES 40/41 Alkan Yilmaz

PAGE 42 JC Sancho
PAGE 44 Comissió Tàpies, VEGAP, Madrid, 2023
PAGE 45 TOP Bisimages for AceboxAlonso
PAGE 45 BOTTOM (GRAPHICS) Alejandro Bernabeu
PAGE 45 BOTTOM (PHOTO) Bisimages for AceboxAlonso
PAGE 46 TOP Ute Zscharnt for David Chipperfield Architects
PAGE 46 CENTER LLPS architects, Eduardo Pérez
PAGE 46 BOTTOM LLPS architects, Eduardo Pérez
PAGE 49 TOP Anish Kapoor, VEGAP, Madrid, 2023; Photo: © Tate
PAGE 49 CENTER JC Sancho
PAGE 49 BOTTOM Sancho-Madridejos
PAGE 50 TOP Mike Master
PAGE 50 BOTTOM Wijdane Jouhari
PAGE 51 Jorge Bernabeu
PAGE 52 TOP Soriano y Asociados Arquitectos
PAGE 53 TOP Soriano y Asociados Arquitectos
PAGE 53 BOTTOM Luis Gordillo

PAGE 54 Baukunstarchiv NRW
PAGE 57 TOP Baukunstarchiv NRW
PAGE 57 BOTTOM ETH-Bibliothek Zurich, Photo archive / photo: Jack Metzger / Com_C16-070-001-005 / CC BY-SA 4.0
PAGE 58 TOP Christoph Ruckstuhl (https://www.atlasofplaces.com/architecture/viamala-bruecke/)

PAGE 58 BOTTOM ETH-Bibliothek Zurich, Photo archive / photo: Comet Photo AG / Com_FC30-0029-006 / CC BY-SA 4.0
PAGE 60 TOP Baukunstarchiv NRW
PAGE 60 BOTTOM LVR-Amt für Denkmalpflege im Rheinland, Jürgen Gregori

PAGE 62 Paul Gauvreau archive
PAGE 66 TOP Paul Gauvreau
PAGE 66 TOP (GRAPHIC) Paul Gauvreau archive
PAGE 66 CENTER Bill, Max: Robert Maillart. Bridges and Constructions. Pall Mall Press, London, Switzerland, 1969
PAGE 66 BOTTOM Paul Gauvreau

PAGE 70–78 ALL RENDERINGS Chair of Structural Analysis, Technical University of Munich
PAGE 74 Archive of Carlos Lázaro
PAGE 77 falconaumanni. CreativeCommons license: CC BY-SA 2.5, https://commons.wikimedia.org/w/index.php?curid=9996616

PAGE 80 Pierluigi D'Acunto, Lukas Ingold, and Ole Ohlbrock
PAGE 83 TOP LEFT ETH-Bibliothek, Photo archive, photo: Heinz Baumann
PAGE 83 TOP RIGHT SOM Archive, photo: Ezra Stoller
PAGE 83 CENTER Sutherland, I.E. "Sketchpad, A Man-Machine Graphical Communication System," PhD thesis, MIT, 1963, p.11
PAGE 83 BOTTOM Schek, H.J. (1974) "The force density method for form finding and computation of general networks," Computer Methods in Applied Mechanics and Engineering 3(1), p. 131.
PAGE 84 Block Research Group / Iwan Baan
PAGE 87 Screenshot from video created by www.supernovavisual.com

PAGE 94 Walter Mair
PAGE 96 Thomas Flechtner
PAGE 97 Walter Mair
PAGE 98 Mikael Olsson
PAGE 101 Maxime Delvaux
PAGES 102/103 Maxime Delvaux

PAGE 104 Cristóbal Palma
PAGE 106 TOP Felipe Fontecilla
PAGE 106 BOTTOM María José Pedraza C
PAGE 108 TOP Cristóbal Palma
PAGE 108 BOTTOM Cecilia Puga, Paula Velasco Architects
PAGE 110–113 Cecilia Puga, Paula Velasco Architects

PAGE 117 TOP Jürg Conzett
PAGE 117 CENTER Roland Bernath
PAGE 117 BOTTOM www.mc2.es/proyecto/puente-del-milenario
PAGE 118 "werk" Nr. 9/1969: Christian Menn: "Viamala-Brücke der N13," page 616
PAGE 119 Zorzi, Silvano; Lonardo, Lucio: Ponte sobre el Rio Guayllabamba, Anteproyecto, Milan, February 1968, Archivio Silvano Zorzi, Polytecnico di Milan
PAGE 121 TOP Culmann, Carl: Die graphische Statik, 2nd ed., Zurich, Verlag Meyer & Zeller, 1875, page 283
PAGE 121 CENTER/BOTTOM Jürg Conzett
PAGE 122 Jürg Conzett

PAGE 126 Karamuk Kuo (rendering David Klemmer)
PAGE 128 TOP Roland Pawlitschko

PAGE 128 BOTTOM Pep Daudé / FOUNDATION Junta Constructora del Temple Expiatori de la Sagrada Família (model: Colección Patrimonio Fundación "la Caixa")
PAGE 131 TOP/BOTTOM Karamuk Kuo
PAGE 132 TOP/BOTTOM Laurian Ghinitoiu
PAGE 133 TOP Mikael Olsson
PAGE 133 BOTTOM Mikael Olsson

PAGE 138 www.hochbau-fotografie.de
PAGE 140 TOP www.hochbau-fotografie.de
PAGE 140 BOTTOM Cheret Bozic Architekten / knippershelbig
PAGE 142 Cheret Bozic Architekten / knippershelbig
PAGE 145 (DRAWINGS) knippershelbig
PAGE 145 (PHOTOS) Schaffitzel Holzindustrie

PAGE 146–150 ALL SKETCHES Tullia Iori

PAGE 154 Anna Maria Essig
PAGE 157 Henrikke Omre and Mie Aspelin
PAGE 158 TOP Anna Maria Essig
PAGE 158 BOTTOM http://broer.no/bro/
PAGE 161 TOP/BOTTOM Åke E:son Lindman

PAGE 162 TEN Studio
PAGE 164 TOP Filip Dujardin
PAGE 164 BOTTOM Auguste e Gustave Perret
PAGE 169 TOP Roberto Gargiani
PAGE 169 BOTTOM Atelier Kempe Thill

PAGE 174 Fenwick Iribarren Architects
PAGE 176 schlaich bergermann partner
PAGE 177 TOP Fenwick Iribarren Architects
PAGE 177 BOTTOM Supreme Committee for Delivery & Legacy
PAGE 178 Fenwick Iribarren Architects
PAGES 180/181 Supreme Committee for Delivery & Legacy

PAGE 182 Taiyo Onorato and Nico Krebs
PAGE 185 ALL Roland Bernath
PAGE 186 Edelaar Mosayebi Inderbitzin Architekt:innen
PAGE 187 ALL Edelaar Mosayebi Inderbitzin Architekt*innen
PAGE 188 ALL Roland Bernath
PAGE 190 ALL Roland Bernath

PAGE 192 GNWA Gonzalo, Neck, Weri Architectes
PAGE 195 TOP Archivio Pier Luigi Nervi
PAGE 195 BOTTOM Holedeck
PAGE 197 Duarte M. Viula Faria

PAGE 198 ZRS Architekten Ingenieure
PAGE 200 TOP ZRS Architekten Ingenieure – photo: Malte Fuchs
PAGE 200 CENTER LEFT / RIGHT ZRS Architekten Ingenieure – photo: Emmanuel Heringer
PAGE 200 BOTTOM ZRS Architekten Ingenieure – photo: Malte Fuchs
PAGE 201 Institution of Structural Engineers
PAGE 202 ALL Druot, Lacaton & Vassal

PAGE 204 Bruther Architects
PAGE 207 Brand, S. (1995) How Buildings Learn: What Happens after They're Built. Penguin Books, London
PAGE 210 TOP Filip Dujardin / Bruther Architects
PAGE 210 BOTTOM Mario Rinke

APPENDIX

THE REALIZATION OF THIS PUBLICATION WAS MADE POSSIBLE THANKS
TO THE GENEROUS SUPPORT OF:

ETH zürich

D**ARCH**
Departement Architektur

Fundación
Agustín de Betancourt

We extend our gratitude to the following architecture and engineering firms for their generous financial support:
Miebach Oberholzer Architekten, ZPF Ingenieure, Graber & Steiger, Atelier Burkhalter Sumi, Deon Architekten,
Giuliani Hönger – Architekten, Penzel Valier, Dr. Deuring + Oehninger, Jan Kinsbergen Architects,
Halter Casagrande Architekten.

EDITORIAL TEAM: Pierluigi D'Acunto, Patrick Ole Ohlbrock, Roland Pawlitschko
COPY EDITING: Alison Kirkland

PROJECT MANAGEMENT: Alexander Felix, Katharina Kulke
PRODUCTION: Amelie Solbrig
LAYOUT, COVER DESIGN AND TYPESETTING: Robert Müller, mueller–mueller.net

PAPER: Magno Natural, 120 g/m²
PRINTING: Grafisches Centrum Cuno GmbH & Co. KG, Calbe
IMAGE EDITING: LVD Gesellschaft für Datenverarbeitung mbH, Berlin

LIBRARY OF CONGRESS CONTROL NUMBER: 2024930499

Bibliographic information published by the German National Library
The German National Library lists this publication in the Deutsche Nationalbibliografie; detailed bibliographic data are available on the Internet at http://dnb.dnb.de.

This work is subject to copyright. All rights are reserved, whether the whole or part of the material is concerned, specifically the rights of translation, reprinting, re-use of illustrations, recitation, broadcasting, reproduction on microfilms or in other ways, and storage in databases. For any kind of use, permission of the copyright owner must be obtained.

ISBN 978-3-0356-2795-4
e-ISBN (PDF) 978-3-0356-2889-0

© 2024 Birkhäuser Verlag GmbH, Basel
Im Westfeld 8, 4055 Basel, Switzerland
Part of Walter de Gruyter GmbH, Berlin/Boston

WWW.BIRKHAUSER.COM